# AFROCENTRICITY: GENERATIONS OF THEORY IN PRACTICE

AFROCENTRICITY: GENERATIONS OF THEORY IN PRACTICE

Copyright © 2025 by Universal Write Publications, LLC

Library of Congress Control Number: 2024926439

PRINT: ISBN: 978-1-942774-38-9
eBOOK: ISBN: 978-1-942774-43-3

Printed in the United States of America.

Mailing/Submissions:

Universal Write Publications, LLC
421 8th avenue, Suite 86
New York, NY 10116

Website: UWPBooks.com

This book has been partially supported with a financial grant from SAGE Publishing.

# AFROCENTRICITY: GENERATIONS OF THEORY IN PRACTICE

Aaron X. Smith, PhD

Editor

Assistant Professor of Africology and
African American Studies

Temple University

Universal Write Publications, LLC
New York, NY

# Dedication

This book is dedicated to Molefi Kete Asante, the scholars he has influenced throughout the world, and more specifically the authors who contributed so selflessly and thoughtfully to this Afrocentric compendium.

# Table of Contents

# *Foreword*

Imagine reading and processing a single, *grand* philosophy, idea, or paradigm that enhances the worldview and cultural logic of the current
generation. It gives them a new energy and enthusiasm to go back and
evaluate the collective histories and traditions of African people accumulated since the beginning of time. Then, it compels them to use their
intellectual and individual talents to teach local, regional, national, and
global communities about African agency, personhood, classical cultural
reference points, universalism, power, and victorious consciousness for
the sake of the memorial past as well as the bright future of African people, whether living, those who have transitioned, or those yet to be born.
*This is Afrocentricity.*

*Afrocentricity: Generations of Theory in Practice* is the first edited collection that primarily features the methodology of historically reflective
autoethnography to interpret the impact of Molefi Kete Asante's groundbreaking *theorization* of the concept of Afrocentricity. His idea formation
began in the mid-1960s, then he cemented the Afrocentric vision by the
publication of foundational, defining key texts that appeared between
1980 and 1987. From Asante's earliest, groundbreaking work on
Afrocentricity to his accumulated present corpus of works, the paradigm
has influenced thousands of publications and research projects that have
normalized and fortified the future of Afrocentricity. Before Asante's
theorization and innovation, Afrocentricity was a basic, but invigorating
adjective or description, waiting to be processed into the influential paradigm that it has become today. A cursory glance at Google's Ngram
function allows us to see that there were traces of the term Afrocentricity
in published intellectual discourse between 1897 and 1903, then again
from 1959 to 1971, then an explosion from 1980 to the present, with the
height of its appearance being in 2000. However, between the lines of
what we can trace through Google's Ngram, are a host of implications of

Asantean Afrocentricity that compel us to pay attention to Asante's and his Afrocentric proteges' and contemporaries' models of comprehensive institution building that has paralleled the flagship creation of the first doctoral program in Africana Studies at Temple University in 1988.

In 1991, the year that Temple University's African American Studies program graduated its first doctoral student, Niyi Coker, I was in my third year at William & Mary, thriving in a BA program in History, yet simultaneously hostage to a curriculum that never offered immersion into the history of Africa and the Diaspora. One year earlier, in summer of 1990, I had attended a special summer session of doctoral studies in History at Virginia Tech, under the auspices of a Commonwealth of Virginia grant to encourage African American students to pursue doctoral degrees in History. At the end of our grueling baptism into the workload of doctoral study, a rigor that agreed with most of us, we had an intimate luncheon and rap session with famed poet Nikki Giovanni. Our parting sentiment as our group dispersed was that while we appreciated the training in History from Virginia Tech's dedicated professors, we also lamented the scarcity of opportunities to engage in immersive study of the Black world. Collectively, we pledged to pursue doctoral degrees in African American Studies, instead. The caveat of this pledge was that, at the time, Temple University was the *only* place in the world where we could go to fulfill this pledge.

In 1991, when I shared by ambition to earn a PhD in African American Studies from Temple University with my mentor and recommendation letter-writer—Carroll F. S. Hardy, the famed associate vice president of student affairs who managed the campus' Multicultural Affairs at William & Mary and the founder of the Stuart Educational Leadership Group, Inc., that convened the National Black Student Leadership Development Conference for a 27-year run—she gave me a unique perspective as advice. In 1991, there were several nationally publicized articles on Temple's Afrocentric doctoral program that disparaged the approach and the degree as "religion" (Harriston, 1991) instead of scholarship, as "irrelevant" and "too politicized" (Magner, 1991), or as an approach that was "bogus," "pseudoscientific," and that made scholars "uncomfortable" (Early, 1991).[1] Dean Hardy, as we affectionately called her, advised me to not to earn the PhD in African American Studies but to try to study the Black experience through a field such as American Studies which would allow me to be more marketable. She also shared the general critique that Temple's program was troubled and unstable and that it would not be easy. The negative national press prompted such advice from mentors all around the country.

However, I had faith in this inaugural doctoral program and in my own ability to be invincible and to forge a path that would allow me to train and teach in immersion African American Studies departments. Again, Temple University was the *only* place in the world to earn this credential.

Temple's curriculum was astonishing because of its Afrocentric immersion. It differed from the training I received in my MA in African American Studies from the University of Maryland, Baltimore County, which was important and comprehensive, but not structured on a disciplinary paradigm for Black Studies. The MA program covered coursework on Black Intellectual Thought, Oral History, Black Literary Theory, Black Folk Culture, Black Cinema, Comparative Black Fiction, Comparative Black Poetry, and Comparative Black Drama. In comparison, the *disciplinary* coursework in Temple's *Afrocentric* African American Studies doctoral program offered even more immersion in grounded African and Diaspora worldviews and history. When I compare the MA coursework with the PhD coursework, there is a radical difference that Afrocentricity allows. What other department in the early 1990s could boast of an immersion curriculum with courses on Proseminar in African American Studies, African Civilizations, Research and Writings of W. E. B. Du Bois, Readings in African American Social Thought, Seminar on the African American Woman, Teaching African American Studies, African American Theater, the Afrocentric Idea, African Aesthetics, Seminar on Martin Luther King Jr., and Research Methods in African American Studies?[2] For the detractors from the late 1980s and early 1990s who questioned whether graduate students could gain a "proper" academic competency without taking the foundational courses of traditional disciplines, Temple University's doctoral program astoundingly modeled not only the possibility of what doctoral study could be in an immersive Africana worldview but also what the new normal and standard curriculum should be to train scholars to lead the future's Africana and Africology departments as a *discipline*.

In addition, the curriculum included informal seminars and training through Temple's commitment to host scholars and theorists such as Marimba Ani, John Henrik Clarke, and Asa Hilliard as well as formal, institutional creations such as the Cheikh Anta Diop International Conference, held annually in Philadelphia as an intergenerational training, mentoring, and leadership development appendage of the doctoral program. The article that my co-author, Bayyinah S. Jeffries, and I wrote for the 20th anniversary of the Diop Conference, "Ritual, Leadership, and Community-Building: The Cheikh Anta Diop International Conference" (2008), itemized how this conference paired with and functioned as a think tank, training ground, and professional rites-of-passage event for Afrocentric scholars and community development activists from around the world.

The all-plenary format—with the discipline's exemplars in the front rows— Molefi Kete Asante, Maulana Karenga, Clenora Hudson Weems, Charshee McIntyre, Kofi Opoku, Freya Rivers, Asa Hilliard, and more—forced emergent scholars to have courage, to be prepared, and to boldly accept opportunities for trial by fire, as the exemplars asked questions and gave peer review from the floor, allowing us to benefit from their wisdom and input in unprecedented ways. This was in comparison to the usual conferences in which it would be difficult to have prolific, senior, and famous scholars in our scattered conference rooms at the least desirable morning and late afternoon presentation slots. From such an audience with Afrocentric exemplars, each generation had the opportunity to meet, network, and excel literally sitting at the feet of the elders, as Asante nurtured and rewarded excellence and innovation for many of us by tapping us to deliver our first keynote addresses, by encouraging us to submit our groundbreaking research to *Journal of Black Studies*, and by giving awards for exemplary scholarship for books and articles. This trajectory is *comprehensive* Afrocentric institution building. Evidence of the intergenerational impact of this multilayered Afrocentric system of professionally developing the scholars who will be stabilizing the nation's Africana Studies departments in the future is the legacy of James L. "Naazir" Conyers Jr., a 1992 graduate of the doctoral program, who used the Diop Conference to network and collaborate on over two dozen edited collections that were responsible for giving generations of Afrocentric scholars opportunities to publish innovative work that continues to stabilize the discipline. Also, 1996 graduate of the doctoral program, Katherine Bankole-Medina, swiftly created the journal *Africological Perspectives*, which published grounded Afrocentric scholarship from within and beyond the Temple School.

Finally, Temple's African American Studies department hosted Black Studies professional organizations to provide on-campus or near-campus immersive Afrocentric events in Philadelphia such as the African Heritage Studies Association (AHSA) and National Council for Black Studies (NCBS). Thus, to have matriculated in Temple's Afrocentric doctoral program meant that students lived a multilayered, well-rounded, culturally reinforced, and rigorous graduate student academic life that functioned as a prosperous and successful village, where there were even opportunities such as the Pan African Studies Community Education Program (PASCEP) to model how to make university-generated knowledge accessible to the community.

Beyond developments that sustained the Temple School of Afrocentric thought, there are philosophical and structural dimensions of Afrocentricity that have been invaluable to sustaining the discipline. Informally, Asante advanced two notable philosophies that are part of the virtual handbook of disciplinary Africana Studies. The first is the standard question that he would ask at dissertation defenses: "*Why couldn't this study have been developed and completed from within another department or a traditional discipline?*" This inquiry challenged scholars to itemize exactly how the Afrocentric paradigm and other intellectual priorities of the Temple doctoral formula give the immersive degree in African American Studies a level of exceptionalism that is required to maintain disciplinary autonomy and distinction within the academy. As many of us know, without this understanding of the need for *immersion* and a discipline-based paradigm, Africana Studies departments struggle in terms of efficiency, mission, and clarity of leadership.

The second standard philosophy of Asante's Afrocentric vision is a charge to newly minted scholars: "*Your job is to create the textbooks that will stabilize the discipline.*" When a scholar matriculated in an Afrocentric doctoral program, a foundation of this training has been the understanding that the discipline requires autonomy in the academy because it is grounded in its own paradigm, priorities, worldview, logic, scope, and assumptions. In my own scholarship, the monograph *Literary Pan-Africanism* (2005) is the basis of my eponymous graduate course; the monograph *Black Cultural Mythology* (2020) provides the conceptual framework for my course on Africana Cultural Memory; and my critical anthology *Literary Spaces: Introduction to Comparative Black Literature* (2007) is a core text for my course on Africana World Literature. Asante's insistence on scholarly productivity that generates texts that promote Afrocentric conceptualizations has been a saving grace for the nation's Africana Studies programs because these types of texts model not only African/Black knowledge or content, but they also exemplify Africana disciplinary competencies.

As a final anecdote, I am honored to share that my training in Temple's Afrocentric doctoral program "planted the seeds of Redwoods." This metaphor reflects how, despite the rigorous coursework and challenge to achieve intellectual excellence that framed all the activity of my training in Temple's doctoral program, I embraced the challenge. After graduating and starting my first job in an autonomous Africana Studies department, I nurtured and tended the seeds of Afrocentricity that were the core of much of my coursework. Not only did I need to understand and digest Afrocentricity in its pure, structural, and textual forms (i.e., cosmology, axiology, ontology, epistemology, and aesthetics), but I also needed to translate it and operationalize it in my pedagogy to ensure that I was a proper steward of this gift of perspective. From this post-doctoral vision to interpret Afrocentricity—a process that Asante has always encouraged because he was aware that Afrocentricity is the foundation of diverse tributaries as each generation will add to it—I developed an Africana Studies rubric grounded in critical Afrocentric priorities. I teach this rubric in *every* course, and my students and I effortlessly subject every content area to this disciplinary rubric. It includes the following principles:

1.   Africana studies is the scientific and systematic study of people of African descent since the beginning of time.

2.  We have the privilege to draw on any episode of African history and experience to reinforce contemporary and future groundedness and objectives.

3.  The goal of this course is to train you to be masterful communicators with a high cultural competency.

4.  The credo of this course (and discipline) is that you will strive to create knowledge and inspire behaviors that will increase the life chances and life experiences of people of African descent, in particular, and of humanity, in general (borrowed from Terry Kershaw's [1998] Afrocentric methodology).

5.  We do not engage in trauma studies; instead, we view the Africana experience as one grounded in epic intuitive conduct and hyperheroic survival that allow us to focus on victorious consciousness.

6.  The discipline has an academic enterprise, which is the privilege to be in classrooms, learning and thinking while the rest of the world works a nine-to-five job, as well as a practical enterprise, which means that, at any time, as applied and functional instruction, we will pivot from exploring academic content to creating ideal programming that allows this content to be accessible for the community.

7.  We are an autonomous discipline that offers an immersive experience in Africana experiences with the goal to understand Black joy, Black prosperity, Black self-actualization, Black self-determination, and Black problem-solving.

8.  We work at the intersection of approximately eighteen subject areas: Black History, Religion, Economics, Politics, Sociology, Psychology, Creative Production, Culture, Aesthetics, Communication, Community Development, Philosophy, Pan-Africanism/Transnationalism, Education, Language/Linguistics, Geography, Gender, and Health/Science/Technology.

9.  Key concepts of the Africana experience are worldview, logic, continuity, anteriority, resistance, cultural memory, survival, and genius.

Many of these parameters are familiar to us because, after sixty years of agency-driven theory and practice in Afrocentric African American Studies, the language that stabilizes the discipline is collective and representative of the best idea formation that Asante and his Afrocentric contemporaries have invested in all of us. We go forth in clarity, rigor, innovation, and excellence because that is what we have been trained to do, and this autoethnographic volume of some of the most contemporary and innovative Afrocentric idea formation is a testament of the impact of Asantean Afrocentricity that is a transnationally utilized foundation of agency-driven curricula that address the experiences of African people.

Christel N. Temple, PhD

November 6, 2024

Pittsburgh, PA

## NOTES

1. See Early (1991). This article was based on the syndication of the *Newsweek* cover article by Henry Louis Gates that disparaged Temple's doctoral program, even though the issue included a perspective from Molefi Kete Asante.
2. Both of these lists of courses come directly from my transcripts.

## REFERENCES

Early G. (1991, October 8). Afrocentrism: Sometimes scholarship, sometimes religion. *Michigan Citizen*, A-2.

Harriston, K. (1991, March 10). As Howard University plans its future, Afrocentricity question looms. *Washington Post*, b01.

Kershaw, T. (1998) Afrocentrism and the Afrocentric method. In J. C. Hamlin (Ed.), *Afrocentric visions: Studies in culture and community*. Sage. https://sk.sagepub.com/book/edvol/afrocentric-visions/chpt/afrocentrism-the-afrocentric-method

Magner, D. (1991). Ph.D. Program stirs debate on the future of black studies. *Chronicle of Higher Education*, 37(40), A1.

# *Preface*

The disciplinary foundations of Afrocentric education grew exponentially in the 1980s and 1990s as Molefi Kete Asante endeavored to share the great news about the power of African agency and perspective within the academic and cultural revolutions he advocated for and symbolized. Throughout the next few decades, the world has witnessed the transformative ramifications of his innovative approaches to learning and actualizing from an African perspective: utilizing the ancient principle of Maat from Kemet, compelled by wise ancestors to create a collection of thoughts and concepts relating to the power, impact, and legacy of Afrocentricity. From the creation of the first PhD program by Asante at Temple University in the Fall of 1988 to elements of related theories that impacted fashion, music, and other aspects of pop culture. It was imperative to concretize an updated scholarly understanding of Afrocentricity from within the field.

Considering the consistent attempts from imitators and invaders to revise African history and minimize African contributions to civilization in general and education more specifically, it became vital to create an intellectual hedge of protection against such present and future onslaughts. From the invasion of Kemet by the Hyksos (1720–1710 BCE) and the intentional desecration of decidedly African iconography as a prominent manifestation of subjugation, I recognize a destructive pattern of Eurocentric distortion, suppression of African realities. Today, we continue to endure similar incursions to our peace and Afrocentric cultural identity under the guise of resisting Critical Race Theory, racist fears demographic shifts that could result in the Browning of America and even the banning of books. These struggles, which continue to this day, are a testament to the ongoing invasions and anti-Black attacks that Afrocentricity faces.

This work serves as a well-deserved celebration of the determination, courage, and intellectual prowess of Molefi Kete Asante and other great Afrocentric scholars. Together, they have created robust cultural and historical matrices that accurately reflect the history and ancestral empowerment through Afrocentric agency. The risk of African thoughts and ideas being usurped, exploitatively commodified, relegated to the margins, or callously appropriated remains ever present. This work was created to provide a corrected record of Afrocentric impact from the past, present, and potential future, and to reaffirm and reimagine all things Afrocentric.

For these and other reasons, Afrocentricity continues to grow in power and importance worldwide. This book was born from a need to reassess, reaffirm, reintroduce, and reimagine all things Afrocentric. I endeavored to solicit a variety of scholarly voices for this work. The contributors accurately reflect the growing diversity of thought and identity within traditional and emerging Afrocentric spaces. This text includes voices from the African continent to the Americas, representing females and males, and the increasing fluidity of perspective and identity. This diversity has added growth and excitement around where Afrocentricity is headed. This collection was formed to provide a triumphant historical reflection, a salient contemporary representation that will maintain relevance into the distant future.

This phenomenal, innovative think tank has held various informative and enriching events over the past 11 years—topics of discussion range from historical to political and cultural. Guest speakers at the institute included Zizwe Poe, Maulana Karenga, Marc Lamont Hill, James Smalls, Adelaide Sanford, and Samia Nkrumah. The institute helps address complex societal problems through the analytical and actionable lens of Afrocentric thought. This independent institution promotes an African culture in intellectual location as a standard for engaging concerns around health, wealth, electoral politics, international affairs, demographic shifts, and academic questions. The production of applicable Afrocentric scholarship is also strongly encouraged at the Molefi Kete Asante Institute. This book was encouraged by the great mission of academic agency, resulting in Asante becoming the author of over 100 books.

What better way to honor such a diligent producer of scholarly work than by creating an additional work that centers on what he has provided to the world? As the website explains, "The Molefi Kete Asante Institute was the brainchild of Ana Yenenga Asante, who sought a library and repository for thousands of books and many honors collected by Molefi Kete Asante. After much discussion, it evolved into a think-tank, bringing together ordinary African people with experts, scholars, and workshop leaders to offer solutions to contemporary challenges. Named for the most published African American scholar, Molefi Kete Asante, the institute bases its projects, mission, activities, and applications on Asante's vision of African agency in defining the African narrative. The institute was founded by Molefi Kete Asante and his wife, Ana Yenenga Asante, in 2011" (https://www.themkainstitute.com/new-page).

Lastly, the most influential party responsible for this book becoming a reality was the urging of Universal Write Publications founder Ayo Sekai. Dr. Sekai first reached out with an opportunity to act as a conduit to help manifest the beautiful brainchild this book has become. With over two decades of experience in research and educational publication, Dr. Sekai's expert opinion is esteemed. This text provided an outlet to become a vessel to collect and communicate the ideas held here. With the call answered, the ancestors helped assemble a capable team who created a collection of testimonies, analyses, and historiographies, which delivered an informative and inspiring presentation of *Afrocentricity: Generations of Theory in Practice.*

# Acknowledgments

Thank you to all supporters and developers of Afrocentric ideas. To my family and friends from Montclair, New Jersey, to all the traveling brothers and sisters, to the alumni of Temple University and the many institutions which helped in my overall development including the Christian Church of Philadelphia, the Molefi Kete Asante Institute, the Triumph Baptist Church, Frost Valley Summer Camp, the Freedom Schools of Philadelphia, Herbert E. Millen Lodge #151, and Phi Beta Sigma Fraternity Incorporated.

A special thank you to my parents and the Afrocentric innovators of tomorrow for all the positive Afrocentric expression you will bring into the world.

# Note from the Publisher

Universal Write Publications (UWP Books)
Ayo Sekai, PhD
Founder & Publisher

It is with profound reverence, ancestral pride, and an unwavering commitment to historically corrective and narrative-affirming scholarship that Universal Write Publications presents *Afrocentricity: Generations of Theory in Practice*, edited by Dr. Aaron X. Smith, with a powerful foreword by Dr. Christel N. Temple.

This volume is a landmark declaration of intellectual sovereignty. A sacred testament to the transgenerational force of Afrocentricity and to the scholars, cultural workers, and thought leaders who have carried this theory into praxis with love, precision, and cultural fidelity.

At the center of this work is the living legacy of *Dr. Molefi Kete Asante,* whose audacious brilliance redefined academic discourse by placing African people at the center of their own historical, cultural, and philosophical narratives. We are all his students. We have learned from him, been taught by him, and impacted by his teachings. This is also true for me. In addition to serving on my dissertation committee, he published 14 of his powerful titles with UWP, launching its foundation as an academic press. *Afrocentricity, as envisioned by Dr. Asante, is not a trend nor simply a critique of Eurocentrism. It is instead a paradigm shift, an assertion that African agency is essential and not optional. That our memory is foundational, not marginal. That our cosmologies are roadmaps to liberation, not relics.*

There are many values to calling oneself an Afrocentric Scholar. One task must be the proper orientation to western ideas. They are not superior to what our ancestors have thought and practiced. Afrocentricity is inherently a critique of the race paradigm advanced by all western epistemologies. Thus, all disciplines in the west are immersed in the idea of white racial domination. Our research and analysis must ask different questions, use a new language, and reject the so-called western gaze. The African Brazilians understand that the real identitarians are those who seek to stifle African agency. African people asserting their culture are working from a subject rather than an object position. I think it might be useful to center our thinking from this perspective.  Much can be learned by supporting a paradigm shift, which is at the core of our work. What questions can we answer that advance maaticity?—Molefi Kete Asante, PhD

In an academic climate that often commodifies Blackness while silencing Black scholars, this book stands in loving defiance that says, "We remember who we are." It says: *We do not require validation from institutions rooted in our erasure.* It affirms what Dr. Asante taught us, that Afrocentricity is not about imitating the West, but about recovering African ways of knowing, being, and becoming. It is about agency.

We extend our deepest gratitude to the contributors of this volume, whose voices span *the African Diaspora, Brazil, Asia, Africa, the Caribbean, and the United States.* These scholars have not only offered theoretical brilliance but also lived wisdom. They have opened their intellectual and spiritual archives to bear witness to the many ways Afrocentricity has shaped their lives, their classrooms, and their communities.

From essays exploring Afrocentricity in curriculum, identity formation, and community activism, to those mapping new frontiers in Pan-African political thought and diasporic solidarity, this volume is both a tribute and a toolkit. It honors not only where Afrocentric theory has been, but where it must go. *To that end, I would like to acknowledge one additional person who moves in silence, ushering in the birth of this book. When history is written, Geane de Lima will stand as an Afrocentrist.*

As a Black, woman-owned, doctor-led press, Universal Write Publications is proud to offer this book as a mirror, a monument, and a map. It mirrors the intellectual excellence of African people. It stands as a monument to the scholars who carved paths where none existed. *And it offers a map to a future where our ways of knowing are institutionalized without being diluted, where Afrocentricity is taught as necessary and imperative in all subject areas of learning, instead of tolerated as an alternative.*

To the students reading this, know that this book is a gift prepared for you by those who came before you. To the educators and activists, use this volume as both a guide and a source of inspiration. Afrocentricity is not going away. It is evolving, and this title is indicative of its impact, the generational passing of the baton, and those who will continue to develop this work in perpetuity.

We are honored to be stewards of this critical moment in Africana thought. May this volume be studied, cited, shared, and cherished as the foundation it is.

In enduring gratitude and scholarly revolution.

**Dr. Ayo Sekai**

PhD, Political Science

# Introduction

## The Legacy of a Critical Cultural Contribution

How does one person author over 100 books? How does a person use denial and resistance to fuel them in a manner that catapults them to greatness while etching their names in the annals of history? How do we use opposition to create opportunities for positive transformation and the realization of our most ambitious aspirations? How do we muster the boldness to envision the world anew and passionately pursue every method of molding those dreams into lasting, tangible realities? This work tells just such a story and many others. Afrocentricity, a transgenerational and transdisciplinary movement centering on African agency and truth, has taken the academic world by storm! The newness of the Afrocentric ideas, concepts, and facts led by Molefi Kete Asante introduced was as shocking to narrow Eurocentric academic sensibilities as the fact the carriers of the messages were overwhelmingly Black.

"Afrocentricity is a paradigmatic intellectual perspective that privileges African agency within the context of African history and culture transcontinentally and transgenerational this means that the quality of location is essential to any analysis that involves African culture and behavior whether literary or economic whether political or cultural in this regard it is the crystallization of a critical perspective on facts" (Asante, 2007, p. 3). The creation of a significant branch of disciplinary study is a distinction that few individuals can boast of. Enter Molefi Kete Asante and Afrocentricity. As the creator of the first doctoral program in African American studies internationally, his ideas and concepts are only rivaled by his innovation and persistence. The inspiration, scholarly publications, and reimaginations of history and contemporary realities resulting from the promulgation of Afrocentricity are vast and compelling.

The increasing emphasis upon and appreciation for diverse perspectives and the inevitability of demographic shifts create greater need and opportunities to discuss and learn about Afrocentricity. Recently, congressional hearings in parent–teacher conferences have been the site of contentious debate, sometimes descending in chaotic fervor based upon xenophobia related to critical race theory. "This comprehensive movement in thought and life created primarily, though not exclusively, by progressive intellectuals of color dash compels us to confront critically the most explosive issue in American civilization: the historical centrality and complicity of law and upholding white supremacy and concomitant hierarchies of gender, class, and sexual orientation). (…) Critical race theory there's an intellectual movement that is both particular to our postmodern (and conservative) times and part of a long tradition of human resistance and liberation" (Crenshaw et al., 1995, p. xi).

Although the concept popularized by Kimberly Crenshaw and inspired by Derrick Bell has reportedly never been taught in K-12 institutions, cultural consternations focusing on these demographics persist. These conflicts and fears of unavoidable changes in education and the nation have created a more intensified need to understand and potentially infuse Afrocentricity into broader academic conversations. New levels of involvement and engagement along racial lines have effectively permeated industries from higher education to presidential politics. There is a growing problem of intellectual narrowness plaguing our nation, which Afrocentricity can help to remedy. The broadening of academic imagination from the expansion of appreciation for diverse intellectual perspectives stands for a positive direction where Afrocentric thinkers can play critical roles in facilitating progress. While several conservative and racially insensitive politicians have petitioned to have books banned, which would serve to open the minds of millions of readers, Afrocentric scholars remain on a decidedly more empathetic and inclusive mission.

The importance of agency and achieving African diasporic liberation through self-determined outlooks and historical contextualization are magnified by the currently polarized racial climate and pop culture propaganda. We need to learn about, talk about, and utilize Afrocentric methods in a way that adequately addresses the challenges we face today. When Afrocentricity first began to gain popularity, there were several demographic shifts in legislative precedents simultaneously changing the face of America. As a comparative chronological analysis, we can highlight the immigration acts of 1986 and 1990, marking the evolution of Afrocentric thought and practice. "In October 1986, the U.S. Congress passed the Immigration Reform and Control Act (IRCA) and President Reagan signed the legislation into law in November of that same year. One of IRC's main objectives is to reduce the number of illegal immigrants coming to and residing in the United States" (White et al., 1990, p. 93). As the 1986 act sought to remedy unauthorized immigration through a multifaceted amnesty program, which included enhancing border enforcement and extending guest worker visa programs, Asante was well on his way to popularizing Afrocentric discourse in the states. Afrocentricity, the theory of social change, written in 1980, evidences a decidedly different academic tone, moving African Americans from the periphery of Eurocentric analysis into positions of their historical centrality. This academic shift was 6 years before the immigration reform and Control Act of 1986. So, as many new Americans were coming from Africa and the Caribbean with dreams of being naturalized, countless Africans in the Americas were coming into new levels of consciousness through their desire to be re-Africanized. The immigration act of 1990 establishes revisions by implementing H-1B visas available to temporary workers with specific skills.

This legislation also offered more significant opportunities for conversions from temporary to permanent status. For those not possessing such skills, the diversity visa lottery offered added opportunities to take part long term in perfecting our union. A year after this groundbreaking legislation passed, Asante released what could be argued as one of the most consequential of his early works, the Afrocentric idea, in 1987 (Asante, 1987). Here, Asante powerfully juxtaposes the problematics of European cultural hegemony and the residual oppression and exploitation of African people and culture, which has traditionally accompanied White collectivity within diverse spaces. A pivotal component of this chronological repositioning requires a recalibration from a Greek foundation to a more historically accurate African one. In the seminal work, Asante encouraged asserting Afrocentric agency by maintaining a victorious consciousness within and among us. Three years later, in 1990, Asante further developed his Afrocentric theoretical principles and positions in the *Kemet, Afrocentricity and Knowledge*. The release of this book comes just years after a new wave of members of the diaspora began an enhanced journey of citizenship. So, while people worldwide were blessed with the ability to travel to America in search of opportunity, contrastingly, hearts, minds, and spirits within the nation's borders were diligently searching for the opportunity to be self-determined and regarded for the fullness of their African descendants of humanity. Understanding the significance of the power of perspective as it relates to the chronology presented further informs the reader of why returning to and developing these Afrocentric conversations is vital now. Without the type of context previously provided, some may mistakenly assume that there is less of a need to continue discussing these concepts that were popularized decades ago. However, new generations of educators, readers, and truth seekers have emerged since the original Afrocentric renaissance. Others here yet focused on entirely different goals and dreams because they possess profoundly different world views than today. Although Asante's work had long established an international reach and transformed its sphere of Afrocentric influence, by this time, geographical changes, cultural shifts, and critical events were significant within the larger conversation of the value offered through new iterations of Afrocentric conversations. Active police brutality committed on people of African and Caribbean descent and America's engagement with leadership and unrest, which recently sought to utilize Kenyan soldiers to quell uprisings in Haiti, all serve to lift the veil of Eurocentric idealistic perceptions of America, which Asante endeavored to dispel. Asante's location theory is one of the primary methodological weapons used to dismantle Eurocentric obstacles to African agency. A primary differentiation between Afrocentric and Eurocentric analysis can be found in introspection. "The Afrocentric method insists that the researcher examines herself or himself in the process of examining any subject. Thus, the process of examination involves introspection and retrospection. Introspection means that the researcher questions herself or himself in regard to the topic under discussion period one might write down all one believes and thinks about a topic prior to beginning the research project the reason for this is to ascertain what obstacles exist to an Afrocentric method in the researchers own mind. Retrospection is the process of questioning oneself after completing the project to ascertain if any personal obstacles exist to a fair interpretation" (Asante, 1997, p. 88).

Afrocentricity is not outdated; instead, Afrocentricity utilizes the past to understand the present better and shape a more liberated, victorious future for African people. If understood and applied appropriately and effectively, the theoretical model point of Afrocentric thought can provide pragmatic and therapeutic remedies when many expect national and international racial reckoning to occur. Afrocentricity can be a cultural calm in a societal storm. It is the role of scholars such as those commissioned for this work to continue providing context and creative presentation of possibilities for Afrocentric ideas for the public's benefit. Through this innovative and effective teaching, Afrocentricity has been communicated in a way that imbued greater independence and pride in scholarly accuracy for students and educators worldwide. As a protege of Dr. Asante, I have always been vigilant in protecting the man, his ideas, and his legacy. I have been blessed to earn a master's degree and a doctoral degree in African American studies from Temple University in addition to three other degree programs I completed at Temple.

While taking classes with Dr. Asante and other leading Afrocentric scholars, I recognized a responsibility to keep the torch of Afrocentric innovation brightly lit throughout generations and diverse spaces. The creation of this work in cooperation with the many brilliant authors who gathered to make this text a reality has been the labor of love. Within these pages exists a palpable degree of affection and appreciation for a man whose profound scholarly contributions have inspired generations and helped to transform the world of Black consciousness and culture. Through lived experience and decades of intense study in addition to the production of scholarship, including manuscripts, edited volumes, encyclopedia entries, and book reviews in scholarly articles in academic journals, I arrive here prepared and confident in my qualifications. This book was created with an understanding of the confidence that must be coupled with the victorious consciousness necessary to liberate hearts and minds through Afrocentric locations. I am profoundly passionate about this text as it was envisioned to be a tribute to the mind of a man who has given so much meaning to the lives of others.

This work is also designed to assess the impact, effectiveness, and outreach of the theoretical framework of Afrocentricity. A further endearing motivation is this work's role in shaping and further cementing the glorious legacy of an incomparable intellectual in the powerfully lasting impacts of his Afrocentric contributions. Like the other authors who accepted the invitation to participate in this project, I have a remarkably esteemed and deferential pasture toward the love of light and learning that Molefi Kete Asante embodies.

Perhaps the opportunity to provide half was most inspiring to future generations. Young scholars and the yet unborn will one day carry on the grand traditions of ancient African scribes like Djehuti while breaking down mathematical equations like Seshat in efforts to positively impact and transform their environment. This work was partly written to inform and encourage our young people about their infinite power using Afrocentricity to help them recognize the strength of their incomparable history and present-day positive potential. Therefore, the uniqueness of the compositions comprising this work was intentionally organized to deliver a new contribution reflected upon existing scholarship. This work is infused with our hope in energy, which manifests the ardent desire to stray from the negative stereotypical pathological perceptual distortions that would serve to culturally dislocate, pervert, and paralyze the potential of our progeny.

We recognize and appreciate that today's avid readers are destined to be great leaders of tomorrow. To achieve all that is intended for their life regarding their destiny, purpose, and potential, we must feed their minds and their imaginations about the possibilities within their power to create and maximize. Lessons of their ancient greatness and modern manifestations of the same tradition to an Afrocentric lens represent an ideal balance of inspiration and applied intelligence to serve as a launchpad for future generations to believe and achieve within a paradigm of victorious consciousness and Afrocentric self-love. While writing for and editing this work, I paid particular attention to my elders' contributions and previous sacrifices and my responsibility to leave this world of Afrocentric understanding in a better position than how I found it for those who would come after me.

This book is another tool that can encourage us to spend more time training young people in an Afrocentric cultural and historical context while promoting options for parents and other adults to spend less time criticizing the children and more time creating spaces for them to grow positively. It is widely understood in academic circles that books can transform the mind in ways that can help develop the power to transform the world around us. This book not only discusses and describes Afrocentricity and the impact of its founders but also elucidates the proof, the theoretical principles, and the examples of success each author brings through their contribution and record of scholarship. Bringing together various creative minds to display various aspects and elements of Afrocentricity's power was not a simple task.

It was imperative that the "location" of the authors selected was of paramount importance rather than prioritizing scholarly efficiency or status in the discipline. It is also important to note how vital it is to have publishing houses such as Universal Write who recognize the importance and lasting value of Molefi Kete Asante and the work he has delivered to the world. The self-determination, agency, and professionalism exhibited by representatives of this publishing house made for the ideal partnership between protégé and publisher to appropriately commemorate decades of Afrocentric determination. This work's timeliness must also be articulated in the context of a valuable self-generated update from within the Afrocentric community. These current self-assessments help to exemplify the agency advocated by proponents of Afrocentric thought while protecting Afrocentric scholars and their ideas from the consistent misrepresentation of members of the community, their work, and even the title Afrocentricity that is commonly mislabeled Afrocentrism. This irresponsible and possibly intentional misrepresentation of theory is rooted in a 1997 questionnaire disseminated by high-school teacher Erich Martel on behalf of the popularly anti-Afrocentric scholar, Mary Lefkowitz. "The term Afrocentrism or Afrocentric as employed in this questionnaire refers to undocumented or misrepresented historical and scientific claims and assertions about ancient Africa, ancient and their influence on the formation of other world cultures and civilizations, especially that of ancient Greece ... these claims are largely made by writers who have not been trained in the research methodologies and skills required to objectively assess the evidence provided by the ancient text, art, technology, philosophy, theology, and cultural exchange nor the voluminous commentary upon them from ancient to modern times" (Asante, 1998, p. x.).

This book is an example of Afrocentric scholars speaking for themselves about themselves from an educated perspective rather than an antagonistic, uninformed, or predatory vantage point, which is all too often the case when Afrocentricity becomes the topic of conversation among the unenlightened. This for us-by-us standard will provide several benefits to the reader concerning the accuracy of information and correctness of historiography and conceptual clarity without contradiction, as all authors involved are well acquainted with Afrocentric theory and related literature. The understanding that Afrocentric thought, like other forms of analysis within the Academy, has grown beyond its walls is not in any way a fad or intellectual trend but the foundational element of a growing discipline that is here to stay while also boasting roots more ancient than all aspects of the traditional Eurocentric canon combined. Throughout the past decades of Afrocentric engagement, many read the material and see it as slightly exciting or inspiring. At the same time, others have always been galvanized to alter their life mission or adopt new manifestations of purpose that they seek to bring into the world because of encountering Afrocentric knowledge.

## AFROCENTRICITY MEETING THE CURRENT MOMENT

Throughout the difficulties of curriculum struggles, labor strikes, demographic shifts, and rising tuition costs, the world of higher education is entirely different when analyzed from the inside out. A significant issue of concern within higher education is the overall depersonalization and subsequent dehumanization of the learning process. The rate of technological advancement coupled with the recently imposed distancing and introversion of the pandemic have created a perfectly imperfect storm of unemotional, dispassionate dissociation. This tragic aloofness has found its way into the hallowed halls of academia, climbing the ivory tower with the skill of the Hadera plant often affiliated with certain elite institutions of higher learning.

This depletion of interconnectedness represents the problematic reality I seek to address and assist in some way with remedying and reconnecting what I view as brokenness within the college and university system. The methodological framework or blueprint I would rely upon to interrogate and explain the focus of my research could be effectively improved through a research approach that looks at the whole human being in our attempts to extract greater productivity from the faculty and staff while promoting higher scholastic and innovative achievements at all levels throughout the college community. A significant element of my research approach will investigate the connections between inspiration and innovation.

People must care enough to protect, inspire, instruct, and inform. Many scholars have generally analyzed the transformative potential of optimism (McLean, 2028; Peale, 2007; Ventrella, 2012), while others are more in line with my research interest who engaged the impacts of positive thoughts in academia more specifically (Nes, 2016; Yu & Luo, 2018). I seek to build upon research on the relationship between positive perspectives, positive actions, and positive outcomes, such as more equitable policy creation, programmatic and institutional outlets for support, and more inclusive curricula. The lofty and imaginative rhetoric attached to the stated purpose and spirit of most colleges and universities only needs to be actualized through compassionate and sincerely empathetic implementation to realize many aspects of my study's purpose.

I endeavor to answer the question: How do we transition from mere words to ways of being and from mottos and mission statements to truly empathy-centered educational institutions and experiences for those these systems are proposed to serve? It may seem romantic to assume that love and essential adherence to the golden rule can remedy most challenges in modern colleges and universities. My research approach in this regard is aspirational yet possible. With a practical application of Afrocentric methodology, I am confident that through engaging interviews, ethnographic analysis, curriculum changes, and perhaps most impactful, transfigurative, theoretical approaches. I sincerely pray that there will be those who read the words of this book and are motivated to learn more about African history, travel throughout the diaspora, and create systems and programs that promote Afrocentric thinking, living, and education. Someone may use this book, among others, as a catalyst to start their Afrocentric school or to include this work within the curriculum of Afrocentric institutions. For some, this book represents a whole new world far different from the academic experiences they have collected over the years. This new exposure and collection of insights and potential ways of thinking and being may have a similar impact to those experienced by great thinkers like Malcolm X, who encountered information in a jail cell, allowing him to unlock the chains on millions of minds.

Or perhaps more applicable to the current context and conversation, a young boy or girl reads this work like that young man from Valdosta, GA, who came up through the ranks of traditional education and popular regional manifestations of religion to become the premier Afrocentric scholar of an era. It has been said before that the role of a great teacher is to train their replacement. Whether directly or indirectly, all participants associated with this work can humbly affirm that we are students of Dr. Molefi Kete Asante. Here, we stand as diligent students to submit our reports. Our submissions include Ma'at, Afrocentricity's genealogical impact, legacy, personally transformative potential, and inclusive future. As the reader, we are a critical component to this future, and we welcome you to engage with, critique, find enlightenment and inspiration from this work we proudly present to you, Afrocentricity generations of theory and practice.

## REFERENCES

Asante, M. K. (1987). *The Afrocentric idea*. Temple University Press.

Asante, M. K. (1998) *The Afrocentric idea, revised and expanded*. Temple University Press

Asante, M. K. (2007). *An Afrocentric manifesto: Toward an African renaissance*. Polity.

Crenshaw, K., Gotanda, N., Peller, G., & Thomas, K. (Eds.). (1995). *Critical race theory: The key writings that formed the movement*. The New Press.

White, M. J., Bean, F. D., & Espenshade, T. J. (1990). The US 1986 immigration reform and control act and undocumented migration to the United States. *Population Research and Policy Review, 9*, 93–116.

# A Brief Annotated Bibliography of Asante Books That Deal With Afrocentricity

## ASANTE, MOLEFI K, *AFROCENTRICITY* (1988)

This text presents Asante's theory as "A philosophical paradigm used to generate theories and methods of analysis and correctives to the social economic and cultural conditions of African people" (abstract). In this work, Asante urges the reader to appreciate the necessity of merging around self-determination, self-love, and transcontinental and transgenerational cohesion as continental in the diasporic African people. Asante delivers a prolific Pan-African panacea for cultural and intellectual dislocation. Here, Asante reiterates the importance of appreciating the power of perspective when approaching information to interpret reality to increase African agency.

The impetus revolves around the idea of African peoples being centered within their own historical, contemporary, and futuristic narratives. This perceptual pivot has transformed the discipline of African American Studies. Agency is emphasized as a key agent of positive change for Africans in pursuit of knowledge of self and greater harmony with their environment. This text offers a meticulous theoretical road map, assisting willing journeymen and women in pursuing self-discovery, self-empowerment, and Pan-African liberation. This work also notes the deficiencies of critical opinions of Afrocentric theoretician's failure to engage the scholarship or display the expected academic rigor of utilizing quotes from Afrocentrists.

## ASANTE, MOLEFI K., *THE AFROCENTRIC MANIFESTO* (2007)

This title symbolizes an additional installment of Afrocentric transformation utilizing a manifesto's urgent and persuasive stylized structure.

Asante's declarations are less like a typical manifesto that argues political stances and takes a cultural position opposing the marginalization and appropriation of African history and related information. Asante posits thoughts within the more extensive historiography of profound African creatives of manifestos, including Frantz Fanon, Amilcar Cabral, and Maulana Karenga. Asante presents innovative Afrocentric ideas that articulate how Afrocentric location can disrupt Eurocentric hegemony with revolutionary results. One of the aspects that sets this work apart is the systematic nature in which Asante systematizes the extensive potential for Afrocentric methodology to impact all educational disciplines.

The expansion of potential for Afrocentric application present in this text provides excellent insight and inspiration regarding implications for future study. The articulation and affirmation of principles that comprise an Afrocentric location provide a creative cultural blueprint for readers to send to themselves within their own cultural and historical contexts, helping them find their way back to themselves intellectually. The emphasis on agency we find throughout Asante's works is present here. The tropes and the examples of the practical application of agency location and Afrocentric deconstruction of various phenomena. Within the analysis of the ideas and concepts of Harold Cruz, Patricia Hill Collins, Paul Gilroy, and others on the topics related to Afrocentricity Asante updates is analysis within the growing zeitgeist of Black Studies. This instalment of Afrocentric scholarship represents Asante reaching a new plateau of Afrocentric development and engagement with far reaching impacts within and beyond the Academy.

## ASANTE, MOLEFI K., *RADICAL INSURGENCIES* (2020)

Molefi Kete Asante presents a unique collection of the usage and practical application of ancient African wisdom within rhetoric, education, politics, and culture. This holistic approach to multifaceted challenges is garnered from select speeches and presentations provided by Asante throughout the years. Beyond the vast subject matter covered by the addresses highlighted is an extensive geographical range as events such as the Chinese communication conference and other gatherings of scholars held in British Columbia and the continent of Africa can be found within the pages of this text. The subjects of interrogation and discussion include the human future, new thoughts on race and racism, African art and restitution, and insurgent African university ultimate Haiti in de-westernizing communication.

Asante's positive, innovative Afrocentric outlooks within the larger context of African rebellion. From continental resistance from early invaders to enslaved Africans running from plantations in the days of Harriet Tubman and Nat Turner. Asante presents this work as a continuation of the struggles for freedom associated with names like Marcus Garvey, W. E. B. Du Bois, and Malcolm X. Radical insurgencies is a word comprised of speeches, thoughts, chapters, and other presentations which would create marching orders for future leaders in pursuit of African liberation from an Afrocentric context. From slave ships to parallels between modern institutions of higher education and enslavement plantations, Asante crafts a call for freedom which begins in the mind and lives throughout every page of this refreshing and rebellious work.

## ASANTE, MOLEFI K., *AFROCENTRICITY: THE THEORY OF SOCIAL CHANGE* (2003)

This work marked a reintroduction of Afrocentricity shortly after the start of a new millennium. This updated and revised version of the original text reflects the widespread impact of Afrocentric thought, which encouraged an expanded edition. Asante describes being moved by testimonials about how his work affected individuals, communities, and institutions, from increased advocacy for Afrocentric agency in educational spaces to religious leaders considering the impacts of Eurocentric imagery and replacing stained glass Messianic images because of Asante's intellectual urgings with so many historical events which occurred from the world of academia to the Global stage.

Asante revisits many previous ideas posted within a new context. The aspects of this work, which deal with future visions also, take on new meaning two decades later. Names such as Malcolm X, for example, went from a figure of the Black addition first emerging from the Nation of Islam to an icon of Black pop culture after the release of the biographical depiction directed by Spike Lee. This book encapsulates a theoretical approach on the rise, centering on the subject place of Africans within literary traditions, ethical paradigms, economic structures, and philosophical understandings.

## ASANTE, MOLEFI K., *THE AFROCENTRIC IDEA* (REVISED AND EXPANDED EDITION, 1998)

This work represents an overall response to criticisms directed at Molefi Kete Asante and Afrocentricity since the theory began to gain widespread popularity. The academic apologetics, which serves to resist mischaracterizations and other negative depictions, displayed courage, and victorious consciousness in the innovative theoretical approach synonymous with its author. Asante goes further by launching their critique of the Eurocentric foundations of academia while pinpointing elements like postmodernism within his critical deconstruction. High-profile thinkers of the day who commented on gates with Afrocentric thought, including Cornell West Paul Gilroy and Mary Lefkowitz, were also addressed.

Asante reiterates the importance of contextualizing culture throughout academic evolution and social change. Asante blends critical analysis with an in-depth pursuit of African truth while locating African culture and thought at the center of his analysis. The text is divided into three parts (the situation, the resistance, and the liberation), which collectively promote a culturally grounded collage of Afrocentric critical thought that highlights the weakness and insufficient lapses in traditional Eurocentric educational approaches and institutions.

## ASANTE, MOLEFI K., *KEMET, AFROCENTRICITY AND KNOWLEDGE* (1990)

This work marks Asante's successful attempt to erect an additional foundational pillar to undergird the emerging growing discipline that would serve the multiple aspects of Black Studies and African intellectual traditions. Easy accessibility to Afrocentricity is prioritized within these pages to enhance the overall experience with the more extensive work. This presentation further reinforced and popularized Africology as a discipline. Asante argues that his vision does not involve simply aggregating topics about Black people into various classes but rather a structured disciplinary approach that involves methodological grounding indicative of previous academic disciplines. Deep philosophical and theoretical questions were tackled from an Afrocentric methodological perspective seeking to remedy age-old dilemmas faced by Black scholars within Eurocentric institutions. From K through 12 education to institutions of higher education, this tendency to marginalize Black history, Black thought, and Black people persists. This text is cited as a love letter to the liberation of the African mind and spirit through a deeper understanding of African history and culture and the reader's relationship to this rich and empowering history.

## ASANTE, MOLEFI K., *AFRICAN PYRAMIDS OF KNOWLEDGE* (2015)

This contribution represents the globalization of the application of Afrocentric location. This text is built on viewing the world and being a global citizen within the Afrocentric context with an understanding of Afrocentricity as a paradigm that produces culturally and historically sound worldviews, centering on African people. After decades of Afrocentric interrogation, the evolution of theory, and the creation of multiple doctoral programs in African American studies worldwide, Asante revisits the impact and current progress of the methodological approach. The transformative potential of Afrocentricity is provided through a salient inventory of its vast impacts and potential for future transformative effects through a contemporary contextualized understanding.

### Afrocentric Thought

The use of ancient African principles in ways of being as a vessel to transform humanity expounded upon theoretical seeds planted decades earlier in previous works made by Asante. In resistance to Eurocentric parochialism and provincialism, Asante offers an Afrocentric remedy rooted in an understanding of human connectivity as old as the pyramids of Africa. These ideas representing the commonalities of the human family were further developed in later works, including *Being Human Being*, written in cooperation with Nah Dove.

## DOVE, NAH AND ASANTE, MOLEFI K., *BEING HUMAN BEING* (2021)

This text represents a modern application of Afrocentric principles that prioritizes the humanity of African people and all peoples worldwide. Molefi Kete Asante and Nah Dove present a powerfully clear and empathetic appeal to greater unity among the human family by deconstructing the intersection of racial hierarchy and problematic patriarchy during an era of extreme polarization, which fuels xenophobia and divisiveness of all types. This work is a breath of fresh, optimistic air that relies on scientific realities rather than social constructions as a common foundation for positive and humane interaction. This work seeks to dispel the destructive myth of race through the analysis of the human genome project, the African roots of all humanity, and the true perils of hierarchical structures disregarding the full humanity of many in the human family. By removing fictitious foundations of human existence, space is created for alternative examinations predicated upon reliable scientific evidence, challenging many cultural norms exhibited along racial lines in contemporary society. Being illusory destructive distractions of race is taken to task by authors who skillfully utilized an Afrocentric methodological lens, making a case for changing our perspectives, our language, and our implementation of racial falsehoods to envision our role on the planet. This text does not represent cultural and racial differences but presents an evolved understanding of these realities, which do not necessitate divisiveness. *Being Human Being* emphasizes the value of education in the fight against racism, patriarchy, and other forms of dehumanization. The authors skillfully articulate the negative results of failing to recognize our collective humanity while denying people the ability to express the same thoroughly.

# CONYERS, JAMES L. (EDITOR), *MOLEFI KETE ASANTE: A CRITICAL AFROCENTRIC READER* (2017)

With the vast abundance of scholarship created by Molefi Kete Asante, which includes over 100 books, a variety of readers would be necessary to encapsulate the magnitude of his scholarly contributions. James L. Conyers Jr. does a phenomenal job in beginning the process of strategically collecting aspects of Asante's writings, creating a brilliantly reflective mosaic of how he has implemented Afrocentric methodology over decades of work in academia and society. This work also provides refreshing insights from the editorial vantage point of scholars familiar with Afrocentricity who are not Molefi Kete Asante. The work is structured in the following categories: motif, history, mythology, and ethos. This work offers a unique opportunity to assess, deconstruct, and critically analyze Asante's work collectively.

The reader format also contextualizes Asante's various works within the more significant growth of the Afrocentric movement, which spans beyond the academy to politics, pop culture, and fashion. The history of great thinkers such as Du Bois Woodson and Clark is built upon through Asante's sizable contribution to the field. Themes of optimism and victorious consciousness, agency, and location can be found in this reader. Emerging scholars like Dr. Raven Moses are building upon the foundational Afrocentric information in this work through studies about amplifying Afrocentric identity.

This work also stands as a powerful testament to the intellectual diligence and scholarly efficiency of James L. Conyers Jr., a proud and productive former student of Molefi Kete Asante; legacy continues to reverberate through the work of the countless students he positively impacted before joining the ancestors.

# CHAPTER 1

## Branches of Igi-Osè: The Genealogical Impact of Afrocentricity

### Eva Bohler, PhD

The psychology of the African without Afrocentricity is a matter of great concern. Instead of looking out from one's own center, the non-Afrocentric person operates in a manner that is negatively predictable. He or she will attack mothers and fathers, disparage the very traditions that gave them hope in times of hopelessness, and trivialize their own nobility.—Asante (2003, p. 3)

## ABSTRACT

The baobab tree, referred to as Igi-Osè by the Yoruba people, symbolizes strength, life, and victory. A similar statement can be made of Afrocentricity, conceptualized by Molefi Kete Asante in 1980 in his groundbreaking work, *Afrocentricity: The Theory of Social Change*. Afrocentricity argues for the agency, centrality, and ultimately the victory of people of African descent, leading to a shift in perspectives on their histories, cultures, and identities. With this in mind, Afrocentricity has been the foundation of research from countless scholars in both Africana Studies and beyond, who see it as the most effective foundation for their scholarship and in many instances; Afrocentricity has also led many of these same scholars to develop various theories, frameworks, and paradigms that have in turn influenced the work of other scholars, creating a "genealogical impact." This is especially apparent today in the work of contemporary scholars. This chapter discusses (a) the ways that Afrocentricity has had an impact on the creation of numerous theories, frameworks, and paradigms; (b) how both Afrocentricity and its "theoretical children" have had wide-reaching impacts on scholarship, especially that of contemporary scholars; and (c) how Afrocentricity has had an impact on my own scholarship, especially how it formed the basis for the methodological framework in my work on Howard Thurman. This chapter aimed to be a significant contribution to the discussion around the invaluable impact of Afrocentricity, especially as it relates to a new generation of scholars.

**Keywords:** Afrocentricity, Africana Womanism, Paradigm, African Womanism, Asante

# INTRODUCTION

The baobab tree, called Igi-Osè[1] in the Yoruba language, is held in high regard on the African continent for its life-giving properties and how it symbolizes life, strength, and victory. The baobab plays an essential role in the African economy and the African ecology, lending itself to uses, including food, clothing, shelter, the burial of the dead, medicinal purposes, and entertainment (Wickens, 1982). As Igi-Osè plays a significant role in the ecology of the African content, the same can be said about Afrocentricity. In 1980, Molefi Kete Asante published *Afrocentricity: The Theory of Social Change* as a groundbreaking advancement in the quest to liberate African people. Afrocentricity advocates for the centrality and victory of African people worldwide, inevitably leading to a shift in perspectives on their histories, cultures, and identities.

Subsequently, it has become a focal point for the research of countless scholars in African Studies and beyond, who see it as the foundation for their scholarship. In many instances, Afrocentricity has led many of these scholars to develop theories, frameworks, paradigms, and scholarly works that have, in turn, influenced the work of other scholars, creating a genealogical impact that continues to expand, especially with the emergence of a new generation of scholars. This chapter is an appraisal of the generational impact of Afrocentricity and discusses (a) the ways that Afrocentricity has had an impact on the creation of numerous theories, frameworks, and paradigms; (b) how both Afrocentricity and its "theoretical children" have had wide-reaching impacts on scholarship, especially that of contemporary scholars; and (c) how Afrocentricity has had an impact on my scholarship, especially how it formed the basis for the methodological framework of my work on Howard Thurman.

This chapter aimed to contribute significantly to the discussion around the invaluable impact of Afrocentricity, especially as it relates to a new generation of scholars. It is important to note that the scholarship discussed in this chapter is an exhaustive list of its genealogical impact but merely a sampling of some essential scholarships that exist because of Afrocentricity.

## AFROCENTRICITY: THE FOUNDATION

Asante's *Afrocentricity: The Theory of Social Change* highlighted the importance of shifting the perspectives around African people. As African people have historically been viewed through the lens of Eurocentricity, Asante (2003, p. 2) notes the problematic nature of this analysis and argues for a necessary shift, defining Afrocentricity as:

> A mode of thought and action in which the centrality of African interests, values, and perspectives predominate. In regards to theory, it is the placing of African people in the center of any analysis of African phenomena ... In terms of action and behavior, it is a devotion to the idea that what is in the best interest of African consciousness is at the heart of ethical behavior. Finally, Afrocentricity seeks to enshrine the idea that blackness itself is a trope of ethics. Thus, to be Black is to be against all forms of oppression, racism, classism, homophobia, patriarchy, child abuse, pedophilia, and white racial domination.

The continual assessment of African people and African phenomena through the Eurocentric lens has consistently led to a devaluing of all things African. African dress, hair, music, food, art, etc. have often been seen and described as not as "sophisticated" as their European counterparts. It is important to note that the descriptor "African" encompasses not just those born on the African continent but also people of African descent throughout the Diaspora, and Asante's use of Africa as the primary descriptor (rather than African American, African Caribbean, etc.) speaks to a shared African origin and the critical role of Africa, not only in the histories of African descent people but also in the history of humankind. Asante (1998) posits that Afrocentricity centers Kemet as the focal point for African perspectives, like how Greece and Rome are the centers for European focal points. This is important because "Without the Afrocentric perspective, the imposition of the European line as universal hinders cultural understanding and demeans humanity" (p. 11).

The Afrocentric perspective pushes back against European intrusion on the agency of African people. Afrocentricity is both living and multilayered, and Afrocentric inquiry is based not only on a rigid, machine-like existence (Yoruba: ero bi aye) but also on how one interacts with the world (Yoruba: nlo pelu agbaye). This forms the basis for an Afrocentric scholar to engage with life and scholarship, as the two are inextricably linked (Asante, 2015). The multilayered aspect of Afrocentricity is displayed in that it is:

> both particular and general inquiry. It is inquiry in the sense that it engages the scholar creatively as a person who lives in the world; it is general because it operates as social inquiry encompassing psychological, cultural, and mythical dimensions of human life, thereby superseding the mechanistic model with its rather static profile. (p. 47)

Afrocentricity engages the human element, moving beyond being merely a method of inquiry and reaching into the daily lives of African people. This life element can be described as the living element of Afrocentricity (Igi-Osè). As it is focused on the agency of African people, its defining characteristics are characteristics that seek their liberation. Asante (2007, p. 41) notes that any Afrocentric project should include the following five characteristics:

> 1) an interest in psychological location; 2) a commitment to finding the African subject place; 3) the defense of African cultural elements; 4) a commitment to lexical refinement; and 5) a commitment to correct the dislocations in the history of Africa.

All five of the minimum characteristics are focused on African agency. A proper psychological location for African people is important because how one views their Africanness is the basis for how they interact with that Africanness and the world around them. The first element of psychological location lays the foundation for the others, as one's psychological orientation will undoubtedly form the basis for the other four characteristics, and any scholarship that purports to be Afrocentric must, at its core, focus on the five characteristics. Additionally, it is important to note the clear lines of delineation between it and other modes of thought. Asante (2007, p. 17) states that:

> Of course, one should realize that it is not simply affecting African styles and manners, but something deeper, more conscious. In fact, it is necessary to separate Africanity from Afrocentricity. The idea of conscientization is at the center of Afrocentricity because this is what makes it different from Africanity. One can practice African customs and mores and not be Afrocentric because Afrocentricity is conscientization related to the agency of African people. One cannot be Afrocentric without being a conscious human being.

Additionally, it is vitally important to distinguish between Afrocentrism and Afrocentricity, as the two have often been conflated. The term Afrocentrism has been used by those who oppose Afrocentricity and view it merely as the opposite of Eurocentrism. Most importantly, Afrocentricity precedes Afrocentrism (Asante, 2007). To this end, I would like to point out that the scholarship discussed in this chapter is the descendants of Afrocentricity, not Afrocentrism. Additionally, one does not have to be of African descent to be Afrocentric, as "Afrocentricity is to a matter of color but of perspective, that is, orientation to data" (Asante, 1993, p. 3). In examining the genealogical impact of Afrocentricity, its theoretical descendants display this orientation to data.

## IMPACT ON AFRICANA STUDIES

While a discussion of the genealogical impact of Afrocentricity discusses its disciplinary impact by default, it is essential to note its effect on the discipline of Africana/Black Studies. The discipline has a liberatory focus, so any output should consider this effect. Abdul Alkalimat (2021, p. 296) notes, "The foundational sustainability of an academic discipline is the productivity that performs its research agenda and feeds its curriculum. The research agenda for Black Studies has always had an antiracist function: it combats the demeaning influence of mainstream scholarship and affirms the humanity of Black people." Afrocentricity, with its liberatory focus on African people, goes hand in hand with the original mission of the discipline. However, it is essential to note that not all departments or programs named "Africana/Black/African American Studies," for example, are Afrocentric in their grounding.

A truly Afrocentric department or program would make, as its focus, discovering the centered place of African people (Asante, 1993). However, this is not always the case, as some clearly need to understand what African American Studies is. It must be remembered that Africana/African American/Black Studies are defined as "not simply the study and teaching about African people but it is the Afrocentric study of African phenomena; otherwise, we would have had African American Studies for a hundred years. But what existed before was not African American Studies but rather a Eurocentric study of Africans" (p. 2). Previous efforts at studying African Americans, historically from a Eurocentric base, most often led to incorrect ideas and perspectives regarding the worth and value of African Americans.

# BRANCHES

## The Afrocentric Paradigm

The Afrocentric Paradigm helped to lay a foundation for the understanding of how to properly define Afrocentricity, especially within the academic context. This was a watershed moment as it helped to remedy the confusion among those who use the word "Afrocentricity," however, clearly misunderstand what it is and what it asserts. There are three aspects foundational to the Paradigm: (a) cognitive; (b) structural; and (c) functional (Mazama, 2003). The cognitive aspect of the Afrocentric Paradigm includes the body concerned with knowledge.

For Afrocentricity, this aspect is expansive and continuing to grow. Mazama provides a detailed roadmap of the cognitive aspect of the paradigm; however, the importance placed on Africa as a reference point for Afrocentricity places it in a different category than other theories. Most importantly, the cognitive aspect of Afrocentricity and the African-centered knowledge that it has produced have been both influenced by knowledge from antecedents such as Frantz Fanon and Cheikh Anta Diop, for example, and influenced generations of scholars coming after (Mazama, 2003), exemplifying the generational history and impact of African thinkers. The structural aspect of the Afrocentric Paradigm relates to where and by whom this knowledge is being developed. For the Afrocentric Paradigm, the founding of the first doctoral program in African American Studies by Molefi Kete Asante in 1988 forms the basis for this structural impact. Mazama (2003, p. 31) argues that:

> The development of the first Ph.D. Program in Africological Studies was critical to the development of the Afrocentric Paradigm. It was a milestone. Not so much because the Ph.D. validated the African experience, but because for the first time we were systematically and consciously building an army of scholars who were going to challenge white supremacy in ways it had never been before, an army of scholars whose aim it was to finally set us free from mental slavery.

Temple's department and the subsequent scholars that it produced and continues to produce have had indelible impacts on the discipline of Africology and African American Studies, the academy, and spaces beyond. In "Temple University's African American studies program @ 30: Assessing the Asante effect," Patricia Reid-Merritt discusses the vast impact of this structural impact. As a result of what she calls the "Asante Affect," Reid-Merritt (2018, p. 573) notes the extensive effect that Temple's Department of Africology and African American Studies in general, and Molefi Kete Asante in particular, have had on the growth of the discipline, in noting that:

> Equally impressive is the level of scholarly commitment to the advancement of the discipline and to concepts, theories, and methods in support of Afrocentricity and Afrocentric approaches. There are journal articles, book chapters, essays, and editorials by PhD holders that are too numerous to name. They explore innovative ideas, revise old conceptions, and advance new paradigms of knowledge in the field.

The structural aspect of the Afrocentric Paradigm is seen in the impact of Temple University's Department of Africology and African American Studies and its impact within the discipline of Africana/Black Studies. The functional aspect of the Afrocentric Paradigm addresses its liberatory element. Mazama (2003, p. 31) notes that "In order to be considered a paradigm, Afrocentricity, it was stipulated above, must prove able to activate our consciousness, to open our heart in such a way that membership in the Eurocentric plantation is no longer an option." For Afrocentricity, knowledge is not produced merely for knowledge's sake, but there must be an end goal toward the liberation of African people.

## Africana Womanism

Africana womanism, conceptualized by Clenora Hudson-Weems, is an Afrocentric theory that birthed out a need to address the faulty nature of feminism, womanism (of the Alice Walker brand), and other related "isms" as they relate to women of African descent. Feminism, which was birthed out of a need to address issues facing white women, is not a viable option for women of African descent. Hudson-Weems (2020, p. 15) argues that Africana womanism is vastly different:

> Neither an outgrowth nor an addendum to feminism, *Africana Womanism* is not Black feminism, African feminism, or Walker's womanism that some Africana women have come to embrace. *Africana Womanism* is an ideology created and designed for all women of African descent. It is grounded in African culture, and therefore, it necessarily focuses on the unique experiences, struggles, needs, and desires of Africana women.

As Africana womanism is grounded in African culture and sees African descent women as subjects rather than objects in their own experiences, it is an integral part of the genealogical heritage of Afrocentricity. Throughout the discussion of its fundamental tenets, Hudson-Weems consistently references Afrocentricity as being one of the building blocks of her theory, as she sees it as placing Africa at the forefront in any analysis of the unique experiences of African descent women, especially in their interactions with African descent men (Hudson-Weems, 2020). Removing the study of the relationships between African descent men and women from a Eurocentric framework and rightly placing it within an African framework underscores the need for unity between the two to advance the collective victory for African people.

## African Womanism

African womanism, as conceptualized by Nah Dove, is an essential contribution to changing the narrative surrounding methods to address issues facing African women and African people. Birthed out of Afrocentricity, African womanism challenges patriarchy and its negative impact on the agency of African women and examines how patriarchy and white are intertwined, both working together to subjugate both African men and women in noting that "European patriarchy underlies the Western social inequalities that affect African women and men in equally perverse ways" (Dove, 1998, p. 517). The historical devaluing of Africa and its people and the spread of European patriarchy are both connected to Eurocentrism and the ways that African people and all phenomena around African people have been misrepresented, underscoring how European patriarchy and Eurocentrism are inextricably linked and displaying the necessity of an Afrocentric framework.

Additionally, African womanism highlights the importance of women in resistance movements, as women have played pivotal roles in both the formation and execution of those movements while still maintaining the role of nurturer, challenging faulty European ideals regarding the humanity of African children. Leaning on its Afrocentric foundations, African womanism argues that European influences have had harmful effects on the lives of African people (Dove, 1998). Like Africana womanism, African womanism underscores the importance of unity between African descent men and women in the overall liberation struggle (Dove, 1998, p. 535; Hudson-Weems, 2020), as "any future and continuing African liberationist theory and activism begin with the effort to recover, herstorically and culturally, the complementary relationship of the woman and the man as the basis for 'ourstory' and self-determination. In this light, therefore, African womanism as Afrocentric theory takes on a central and critical role in that effort." The liberation of African descent people depends on the relationship between the African man and woman, and restoring this relationship to African ideas is vitally important.

### *Invisible Jim Crow* and Agency Reduction Formation

Michael Tillotson's *Invisible Jim Crow: Contemporary Ideological Threats to the Internal Security of African Americans* and its accompanying theory of Agency Reduction Formation are rooted within Afrocentricity. A work that seeks to address the foundational issue facing African people—agency—Tillotson discusses a myriad of ideologies that have been harmful to the well-being of African descent people. As the list of those ideologies is extensive, Tillotson (2011, p. 60) discusses his theory of Agency Reduction Formation, defining it as "Any system of thought that distracts, neutralizes, or reduces the need and desire for assertive collective agency by African Americans."

Agency Reduction Formation is a response to the postmodern train of thought that seeks to devalue the collective identity of African Americans (Tillotson, 2011). These efforts are connected to the overall agency of African Americans. As a solution, "...if African Americans uncritically accept postmodernism, their need for collective resistance as well as the struggle for human equality will be neutralized and the current asymmetrical Black/white structural relationships in America will remain unchallenged and unchanged" (p. 66). In examining Agency Reduction Formation, it is evident that much of Tillotson's criticism of current systems is based on an Afrocentric standpoint regarding how many of these current systems negatively affect the agency of African descent people in America.

While *Invisible Jim Crow* discusses the reductive nature of postmodernism on African Americans, for example, Tillotson (2011, p. 64) argues that "... the uncritical acceptance of postmodernism in its current forms by African Americans, as located within America's cultural, social, and political projects, has the potential to lead to a collective political passivity of African Americans." For context, Brown (2002, p. 59) notes that "central to modernism is the fundamental and democratic belief that human life can only be improved via the application of human rationality." As it relates to postmodernism, it "is also the idea that for modernism's aspirations to improve people's lives, its history shows the opposite" (Brown, 2002, p. 59).

Asante makes a similar argument regarding the incongruency of Afrocentricity and postmodernism in *The Afrocentric Idea*. In his opinion postmodernism and Afrocentricity are in opposition to one another in terms of the issue of culture for African people (Asante, 1998), he argues that as postmodernism seeks to move away from modernism, and moving away from culture is a foundation of postmodernism. Additionally, "Afrocentricity cannot abandon the structuralism of modernism without betraying the achievements of culture. African Americans are a preeminently cultured people within American society, and our contributions to what is called 'popular American culture' are immense" (Asante, 1998, p. 9). Tillotson's analysis of problematic ideologies that have hindered the agency of African Americans and the solutions for restoring this have at its core, the people's best interests.

## Asiacentricity

Yoshitaka Miike's Asiacentricity is another branch from the tree of Afrocentricity. In "The Asiacentric idea in communication: Understanding the significance of a paradigm," Miike (2019) defines Asiacentricity as "the self-conscious act of placing Asian ideas and ideals at the center of any inquiry into Asian peoples and phenomena... Asiacentricity is against the marginalization of Asian views and values within Asian cultural contexts." Culturally, Asiacentricity positions itself as seeing the issues of culture and tradition as foundationally important (p. 51). As it sees the issues of culture, tradition, and ultimately liberation as being foundational, Miike affirms that Asiacentricity draws this directly from Kawaida, stating that "As the metatheory of Afrocentricity does, the Asiacentric paradigm adopts this *Kawaida* ('tradition' in Swahili) vantage point" (p. 55). Karenga (1977, p. 139) notes that:

> Kawaida critically examines various contributions to Black and human history, and makes a selective analysis of what is real and relevant, extracts it, integrates it into its system and then, puts it in the service of Black liberation. Nothing comes into being by itself; every person and thought draws and rises from the sociohistorical context to which they owe their existence.

In examining Asiacentricity, one can see the importance that Miike (2019, p. 55) places on tradition, as he discusses its implication with Asiacentricity in noting that "...by *tradition,* Asiacentrists do not mean the cultural essence in an ancient, pure, and stagnant sense, but they refer to a 'living tradition' that is always invented and reinvented and proactively blending the old and the new." Miike's discussion of tradition within the framework of Asiacentricity is directly drawn from Kawaida in that it is a continual process of analysis. In summary, Kawaida is an ongoing synthesis of the best in African thought and practice in constant exchange with the world (Karenga, 2024). The influence of Afrocentric philosophies on Miike's Asiacentricity is evident and additionally shows how its framework can be applied to other people groups to challenge the effects of Eurocentricity.

*Research Methods in Africana Studies*

Afrocentricity has also contributed to redefining research methods within the discipline. Serie McDougal III's *Research Methods in Africana Studies* seeks to address the significant problem of how research focusing on African descent people has historically been faulty because it has traditionally been centered on Eurocentric methods. This is why using Afrocentric research methods to research African people is imperative. Afrocentric research methodology has at its core, the goal of improving the lives of African people (McDougal, 2014). For this to occur, however, the research must be appropriately located. Asante (2007, p. 25) notes the importance of location, as "location is a principal activity of the Afrocentric analyst." McDougal (2014, p. 107) identifies several Afrocentric paradigms (e.g., Afrocentric Paradigm, Kawaida Paradigm, Pan-African Paradigm, Worldview Paradigms Analysis) and theories (e.g., Two Cradle Theory, African Self-Consciousness Theory, Nzuri Theory) that can be utilized in research on African descent people, along with Intersection Interests Theory (IIT) and asserts that:

> The realm in which an Africana Studies researcher operates is at the intersection of his or her interests and developing expertise and the needs and concerns of the people (people of African descent). The IIT approach is designed to guide researchers in the process of producing research that is interesting and important to them and relevant to the community.

IIT does not require the researcher to abandon their research interests but allows them to marry those interests with those pertinent to African descent people. An Afrocentric researcher will always aim to go beyond the research for research's sake and to conduct scholarship to find solutions for African people. Additionally, placing the well-being of African people at the forefront of research is a departure from Eurocentric research methodology that has historically caused harm (e.g., the Tuskegee Syphilis Study, Henrietta Lacks, and HeLa cells). Afrocentric research methods uphold the importance of identifying what is in the best interest of African people, forming the basis for ethical behavior (Asante,

2003). They place in high regard the importance of not sacrificing well-being for the attainment of data.

## The Demise of the Inhuman

Ana Monteiro-Ferreira's *The Demise of the Inhuman: Afrocentricity, Modernism, and Postmodernism* is another valuable branch of Afrocentricity. Monteiro-Ferreira's work analyzes African and European worldviews (Monteiro-Ferreira, 2014). More specifically,

> Modernism, Marxism, existentialism, feminism, postmodernism, and postcolonialism are addressed in dialogue with Afrocentricity as part of the two-way relationship between theoretical understanding and practice that challenges established and hegemonic approaches to knowledge in the attempt to make sense of the world while navigating the shattered ideologies of Western thought. (Monteiro-Ferreira, 2014, p. xxi)

The theories above are used to examine how they, based on Eurocentric/Western ideology and their beliefs, have been insufficient in addressing the essential need for liberation. Afrocentricity is utilized to dismantle these theories, and the subsequent bias has blurred the lens by which the European researcher has historically viewed non-Europeans (Monteiro-Ferreira, 2014). The usefulness of Afrocentricity goes beyond its benefit for African people, as a similar framework can be applied to other people groups (see "Asiacentricity" by Miike). Within the context of research, it is essential to underscore,

> The fact is that the use of an Afrocentric methodology to primary as well as secondary sources will prove an advantageous analytical and deconstructive procedure with which to divest the European research from the bias of the traditionally hegemonic interpretations of culture and history. It is also important to clarify that there is no incompatibility when using the Afrocentric methodology to the study of Asian, Native American, Eskimo, Aboriginal Australia, or even European peoples. (Monteiro-Ferreira, 2014, p. 35)

Monteiro-Ferreira's application of Afrocentricity ultimately examines how liberation can be achieved by reviewing and challenging systems that are part of European domination.

Black Cultural Mythology

Christel Temple's paradigm, Black Cultural Mythology, is "a renewed approach to stabilizing cultural memory that collectively ensures the preservation and recollection of African American and broader diasporan legacy using conceptual tools to actively engage the culturally relevant past" (Temple, 2020, p. 23). African people throughout the diaspora have relied on mythology as deeply connected to culture. However, European intervention in various forms has often threatened the preservation of diasporic African mythology. In constructing its framework, Black Cultural Mythology recognizes the classical African past (Kemet) and West African traditions as vital to understanding and preserving cultural memory and foundational to African cosmology (Asante, 2015; Temple, 2020). Black Cultural Mythology can also be seen as an act of Sankofa, which is reclaiming what has been left behind, or *gba ohun ti a ti fi sile* in the Yoruba language.

The Afrocentric Dissertation

Afrocentricity has dramatically influenced the work of PhD students, especially those who graduated from Temple University, including three of the individuals mentioned in this chapter—Michael Tillotson, Serie McDougal III, and Ana Monteiro-Ferreira. A review of doctoral dissertations from Temple University's Department of Africology and African American Studies shows an abundance of the word "Afrocentricity" in their titles. Some of these include "Mirroring Isis: An Afrocentric analysis of the works of selected African American female writers" (Barbara Marshall, Temple University, 1993), "From Incipient Afrocentric thought and praxis to Afrocentric thought and Praxis: An intellectual history" (Cecil Gray, Temple University, 1995), "Africological rhetorical theory and criticism: Afrocentric approaches to the rhetoric of Malcolm X" (Jeffrey Woodyard, Temple University, 1996), to more recent scholarship such as "An Afrocentric examination of Afrocentric schools: Status, identity, and liberation" (Naaja Rogers, Temple University, 2023), and "Soul as a gateway to erotic possibilities: An Afrocentric study of Black women's musical narratives as extensions of agency and freedom" (Danielle Macon, Temple University, 2023).

It is important to note that this list is incomplete. The lack of "Afrocentric" or "Afrocentricity" in a dissertation title does not mean it is not an Afrocentric scholarship. For example, "Black mamas on the screen: African matriarchy and African American motherhood in Spike Lee Joints" (Taylor, 2024). As the influence of Afrocentricity has spread far beyond the campus of Temple University, there are numerous dissertations from scholars at various institutions such as "Back to the classroom: Afrocentricity and teacher research in first year writing" (Perryman-Clark, 2010) and "A culturally centered study on hope: Africans as subject and agent" (Chandler, 2011). This speaks of the impact that Afrocentricity has had on generations of scholars.

## Personal Impact

In 2017, I took a course taught by Molefi Kete Asante titled African Philosophical Thought. During the course, Asante discussed theologian, civil rights leader, and African philosopher Howard Thurman, and until that course, I had not heard of Thurman. The discussion piqued my interest, leading me to do more research on who Howard Thurman was. As I did more research, I found myself quite intrigued, and this was a pivotal moment in the development of my scholarship, which led me to eventually settle on my dissertation topic, "Afrocentric analysis of the philosophies of Howard Thurman." In formulating this topic, I was genuinely interested in whether Thurman's philosophies contained anything that could lead him to be included as an Afrocentric philosopher, and undoubtedly, Afrocentricity played a pivotal role in my methodology.

During the process of formulating my literature review, I found that there was a shortage of works examining Howard Thurman from an Afrocentric lens:

> For example, writings such as Walter E. Fluker's *They Looked for a City: A Comparative Analysis of the Ideal of Community in the Thought of Howard Thurman and Martin Luther King, Jr.* and Luther E Smith, Jr's Howard Thurman: *The Mystic as Prophet* has been from a Eurocentric base. (Bohler, 2021, p. 2)

The goal of my work was twofold: (a) to analyze Thurman's philosophies via Afrocentricity and (b) add this Afrocentric analysis of Thurman to the body of literature on Thurman. To do this, I read several of his works and placed them in two categories: community and mysticism. I then examined those works closely to determine Thurman's connection, if any, to Afrocentricity. For example, Thurman places a premium on the importance of community. I determined that the importance of community and human relations as it exists within Thurman's philosophies has a connection to *Njia,* which is "the collective expression of the Afrocentric worldview which is grounded in the historical experiences of African people" (Asante, 2003, p. 30).

In an analysis of Thurman's philosophies, I included a study of his rhetoric, as one's rhetorical condition is a guide by which their location can be determined (Asante, 1998). Additionally,

> The protester must use symbols, myths, and sounds that are different from those of the established order. Otherwise, the protest speaker can never use the language of the established order with as much skill as the establishment. The oppressed must gain attention and control by introducing another language, another sound. (Asante, 1998, p. 127)

I argue that:

> In terms of discussing Thurman's rhetoric, it is important to discuss whether his rhetoric is using the language of the oppressor or whether he is using the language of the oppressed. It is important to note that can also be seen within the mythoforms and whether there is a connection drawn from the culture of the oppressed. Ultimately, the goal should be to create a means of protest that utilizes a different stream of rhetoric that has traditionally been used by the oppressor. (Bohler, 2021, p. 183)

In my analysis, I discovered that, while there were some connections to various ideas in Afrocentricity, there was not enough to consider them as Afrocentric nor sufficient to consider him an Afrocentric philosopher. It is important to note that "to determine that a project is Afrocentric, it must first be centered in Africa, and, while this examination discovered elements within that could be seen as connected to Afrocentricity, Thurman's philosophies are lacking in a number of the required elements for a project to be deemed Afrocentric, but this does not in any way diminish his philosophical contributions, especially to African descended people" (Bohler, 2021). As a result of this research, I was able to implement Afrocentricity as a framework for analysis that I can implement in further study.

As a scholar, I can affirm that Afrocentricity has transformed my scholarship. Before my time at Temple University (for both the Master of Arts in African American Studies and the Doctor of Philosophy in Africology and African American Studies), I assumed that the term "Afrocentric" referred to a style of dress, a genre of literature, and a type of music; however, as I have learned and grown to appreciate, it is much more than merely those expressions, as Afrocentricity is for the victory of African people.

## CONCLUSION

Part of the strength of Afrocentricity is immeasurable, as it has been influential in the development of countless theories, methodologies, and scholarly work, and those theories, methods, and literary works have gone on to influence a newer generation of scholars. This genealogical impact is one that undoubtedly will continue for generations to come. It can be said that part of the strength of Afrocentricity lies in its ability to withstand the test of time and its impact on generations of scholars. As Igi-Osè is solid and resilient, ensuring its survival and its ability to nourish multiple generations of people who depend on it for their survival, the same can be said of Afrocentricity, which has an expansive genealogical impact.

## NOTE

1. Yoruba words and phrases are used throughout this chapter to show the beauty and value of African language. As a woman of African descent, I felt it important to use a language some of my African ancestors spoke.

## REFERENCES

Alkalimat, A. (2021). *The history of Black studies*. Pluto Press. https://doi.org/10.2307/j.ctv2114fqn

Asante, M. K. (1993). *Malcolm X as cultural hero & other Afrocentric essays*. Africa World Press.

Asante, M. K. (1998). *The Afrocentric idea*. Temple University Press.

Asante, M. K. (2003). *Afrocentricity: The theory of social change*. African American Images.

Asante, M. K. (2007). *An Afrocentric manifesto*. Polity Press.

Asante, M. K. (2015). *African pyramids of knowledge: Kemet, Afrocentricity and Africology*. Universal Write Press.

Bohler, E. D. (2021). *An Afrocentric analysis of the philosophies of Howard Thurman* [Doctoral dissertation]. Temple University.

Brown, S. (2002). Postmodernism. In G. Blakeley & V. Bryson (Eds.), *Contemporary political concepts: A critical introduction* (pp. 54–72). Pluto Press. https://doi.org/10.2307/j.ctt18fs3n8.7

Chandler, D. R. (2011). *A culturally centered study on hope: Africans as subject and agent* [Doctoral dissertation]. University of Wisconsin—Madison.

Dove, N. (1998). African womanism: An Afrocentric theory. *Journal of Black Studies, 28*(5), 515–539. http://www.jstor.org/stable/2784792.

Gray, C. C. (1995). *From incipient Afrocentric thought and praxis to Afrocentric thought and praxis: An intellectual history.* Temple University.

Hudson-Weems, C. (2020). *Africana womanism: Reclaiming ourselves* (5th ed.). Routledge.

Karenga, M. R. (1977). Kawaida and its critics: A sociohistorical analysis. *Journal of Black Studies, 8*(2), 125–148. http://www.jstor.org/stable/2783872

Karenga, M. (2024). *Philosophies, principles, and program.* Us Organization. https://www.us-organization.org/30th/ppp.html

Macon, D. S. (2023). *Soul as a gateway to erotic possibilities: An Afrocentric study of Black women's musical narratives as extensions of agency and freedom.* Temple University.

Marshall, B. J. (1993). *Mirroring Isis: An Afrocentric analysis of the works of selected African American female writers.* Temple University.

Mazama, A. (2003). The Afrocentric paradigm. In A. Mazama (Ed.), *The Afrocentric paradigm* (p. 31). Africa World Press.

McDougal III, S. (2014). *Research methods in Africana studies.* Peter Lang Publishing.

Miike, Y. (2019). *The Asiacentric idea in communication: Understanding the significance of a paradigm.* https://hilo.hawaii.edu/documents/depts/communication/YoshitakaMiikeSeinanStudiesinEnglishLanguageandLiteratureVol.60No.1July2019pp.49-73.pdf

Monteiro-Ferreira, A. (2014). *The demise of the inhuman.* SUNY Press.

Perryman-Clark, S. M. (2010). *Back to the classroom: Afrocentricity and Teacher-research in First-year Writing.* Michigan State University.

Reid-Merritt, P. (2018). Temple University's African American studies PhD program @ 30: Assessing the Asante affect. *Journal of Black Studies, 49*(6), 559–575. https://www.jstor.org/stable/26574581.

Rogers, N. N. (2023). *An Afrocentric examination of Afrocentric schools: Status, agency, and liberation.* Temple University.

Taylor, M. B. (2024). *Black mamas on the screen: African matriarchy and African American motherhood in spike lee joints* [Doctoral dissertation]. Temple University.

Temple, C. N. (2020). *Black cultural mythology.* SUNY Press.

Tillotson, M. (2011). *Invisible Jim Crow: Contemporary ideological threats to the internal security of African Americans.* Africa World Press.

Wickens, G. E. (1982). The Baobab: Africa's upside-down tree. *Kew Bulletin, 37*(2), 173–209. https://doi.org/10.2307/4109961

Woodyard, J. L. (1996). *Africalogical rhetorical theory and criticism: Afrocentric approaches to the rhetoric of Malcolm X.* Temple University.

# CHAPTER 2

## The Asantian Perspective: Critical Insights into Molefi Kete Asante's Conceptualization of Afrocentric Theory

Louis Walee, PhD

### ABSTRACT

Afrocentricity is a socio-intellectual theory that privileges the centrality of events and phenomena that make up the African experience. As a theory of agency, cultural centrism, and human freedom, Afrocentricity asserts that people of African descent are subjects in their own historical and cultural narrative and are capable of self-determination, an essential part of human agency. As a paradigm encompassing various assumptions, concepts, and theories, Afrocentricity is best conceived and operationalized as a meta-paradigm in the discipline of Africology, representing the most recent intellectual and disciplinary advancement of what has historically been called Black Studies, African American Studies, and Africana Studies among other nomenclature.

The originator of the Afrocentric idea is Molefi Kete Asante, full professor and long-time chair of the department of Africology and African American Studies, which is the first PhD program in African American Studies in the world at Temple University in Philadelphia, PA. As the architect behind Afrocentricity, Asante's theoretical perspective on the African and broader human reality has been widely acclaimed and recognized as an intellectual formation integral to the disestablishment of hierarchical systems of hegemonic discourse and, therefore, toward the greater possibility of inaugurating genuine human freedom.

This chapter seeks to accomplish three objectives: The first is to define Molefi Kete Asante's conceptualization of Afrocentric theory properly; the second objective is to locate the impact Afrocentricity has had on the discipline of Black Studies (Africology); and the third is to provide conceptual clarity and clear definition, which is needed to address and rectify the conceptual distortions concerning Afrocentricity and disciplinary Black Studies (Africology). Ultimately, this chapter aims to illustrate and celebrate the merits of Asante's intellectual formations about the discipline and the epistemic prominence and applicability of Afrocentricity as a theory of social change designed to improve the quality of African and broader human life on this earth.

**Keywords:** Afrocentric Theory, Afrocentricity, Eurocentric Criticism, Doctoral Program

## THE CATALYST: MOLEFI KETE ASANTE'S AFROCENTRIC IDEA

Afrocentricity is a paradigmatic intellectual perspective that privileges African agency within the context of African history and culture trans continentally and trans-generationally.—Molefi Kete Asante, *An Afrocentric Manifesto: Toward an African Renaissance* (2007, p. 2)

I have often said that *the catalyst must be courageous*, meaning that the impulse or driving force behind a particular event must be unyielding at its inception. My line of thinking here is that for anything of merit to exist and gain recognition, it must ensure its presence is felt. With this quality of fury, it is easy for any assumption, belief, idea, or sentiment theory to fully take off and reach escape velocity (so to speak). With the emergence of Afrocentricity, we are presented with a catalyst whose dynamism, zeal, and expansiveness are usually felt by its quality of moral and intellectual integrity, sensibility, and genius. Afrocentricity is a socio-intellectual theory created by Molefi Kete Asante, the world's leading theorist on Afrocentric theory (Karenga, 2007; Zulu, 2008), who defines *Afrocentricity* as "a mode of thought and action in which the centrality of African interest, values, and perspectives predominate. Concerning theory, it is the placing of African people at the center of any analysis of African phenomena" (Asante, 2003, p. 2).

A centric theory is the one concerned with the quality of cultural and historical centeredness or groundedness of a particular group of people (Asante, 1990; McDougal III, 2017). Afrocentricity asserts the centrality of experiences that constitute the lives and reality of African people as its primary metaphysical assumption and theoretical focus. Afrocentricity looks to examine the assumptions, beliefs, experiences, habits, inclinations, ideas, interests, perspectives, sentiments, thoughts, and values that predominate the conscious and subconscious minds of African people, both transgenerationally and transnationally, from the cultural, historical, and psychological standpoint of African descendant people themselves.

As such, the theory locates *African people*, that is, those bearing full or partial ancestry to the African continent and possessing cultural, historical, and psychological characteristics particular to African humanity (self-cite), as subjects, as human beings worthy of admiration, consideration, and respect regarding the human experience as opposed to objects, inhuman or depersonalized beings (Asante, 1992). Afrocentricity is also a theory of *agency*, which refers to the quality of "playing a self-conscious and active role in shaping one's destiny" (McDougal III, 2017, p. 41), and the theory regards African people as *agents* or as humans who are capable of self-determining and acting on behalf of their own best interest (Asante, 2007).

Where centrism grounds one in their history and culture, the agency provides the cultural and psychological resources necessary to establish true human freedom (Asante, 2007). Finally, Afrocentricity is a theory of conscientization and is a perspective that is concerned with African consciousness, particularly *victorious consciousness* or the state of "knowledge and awareness that African people have been victorious in the past and will be victorious in the future" (McDougal III, 2017, p. 41). Essentially, it is difficult to have a centric understanding of one's history and culture and exercise agency if one first lacks a quality of consciousness informing who they are, where they have come from, and what is possible (to achieve; McDougal III, 2017). As a theory with various facets that seeks to illuminate the African self-image and conceptualize (or reconceptualize) the deeper cultural-historical experience of African people (Asante, 2006). Afrocentricity, according to Karenga (1988, p. 404), is:

> A quest for and an expression of historical and cultural anchor, a critical reconstruction that dares to restore missing and hidden parts of our historical self-formation and pose the African experience as a significant paradigm for human liberation and a higher level of human life.

Afrocentricity is also a theory of social change (Anderson, 2012; Asante, 2003, 2007) that, as an area of primary focus, seeks to consciously advance people of African descent in every dimension of society (Karenga, 1988; McDougal III, 2014, 2017; Tillotson & McDougal, 2013); moreover, Afrocentricity seeks to reconstruct societal relations by attacking infrastructures that advance hierarchies (i.e., racism, classism, sexism) which restrict genuine human agency, expression, and freedom, and ultimately hinders the ability to advance a genuine initiative centered around cultivating cultural pluralism, as "a fundamental steppingstone to any multicultural project" (Asante, 1992, p. 21).

Afrocentricity is a revolutionary theoretical perspective that can initiate a true cultural pluralistic (or multicultural) project because the theory is nonhierarchical, non-hegemonic, and antiracist (Asante, 1991) and instead it aims at establishing a centered position where all members of society can coexist in a condition of harmony, peace, and mutual understanding (Asante, 1991, 1992). Thus, as a theory of social change, Afrocentricity can be defined and perceived as "a model for intercultural agency in which pluralism exists without hierarchy and respect for cultural origins, achievements, and prospects is freely granted" (Asante, 1998, p. xii, 42).

## VISION AND PURPOSE: MOLEFI KETE ASANTE'S INTELLECTUAL CONTRIBUTIONS TO BLACK STUDIES

I am a child of the Black Studies Movement, having been born to it in the late night and early morning labors of love and emotion that saw young men and women at UCLA, members of the Harambee Club, and later SNCC-UCLA of which I was chair, totally absorbed in the creation of the new, the novel, the radical.—Molefi Kete Asante, *African American Studies: The Future of the Discipline* (1992, p. 22)

Born in Valdosta, Georgia (Asante, 2007, 2020a), Molefi Kete Asante was a member of the student protest movements that characterized the Black Freedom Struggle of the 1960s, which called for the creation of a social and academic enterprise to represent the communal, political, and intellectual needs of African Americans, Black Studies (Asante, 2018, 2020a; Karenga, 2007). An avid learner, philosophical, and visionary, Asante would earn his PhD as a junior professor at the University of California, LA (UCLA) at the age of 26, receive the status of full professor at the State University of New York at 30 years of age, and create the first doctoral degree-granting academic department in African American Studies in the world at Temple University in 1988 in Philadelphia, PA (Asante, 1992, 2007; Karenga, 2007; Zulu, 2008).

As one of the world's leading theorists and disciplinary experts regarding Black Studies, Afrocentricity is arguably Asante's most potent intellectual contribution to development, maintenance, and maturation. However, often, the impact of Asante's scholarly contributions has not been thoroughly located nor examined, whether unintentionally or otherwise, which I argue dismisses Asante's critical influence, creative genius, and, quite frankly, the necessity of Asante's theoretical formations, which where undoubtedly needed to create a concise and clear picture of what Black Studies is, why it exists, and how it functions as a modern academic discipline with a particular theoretical (Afrocentric) basis.

*(A) Epistemic Identity*

To provide a corrective to this precedence, and to give Asante his flowers, I list the five areas of conceptual or functional impact: epistemic identity, doctoral program, naming, Eurocentric critique, and conscientization, which Asante has provided about the discipline. I start with the restatement that (A) one of the most salient conceptual contributions Molefi Kete Asante has provided toward Black Studies disciplinarity is epistemic identity as specifically located in the Afrocentric Idea, that which became, according to Karenga (1988, p. 403) "a fundamental building bloc in the conceptual edifice of the Black Studies paradigm" as "a Black Studies philosophy must begin self-consciously and self-definitionally as an Afrocentric enterprise."

Afrocentricity necessitates the examination of African phenomena that abide by a "conscious process by which a person locates or relocates

African phenomena within an African subject content or agency and action" (Asante, 2002, p. 97). Therefore, it is with this unique and distinct definitive perspective that the study of African culture, history, people and life be solely based upon (Karenga, 1988). Asante advanced an epistemic position that fundamentally changed the way African phenomena were viewed, both within Black Studies and all other academic disciplines, because he asserted, kept, and defended the perspective that phenomena be apprehended from the standpoint of African people as both subjects and agents in their own cultural and history narrative:

> No intellectual of African descent or otherwise in the late 20th century and early 21st century had been this committed to a centric perspective about African humanity. Thus, the Afrocentric Idea is a quality of thought that is still a conceptual foundation of Black Studies and the field's future.

### (B) Doctoral Program

Secondly, because of the consistency, grit, and vision of Molefi Kete Asante (B), we now have the first PhD program in African American Studies. Where Nathan Hare, the late "Godfather of Black Studies," was responsible for creating the first Black Studies Department at San Francisco State University, which was formerly called San Francisco State College, in 1968 (Asante, 2007; Hare, 1968; Karenga, 2005); 20 years later Asante brought the movement for Black Studies full circle with the creation of the world's first doctoral degree-granting academic discipline in Black Studies at Temple University in Philadelphia, PA (Asante, 2018). As Asante explains in his *Journal of Black Studies* (*JBS*) article "The relentless pursuit of discipline: An Africological march toward knowledge liberation," the path toward the creation of the first doctorate in African American Studies was indeed an arduous process; however, regarding this endeavor, Asante (2018, p. 540) states that he and his fellow Afrocentrist "understood the Afrocentric mission to create a discipline" and thus nothing could stand against the movement for a doctorate program in Black Studies.

### (C) Naming

Speaking of Black Studies, therein lies a third contribution (or critique) Asante raised about the discipline (C) that of naming. Asante has preferred to refer to the academic discipline that emerged in the American academy, Black Studies, as *Africology*, which can be defined as "the Afrocentric examination of African phenomena related to African people" (Van Horne, 2007, p. 60). Though Asante (2009, p. 12) states, "I think the term Black Studies was quite illuminating because it introduced a new perspective about information," he identifies both disciplinary and conceptual pitfalls regarding the name of the discipline. Firstly, though I, many others, and Asante himself have referred to Black Studies as a discipline, which is a byproduct of scholars in our area being familiar and comfortable with the of our field, technically, Black Studies being called "Black Studies," it is an area or field of study. A field or area of study refers to a scope of examination that is quite open and general in design, meaning that it lacks *discipline*, or a committed perspective shared by a community of practitioners regarding a certain area of inquiry (self-cite). Every discipline, be it anthropology, history, political science, psychology, sociology, or Africology, has its actions, concepts, theories, methods, and paradigms unique to that discipline. Furthermore, every discipline has a particular focus which fuels research interest and guides research which Afrocentric scholar Serie McDougal III (2017, p. 4) cites as the *domain of inquiry*, explaining:

> Every discipline has a domain of inquiry: for example, political phenomena for political science and psychological phenomena for psychology. The domain of inquiry refers to the specific aspects, subsets, or dimensions of reality on which a discipline focuses its thought.

Africology is the preferred word used by Asante and others to refer to Black Studies, also called African American Studies, Africana Studies, and Pan-African Studies. Henceforth, these names are often used interchangeably to refer to the same field (despite specific conceptual differences between each name). It is not simply the study of African phenomena that makes for an intellectual project; it is the *Afrocentric* examination of African phenomena that makes for an Africological enterprise (Asante, 1992; Tillotson & McDougal, 2013). Here, the keyword is "Afrocentric," which identifies and disambiguates the quality of perspective utilized to examine African phenomena (Asante, 2009). It is, in principle, this degree of disciplinary perspective that differentiates Africology from Black Studies, alongside the "ology" suffix which means "the study of" which allows Africology to be quickly apprehended as a discipline similar to others in name construction (i.e., anthropology, sociology, psychology) and the fact the Africology contains all the necessary metaphysical, theoretical, sociological (communal), and conceptual aspects that constitute itself as an academic discipline (Asante, 1992, 2009).

As an area of field of studies, technically, any discipline can teach Black Studies courses without ever having been trained in the intellectual tradition that centers the primacy of the African experience (Afrocentricity) nor having been trained in the assumptions, concepts, theories, methods, methodologies, and paradigms that constitute the discipline (Africology). What Africology did was to create a zone of demarcation where courses offered within the discipline of Africology could not be infringed upon because those courses were offered within the boundaries of Africological disciplinarity. Black Studies, however, as an area or field of study, has faced difficulty in this area; as Asante (2009, p. 15) mentions, "Black Studies carried with it a certain degree of impermeability. However, the name alone is sufficient to prevent encroachment on courses, ideas, and methods. Fields may not infringe upon your discipline's name but still encroach upon your courses." Henceforth, Black Studies courses have often been found offered in anthropology, history, linguistics, sociology, political science, and psychology departments, which fundamentally are not Afrocentric in epistemic orientation (rather Eurocentric) and therefore do not substantiate the quality centeredness, agency, or victorious conscious that characterizes Afrocentric enterprise nor Africological disciplinarity. In raising the question of terminology concerning disciplinarity, as cited in his article "Africology and the puzzle of nomenclature," Asante sought to expose the conceptual ambiguity that came with the name Black Studies, despite its historical significance in Black America and bring to light the epistemic challenges that could hinder the future development of the discipline if the names were not adequately addressed. As such, Asante remains in favor of Africology as the optimal name used to refer to the discipline historically referred to as Black Studies, also called African American Studies, Africana Studies, and Pan-African Studies, among other terminologies, which also extinguishes the issue of having multiple names that essentially refer to the same discipline. Ultimately, Asante (2018, p. 535) remarks that:

A discipline is neither an aggregation of courses nor an administrative unit; it is essentially a unique perspective on facts and information regardless of their origin. Hence, the discipline of Africology is the Afrocentric study of African phenomena trans generationally and trans continentally.

## (D) Eurocentric Critique

Fourthly, (D) Asante has been one of the most outspoken critics of European social, intellectual, and cultural hegemony, historically and contemporaneously imposed on many of the world's cultures. Following a sequence of historical events between the mid and late 15th century, including Europe's emergence from the Dark Ages following the expulsion of occupying Moors, the discovery of maritime maps and naval routes, military development, religious-political arbitration between the Catholic Portuguese and Spaniards and the issuing of the papal bull (religious decree) by the Catholic church, which sanctioned enslavement of indigenous peoples (Clarke, 2011), Europe would begin to impose itself upon the world and its many peoples. This imposition has been located as *Eurocentrism*, which Asante (2005, p. 236) explains here:

> Eurocentrism is a political, cultural, social, and economic world system that emerged with the expansion of Europe during the voyages of conquest from 1492 to 1600. When Europe expanded into Africa, Asia, America, and the Pacific regions after Christopher Columbus's voyages to the Americas, it brought to those regions the religion, language, customs, traditions, and symbol systems of Europe. In one sense Eurocentrism may be seen as the advancement of the European ideal, but in another sense, it may be seen as imperialism, exploitation, and the promotion of greed. These two senses of the same phenomenon have created tension between Europeans and other peoples, particularly when Eurocentrism, as an intellectual tendency, has been imposed upon those peoples.

As a historical consequence of Europe's encroachment upon the world and the various human cultures that inhabited it, there has been a tendency to relate information, knowledge, perspective, imagination, and reality from a Eurocentric standpoint, that is, from the cultural, historical, and psychological location of the European experience. Asante (2007, p. 17) remarks, "Eurocentricity imposes its consciousness as universal, making a particular

historical reality the total, in the European's view, of the human experience." The issue here, of course, is that there are many cultures and
ethnicities in the world who can be identified as Africans, Asians, Native
Americans, Indigenous natives of Oceania, Latinos, Arabs, Europeans, and
Pacific Islanders, among other groups of people.

Thus, to impose a certain quality of perspective upon others, as
Eurocentricity has and continues to do, is condescending, disrespectful,
ethnocentric, immoral, and generally racist in orientation. Asante (1991,
p. 172) has gone on the record before by saying that "unlike Eurocentricity,
Afrocentricity does not condone ethnocentric valorization at the expense
of degrading other groups' perspectives," instead of understanding that
every one of the world cultures has intrinsic value and value to offer
(Asante, 2006). *Culture*, according to Nah Dove (2018, p. 130), is:

> A human endeavour, which all human groups develop in an attempt to
> make sense of their lives and bring order to society. As a powerful pur-
> veyor of ideas, values, and beliefs, culture aids in the shaping of human
> thought and behaviour. Culture is like a glue that binds people in ways
> that they choose. It is a historical entity, grounded in knowledge, providing
> a reservoir of information based on experiences that provide a foundation
> for understanding life and how it may be lived.

As aforementioned, Afrocentricity is a centric theory that privileges the
understanding of culture and history from the purview of the people in
question as subjects and agents. Indeed, through Afrocentricity, and to a
more significant extent, Africological disciplinary "prioritize the needs
and interests of people of African descent" (McDougal III, 2014, p. 244).
Since "any applied study of African people should be geared toward solving problems or meeting challenges that are relevant to people of African
descent" (Tillotson & McDougal, 2013, p. 105), Afrocentricity condones
"a nonhierarchical approach that respects and celebrates a variety of
cultural perspectives on world phenomena" (Asante, 1991, p. 172).

Where *cultural pluralism* (*multiculturalism*) "advocates for a social order
in which the constituent communities of the nation are allowed to coexist
on their cultural terms, not on the exclusive terms of the majority culture,
although cultural diffusion appears inescapable in a multicultural milieu"
(Okafor, 2014, p. 210), so does Afrocentricity as a theory of social

change. Thus, inevitably, Asante (2020b, pp. 122–123) has been tena-
cious in his critique of Eurocentricity, whether in the American academy
or elsewhere, and has remained adamant that for "humans [to] learn to
appreciate each other's talents, creative force, aesthetic imagination, and
properly constructed vision of what the world could be in the future,"
the masquerade of European cultural, historical, and socio-intellectual
universality and superiority must come to an end.

## (E) Conscientization

Finally, (E) Molefi Kete Asante has provided a quality of consciousness
missing in what has historically been called Black Studies and the larger
African world. *Consciousness* refers to an intrinsic state of awareness
(self-cite) that was obfuscated in the minds of many continental and
diasporan African people during the turbulent era that identified the 20th
century. At the same time, the Western world may fixate its historical
sights on World Wars I and II, the Great Depression, the Vietnam War,
and the assassination of John F. Kennedy, African Americans were dealing
with Jim Crow, the Civil Rights Movement, and the Black Freedom
Struggle, while the African Caribbean and continent were wrestling with
colonialism, decolonization, and the issue of nation building.

In the 1980s, Afrocentricity as a socio-intellectual theory of social change
emerged from the vision of Molefi Kete Asante, which sought from its
inception to locate, discern, and provide conceptual clarity regarding the
African consciousness. As Asante (2007, p. 32) states in his book *An
Afrocentric Manifesto: Toward an African Renaissance*, "My aim with
the publication of Afrocentricity was to strike a blow at the lack of consciousness, not simply the lack of consciousness of our oppression but
the lack of consciousness of what victories were possible." As such,
Afrocentricity sought *conscientization*, which refers to the process of
awakening the conscious (self-cite) as a cultural, historical, epistemic,
and psychological corrective to the people of African descent who, over
the last few hundred years, were struggling to regain consciousness of
their identity before the "*Maafa*" (Ani, 1994, p. 583), which is the
Kiswahili word referring to the calamity that was European (and Arab)
colonialism, imperialism, and the enslavement of African people. From a
disciplinary standpoint, Asante created a quality of conversation and

mindfulness around our historical reality and identity as African people. By doing so, we began, as a global people, to consciously and methodically self-examine, as our ancestors had done many millennia before us, ourselves as African people, that is, our assumptions, beliefs, culture, history, habits, ideas, thoughts, sentiments, and values and determine where we who we said we are, or where we are viewing ourselves from the standpoint of other people. Thus, to this end, the process of awakening the conscious was indeed an Afrocentric endeavor, for it sought to approach our self and collective cultural image as African people and determine whether we were acting independently on behalf of our own best interest or not (Karenga, 1988).

Ultimately, Molefi Kete Asante is the world's leading Afrocentric theorist and remains a leading disciplinary expert in what has been called Black Studies (Africology). Asante is the architect of the first PhD program in Black Studies at Temple University, the department of Africology and African American Studies. Furthermore, Asante is the original editor of *JBS*, the author of over 100 books and 300 scholarly articles, has served on over 125 doctoral dissertations, conducted countless professional presentations, and has been the recipient of numerous awards recognizing his commitment to upholding the triple mission of Black Studies, that is, academic excellence, cultural grounding, and social responsibility (Karenga, 2005, 2007; Zulu, 2008). Asante has had significant "skin in the game" of academia, and his contributions to the development, maintenance, and maturation of the discipline are worthy of acknowledgment and praise. Hence, I believe it is pivotal to recognize and cherish the achievements of Asante, which are both iconic and remarkable for any scholar regardless of their field of interest, intending to advance the discipline wherever possible based on Asante's intellectual and disciplinary formations.

## ESTABLISHING CLARITY: RECTIFYING THE CONCEPTUAL DISTORTION OF AFROCENTRICITY AND AFRICOLOGY

With the emergence of Afrocentricity as a distinct quality of socio-intellectual perspective underlying the conceptual base of Black Studies and Africology standing for the conceptual advancement of the discipline, there have been many questions surrounding both Afrocentricity and Africology that require resolution to mitigate any conceptual distortions surrounding both phenomena. As a graduate of the Department of Africology and African American Studies at Temple University, I am familiar with many of the areas of confusion some have regarding both Afrocentricity and Africology and, therefore, am equipped to provide conceptual clarity about this matter. I will explain 12 of the most cited areas of ambiguity concerning theory and discipline.

To start, (1) a principal area of confusion is about the disciplinary nature of Africology, which was also asked about Black/African American/ Pan-African Studies: Is the discipline interdisciplinary, multidisciplinary, or transdisciplinary? The answer is that Africology is neither interdisciplinary, multidisciplinary, or transdisciplinary but *unidisciplinary* (McDougal III, 2017). What differentiates Africology from other disciplines lies in its approach to an area of study, which is *Afrocentric* in orientation, and the discipline's purpose, which is to consciously advance African people in every sector of society and improve the quality of life concerning African humanity on this earth (Hare, 1968; McDougal III, 2017). Since Africology draws its metaphysical assumptions from African cultures (Asante, 2007; Karenga, 2009), it supports a particular quality of perspective rooted deeply in the epistemic matrix that is Indigenous African thought and practice. Henceforth, it does not have the same assumptions, which are inherently Eurocentric, that populate other disciplines such as anthropology, history, sociology, political science, and psychology.

To this end, (2) Africology is its academic discipline appearing from its location (in African historical reality). It is not a subfield of anthropology, history, sociology, or any other so-called "traditional" discipline. (3) In this same line of thought, Africology holds its own distinct and unique conceptual apparatus, theories, methods, and paradigms just as any other discipline (Asante, 2020a; McDougal III, 2017). Critical examples of concepts include *center, location, dislocation,* and *relocation;* theories include *Location Theory, Africana Womanism, Africana Literary Theory,* and *African Womanist Theory;* methods include *Afronographic Methods* and paradigms include the *Afrocentric Paradigm.* Another area in need of conceptual correction is that (4) Afrocentricity is not a reaction or "Africanized" (Black) version of Eurocentricity (Asante, 1991, 1992).

This is true for two reasons: African people are the oldest group of humans on earth. Therefore, Black Studies as a scientific tradition dating back to the remotest periods of African antiquity predates Europe and, consequently, the European intellectual tradition (also called White Studies). Secondly, Afrocentric theory and Africological disciplinarity are not anti-African, for the theory and discipline champions cultural pluralism. Adversely, Eurocentricity accentuates its cultural reality above all others (Asante, 1991, 1992). Henceforth, both perspectives are opposed to one another. Moreover, Afrocentricity is not "anti-White"; instead, it is anti-hegemonic. This is a critical differentiation in interrogation because Afrocentricity, as Asante (2007, p. 111) explains that "there should be nothing incorrect about European people wanting to have motifs, ideas, narratives, concepts that are derived from their history. That is to be expected"; however "what is not to be expected is the idea that Europe somehow has a right to hold a hegemonic banner over all other people. Afrocentricity does not seek African hegemony; it seeks pluralism without hierarchy."

Continuing, (5) Afrocentricity is a culturally responsive theory that is of antiracial theoretical orientation, unlike Eurocentricity, which substantiates *race*, that is a notion that describes varying levels of difference in physical appearance among different groups of people (Chandler, 1999; Welsing, 1991), as the primary social indicator used to criticize and categorize different groups of people artificially. Afrocentricity is also (6) a nonsexist and gender-affirming theory for it "emphasizes the need for partnership between Africana men and women" (Stewart, 2015, p. 108), (7) does not advance class-based differences for it is a humanizing theory centered in a humanizing discipline (Asante, 1992) and (8) while heteronormative in conceptual construction does not condone homo-antagonistic or homophobic behavior and practices (Anderson, 2012; Asante, 2003).

Eurocentricity, on the other hand, appears from a cultural and historical context with severe metaphysical connotations arising in Eurasian antiquity that are indeed chauvinistic, hierarchical, and discriminatory in orientation, such has been shown in the scholarship of Cheikh Anta Diop, particularly his *Two Cradle Theory*. Next, (9) Afrocentricity and Africology are not opposed to any examination of subject matter, be it anthropology, cinema, class, communication, economics, gender, history, language, media, politics, psychology, sexuality, and sociology, among other areas; however, regardless of the subject matter, to comprise an Afrocentric project the quality of theoretical perspective that must be used to examine any subject matter must be Afrocentric. This methodological, foundational grounding clarifies the place of intellectual identity (Afrocentricity) and epistemic disciplinarity (Africology) a scholar is approaching from in their examination of phenomena. Otherwise, any examination that lacks an Afrocentric lens does not constitute a true Afrocentric epistemological endeavor (Asante, 1992, 2007, 2009).

Transitioning, (10) Afrocentricity should not be conflated with Afrocentrism, for they are not the same, and the only similarity between both words is that they contain an "Afro" prefix. Asante (2007, pp. 16–17) clarifies that *Afrocentricity* is "a consciousness, quality of thought, mode of analysis, and an actionable perspective where Africans seek, from agency, to assert subject place within the context of African history" while *Afrocentrism* refers to "a broad cultural movement of the late twentieth century that has a set of philosophical, political, and artistic ideas which provides the basis for the musical, sartorial, and aesthetic dimensions of the African personality." Next, (11) Afrocentricity is not a theory focused only on African American ethnicity. Often, because Afrocentricity was created by an African American, Molefi Kete Asante, it is assumed that Afrocentricity pertains only to the descendants of enslaved Africans in the United States, African Americans, at the exclusion of other African descendant people; however, this is inaccurate.

Afrocentricity is a *theory* that is a particular perspective on some aspect of reality (self-cite) and is "a frame of reference wherein phenomena are viewed from the perspective of the African person" (Asante, 1991, p. 171). Afrocentricity, by its conceptual nature, is not ethnocentric, for it focalizes the experiences of all African descendant groups of people, including, but not limited to, African Americans. This leads to the final clarification (12) that anyone can be Afrocentric in theoretical orientation. Theories are not biologically decided; they are created, expressed, and shared by different people. Regardless of geographical, national, and ethnic origins, anyone intellectually committed to the *Afrocentric Idea* or "a moral as well as an intellectual location that posits Africans as subjects rather than as objects of human history and that establishes a perfectly valid and scientific basis for the explanation of African historical experiences" (Asante, 1998, pp. xii–xiii) can be Afrocentric. Notable examples in academia include Afrocentric scholars such as the late Portuguese theorist Ana Monteiro-Ferreira, the author of *The Demise of the Inhuman*, which challenged global systems of dominance, and Japanese and Chinese scholars Yoshitaka Miike and Jing Yin, who created the concept of *Asiacentricity*, which created a liberatory discourse concerning Asian humanity (Asante, 2007). While this list is by no means exhaustive, it should hopefully provide some conceptual clarity and clear definition needed to address and rectify the conceptual distortions of Afrocentricity and Africological disciplinarity.

## CONCLUSION

This chapter has been constructed to celebrate the genius of Molefi Kete Asante's intellectual contributions regarding the establishment of the discipline historically known as Black Studies, which has been referred to in recent times as Africology, and the epistemic validity and applicability of Afrocentricity as a socio-intellectual theory of social change designed to improve the quality of African and broader human life on this earth. Through an examination of definition and meaning, Asante's intellectual contributions to the discipline and correction concerning the conceptual distortions of Afrocentricity and Africology, hopefully, this chapter has shown the indispensability of Asante's epistemic formations and contributions to the disciplinary Afrocentric study of African life throughout space and time.

Moreover, this chapter has helped provide a quality of consciousness and understanding regarding Molefi Kete Asante's importance as an intellectual scholar, visionary, and warrior who has dedicated his life and profession to improving African humanity. Indeed, many heroes, heroines, elders, and ancestors are worthy of praise, and Molefi Kete Asante easily sits among them. Thank you for all you have done for us as a global people, Professor Asante. Your work will live on, immortalized in the hearts, minds, and spirits of those committed to African agency and human liberation. Thank you.

## REFERENCES

Anderson, R. (2012). Molefi Kete Asante: The Afrocentric idea and the cultural turn in intercultural communication studies. *International Journal of Intercultural Relations, 36*(6), 760–769. https://doi.org/10.1016/j.ijintrel.2012.08.005

Ani, M. (1994). *Yurugu: An African-centered critique of European cultural thought and behavior*. Africa World Press.

Asante, M. K. (1990). *Kemet, Afrocentricity and knowledge*. African World Press.

Asante, M. K. (1991). The Afrocentric idea in education. *The Journal of Negro Education, 60*(2), 170–180. https://doi.org/10.2307/2295608

Asante, M. K. (1992). African American Studies: The future of the discipline. *The Black Scholar, 22*(3), 20–29. https://doi.org/10.1080/00064246.1992.11413041

Asante, M. K. (1998). *The Afrocentric idea* (rev. and exp., ed.). Temple University Press.

Asante, M. K. (2002). Intellectual dislocation: Applying analytic Afrocentricity to narratives of identity. *Howard Journal of Communications, 13*(1), 97–110. https://doi.org/10.1080/106461702753555067

Asante, M. K. (2003). *Afrocentricity: The theory of social change* (rev. and exp., ed.). African American Images.

Asante, M. K. (2005). Eurocentrism. In M. K. Asante & A. Mazama (Eds.), *Encyclopedia of black studies* (p. 236). Sage Publications, Inc. https://doi.org/10.4135/9781412952538.n123

Asante, M. K. (2006). A discourse on black studies: Liberating the study of African people in the western academy. *Journal of Black Studies, 36*(5), 646–662. http://www.jstor.org/stable/40026678

Asante, M. K. (2007). *An Afrocentric manifesto*. Polity Press.

Asante, M. K. (2009). Africology and the puzzle of nomenclature. *Journal of Black Studies, 40*(1), 12–23. http://www.jstor.org/stable/40282617

Asante, M. K. (2018). The relentless pursuit of discipline: An Africological march toward knowledge liberation. *Journal of Black Studies, 49*(6), 531–541. https://doi.org/10.1177/0021934718788646

Asante, M. K. (2020a). Africology, Afrocentricity, and what remains to be done. *The Black Scholar, 50*(3), 48–57. https://doi.org/10.1080/00064246.2020.1780859

Asante, M. K. (2020b). *Radical insurgencies*. Universal Write Publications LLC.

Chandler, W. B. (1999). *Ancient future: The teachings and prophetic wisdom of the seven hermetic Laws of ancient Egypt*. Black Classic Press.

Clarke, J. H. (2011). *Christopher Columbus and the Afrikan Holocaust: Slavery and the rise of European capitalism*. Eworld Incorporated.

Dove, N. (2018). Race revisited: Against a cultural construction bearing significant implications. *International Journal of African Renaissance Studies – Multi-, Inter- and Transdisciplinarity, 13*(2), 129–143. https://doi.org/10.1080/18186874.2018.1538703

Hare, N. (1968). A conceptual proposal for a department of black studies. *Civil Rights Movement Archives*. https://www.crmvet.org/docs/nor/twlf/680429_sfsc_blackstudies.pdf

Karenga, M. (1988). Black studies and the problematic of paradigm: The philosophical dimension. *Journal of Black Studies, 18*(4), 395–414. http://www.jstor.org/stable/2784370

Karenga, M. (2005). Black Studies. In M. K. Asante & A. Mazama (Eds.), *Encyclopedia of Black studies* (pp. 149–151). Sage Publications, Inc. https://doi.org/10.4135/9781412952538.n78

Karenga, M. (2007). Molefi Asante and the Afrocentric initiative: Mapping his intellectual impact. *Los Angeles Sentinel*, p. A-7. https://www.us-organization.org/position/documents/MolefiAsanteandtheAfrocentricInitiative.pdf

Karenga, M. (2009). Names and notions of black studies: Issues of roots, range, and relevance. *Journal of Black Studies, 40*(1), 41–64. http://www.jstor.org/stable/40282619

McDougal, S. (2014). Africana studies' epistemic identity: An analysis of theory and epistemology in the discipline. *Journal of African American Studies, 18*(2), 236–250. http://www.jstor.org/stable/43525547

McDougal III, S. (2017). *Research methods in Africana studies*. Peter Lang.

Okafor, V. O. (2014). Africology, Black studies, African American studies, Africana studies, or African world studies? What's so important about a given name? *The Journal of Pan-African Studies, 6*, 209.

Stewart, J. B. (2015). Black/Africana studies, then and now: Reconstructing a century of intellectual inquiry and political engagement, 1915–2015. *The Journal of African American History, 100*(1), 87–118. https://doi.org/10.5323/jafriamerhist.100.1.0087

Tillotson, M., & McDougal, S. (2013). Applied Africana studies. *Journal of Black Studies, 44*(1), 101–113. http://www.jstor.org/stable/23414706

Van Horne, W. (2007). Africology. In M. K. Asante & A. Mazama (Eds.), *Encyclopedia of Black studies* (pp. 60–61). Sage Publications, Inc. https://doi.org/10.4135/9781412952538

Welsing, F. C. (1991). *The Isis (Yssis) papers*. Third World Press.

Zulu, I. M. (2008). Africology 101: An interview with scholar activist Molefi Kete Asante. *The Journal of Pan African Studies, 2*(2), 79–84. https://www.jpanafrican.org/docs/vol2no2/Africology101.pdf

# CHAPTER 3

## How Afrocentricity Recentered My Public Policy Practice to Highlight Cultural and Historical Dislocation and Intervention

Carm R. Almonor, PhD

### ABSTRACT

Three cases within my legal practice centered African American historical and cultural policy research (Kumah-Abiwu, 2016) within Equal Protection arguments to create new laws: expanding codified scope of recognized kinship for child caretakers; accommodating unique African diaspora migrations within the federal constitutional Right to Travel; and repealing noncustodial parental disclosure laws for benefit recipients in part based on cultural arguments concerning African complementary matriarchy, or Kemetic Maaticity. We successfully challenged three NJ laws and reduced the economic burden of incarceration for thousands of low-wealth families. These cases included *In re Moore* in which my client and I successfully repealed a state law requiring single-parent federal benefit recipients to name the noncustodial parent—a factual impossibility for many, including my client who had conceived during a prior life of sex work. Likewise, *In re Bradshaw* culminated in the repeal of a state law that had barred my client from receiving benefits to care for the child of a drug addicted and incarcerated distant cousin due to inadequate familial degree. Our new *Bradshaw* law supplanted the five-degree kinship requirement with an allowance of any demonstrable consanguinity, thereby recognizing nonnuclear Global South familial cultures and lifting a heavy burden on carceral extended families seeking to prevent family separation, foster care and intergenerational recidivism. Finally, in *Sanchez v. Department of Human Services*, 314 N.J. Super. 11 (1998), my team, clients, and I successfully invalidated the statutory 1-year residency requirement for interstate migrating citizens needing federal welfare assistance. My legal argument successfully invoked the federal Constitutional Fourteenth Amendment Equal Protection Clause and the Right to Travel.

**Keywords:** Afrocentricity, Policy, Law, Culture

# INTRODUCTION

"A riot is the language of the unheard," Dr. King admonished in September 1966. Two days after King's August 1963 "I Have a Dream" speech at the Capitol, the head of domestic surveillance under the FBI's head, J. Edgar Hoover, had already "marked" King "the most dangerous Negro of the future of this Nation." Hoover concurred and designated King, a premier enemy of the state. "But the state of what?" one might rhetorically ponder. Indeed, giving voice to the unheard masses, as King sought, is the essence of a purported democratic state. Hoover was defending a different state—that of enforced, undemocratic hierarchy passed down from two-and-a-half centuries of American enslavement, notwithstanding its founding democratic poetry.

As if responding to his call, less than 20 months (about one and a half years) after the riot explanation, an assassin's bullet felled the pauper King even as he gave voice to the economic oppression of Memphis sanitation workers who had been crushed to death by an underpaying and uncaring segregationist government. Mass civil unrest erupted nationally as prophesied. Both the economic pleas of the Black masses and that of their prophet had been violently silenced. Heaping layers of insult and injury, Nixon joined federal violence to that of Southern segregationist states and vigilantes (Anderson, 2015). As Nixon protégé John Ehrlichman confessed later upon his death bed, the president's Drug War response to civil unrest thinly veiled militaristic scorched earth upon Black communities already betrayed economically by post-*Brown v. Bd.* Southern segregation academies and Northern redlining.

Much as a convict leasing (Blackmon, 2009) dial tone had answered the economic freedom call of 200,000 self-emancipated Black soldiers after they won the Civil War, one million Black World War II soldiers helped to repel global tyrannical white supremacy only to return to the domestic model from which European fascists had found inspiration. Reaching for a blood-earned hand up after fighting in two world wars—a fair share of the whites-only passed GI Bill, Homestead Act, and Social Security Act, for example—Black GIs and their communities instead received a further bloodied hangman's noose of vigilante lynch mobs, scaled whole-town lynchings through resentful race massacres, and convict leasing 2.0, a new state carceral slavery reprise, again exploiting emancipation's prison exception in the U.S. Constitution's Thirteenth Amendment. Through Nixon's "Black" and "Hippie" Drug War, a disproportionately Black and Brown prison population thus mushroomed from 300,000 years in the early 1970s to 2.3 million today. Successive economic and militarized justice bombs, private and public, detonated on Black communities and families repeatedly (Ani, 1994).

Three decades later, I sat in my law office across dozens of wars weary Black, brown, and poor clients as a constitutional legal services attorney, challenging the latest anti-Black economic Maafa, or disaster—a cluster of welfare reform bombs dropped by Democratic President Bill Clinton and his Newt Gingrich-led Republican congressional interlocutors. Three of those cases, each defining distinct aspects of the family, form this chapter's Afrocentric case studies. Each case dually illustrates the Eurocentric policy lens and its Afrocentric retort. The following sections describe dislocations (Asante, 2003b) within the policy frameworks that produced each law before considering Afrocentric solutions in recentered culture and history suggested by the policy arguments and contexts of these successful cases.

## TWO WORLDS IN TENSION, EUROCENTRIC PUBLIC POLICY FRAMES

I was introduced to the methods of public policy analysis as a law student policy drafter in one of two legislative service law school clinics in the nation. I received detailed training from two foremost experts in

international public policy analysis and writing. I went on to become
editor-in-chief of the program for two terms and was then invited to edit
laws for a UN-affiliated program serving francophone policy in Sierra
Leone. The methods learned in those programs further served me
through over a decade as a constitutional lawyer and registered state
legislative agent in the public interest. My law clinic advisor and mentor
had developed the gold standard of methods: in the field—the problem-
solving methodology. It was linear, empirical, behavioral, and
multidisciplinary and paralleled the scientific methods in its precision
and process-based validity. At the heart of the technique, it posed a series
of seven standard and diverse categories of causal hypotheses to explain
demonstrated public policy problems of scale.

These causes ranged from lexical allowances within the language of current law to ideology, practical constraints, and economic incentives and
sanctions felt by identified actors of targeted behavior. The method set
itself aside in its structural comprehensiveness, meant to dispel selectivity
bias in the disciplinary or methodological focus of the researcher. The
two primary alternative methods used in most legislation included ends-
means, in which policymakers deductively filled the political policy
orders of those in power based on no empirical basis other than the
unexamined whim of edict. These included the first Portuguese slave
codes and Catholic race rules formed to justify enslavement in the 16th
and 17th centuries, the post-Bacon's Rebellion adoptions of race laws in
the late 17th century, and the countess segregation laws separating every
quotidian aspect of Southern life.

For these, the naked political power of a few European land aristocratic
white Protestant men and their heirs, not evidence-based broad public
good, determined instant, sweeping public policy. Hence, a rabidly pro-
gun open carry Governor Ronald Reagan suddenly favored restrictions
to open carry under the Mumford Act once faced with armed Black
Panther Party members protesting at the state capital. Meanwhile, today's
senior conservative justices, Clarence Thomas and Sam Alito, married to
documented pro-insurrection activists, have expressly endorsed broad
presidential immunity for Trump's tyrannical acts while curtailing presidential remedial agency deferral through the long-held *Chevron* case. Its
Trump empowerment also contrasts with its previous constraints to the
Obama and Biden administrations' remedial powers for historically
harmed groups, whether through student loan forgiveness, migrant

Dreamer legal status, or child subsidies that halved child poverty before court reversal. Such logically inconsistent winds are the *hot air* of political ends justifying policy means styled legislation.

By contrast, the second status quo alternative, incrementalism, proscribes deliberate observations often by government commissions, such as those of remedial legislation throughout Black history's struggles—from the cultural deficit modeled Moynihan Report that eventually described a cultural cause to Black inequality rooted in single-parent households, to the Kerner Report of 1968, arriving at structural inequalities at the root of racialized "two Americas." These thoughtful ideas have often taken decades to filter into policy, eroding relevance in an ever-changing factual environment (Baldwin, 1993). As importantly, such remedial laws rarely, although sometimes, culminate in impactful laws such as the preventative mandates of Section 5 of the Voting Rights Act of 1965 and the 1970s Bakke case affirmative action and *Roe v. Wade* women's right to privacy in reproductive choice.

Yet, even these grand, rare remedial sandcastles of victorious democratic incrementalism have washed away instantly in angry ends-means hurricanes of despotic political racism and patriarchy (Asante, 2010). Such has occurred throughout periods of racist backlash to Black success, as occurred to end the Voting Rights Act, Section 5, under the Trump–Roberts Supreme Court in 2013 and to end affirmative action and choice nearly a decade later. The Hayes–Tilden Compromise of 1877, ending Reconstruction (Du Bois, 2014) and the Drug War one century later, ending the Civil Rights and Black Power Movements, marked other significant periods of ends-means political autocracy canceling incrementalist, painstaking fruit of Black struggle. These pivotal roles of culture and history are often hidden or undeveloped in these Western policy methods. In ending women's bodily autonomy as a half-century federal right, the 2022 *Dobbs* decision cited medieval selections of Western "history and tradition" roughly 70 times.

Likewise, the infamous *Dred Scott* decision by Roger Taney was led by a majority Southern enslaver court, much like the pro-insurrectionist ties of the Trump–Roberts Court. Blatantly self-dealing patriarchs of material white supremacy swiftly severed prior land-based Black rights to freedom based on Western selective historical reading and normalization of enforced racial hierarchy. Historical traditions of cultural racism (Kendi,

2016) and patriarchy have thus stealthily animated the "ends" of such periods of tyrannical hierarchical correction through emergency ends-means policy edict. Within the empirically cleansed problem solving, the issue lies not in the explicit wielding of universalized Western hierarchical cultural history but in its downplayed importance. While "ideology" broadly guides one area of causal investigation, the method fails to develop specific cultural-historical causal models of ideology. Instead, it relegates history to the role of fixed descriptive context, which is largely irrelevant to the focus on behaviorally mailable policy variables.

## AFROCENTRIC FRAMEWORKS

Several Afrocentric frameworks establish a foundation for recasting public policy, while others represent resulting gifts to policy analysis from Afrocentric theory. Key foundational frameworks include location and reduction formation (Asante, 2003a).

### Foundational Location and Agency Reduction Formation

In location theory, Asante intends that "the reader will be able to adequately locate the text to make judgments about the author's creative abilities as well as the author's philosophical underpinning" (Akbar, 2003, p. 240). He specifically advances this purpose by presenting a figurative spatial concept of place and merging it with Afrocentrism's focus on culture, "a text must fit within a multiplicity of places, each one defined by the dynamic interplay of culture and purpose" (p. 240). Once applied, it encourages students within their learning by anchoring social studies lessons within lived, African American cultural/historical, and physical communal spaces of students. Afrocentrists explicitly and singularly frame educational and other institutional problems as cultural dislocations.

Thus, the inequitable historical policy continuum—outlawing, defunding, and distorting Black education through respective eras of slavery, segregation, and today's mass incarceration—all reflect a deeply endemic white American cultural norm. Asante's location provides a central metaphor, but its application to a people physically torn from their communal moorings through waves of existential migration, from the Middle Passage to Great Migrations, invites literal, physical dislocative interpretation as well. Likewise, within geography, Asante implies the ever-present literal spatial parallels of location.

In *Afrocentricity*, for example, he notes Africa's massive and misrepresented cartographical size—large enough to fit America in Africa four times (Asante, 2012a). This reference to European spatial misrepresentation of Africa relative to its size implies a physical form of *agency reduction formation* commensurate with the cultural phenomenon of identity dislocation and commensurate power dilution introduced by Tillotson (2011). Such locative agency extends to all areas of cultural life, from epistemological to political, moral/axiological, and spiritual. Asante, thus, asserts in *Afrocentricity* that it places "Africa at the center of our existential reality" within an "African cultural system."

Three strengths of the Afrocentric dislocation approach to policy (Akua, 2017) are noteworthy: (a) its cross-disciplinary breadth, concurring with and developing the historical and cultural aspects of other relevant disciplines; (b) its cross-cultural reach to parallel historicized sociocultural continuity in African, European, and other identities, which drive broadly patterned beliefs, values, and behaviors; and (c) its extensive menu of relevant cultural and historical data. Just as Afrocentricity (Asante, 2008) allows an infinite historical range from which to analyze today's problems in dislocated African living, it grants the same expanse for culturally corrective Sankofan recentering. Specifically, Afrocentricity centers on correcting the cultural experiences of free African people with consequential civilizations (Diop, 1974) and cultures for the whole of human history. Hence, it centers Diop's focus on ancient Egypt and Imhotep, the world's first multi-genius who designed the first pyramids and mapped multiple bodily systems many millennia before Hypocrites; it reaches the biblical Candakes, successful warrior queens of Cush; and it encompasses the unsurpassed wealth and undeniable contributions of the latter West African empires and the Moors, who technologically advanced all Southern Europe during a 1,000-year occupation.

Why, with such a vast human history, should humanity limit its historical-cultural database to the relative presence of European colonial enlightenment while isolating, deifying, racializing, and de-Africanizing all Greco-Roman history through the present? Like critical Black scholar

Ta-Nehisi Coates's recounting of encountering Black Studies as a student at Howard University (2015), 1619 founder Nicole Hannah-Jones recounts in the preface to her latest essay anthology the importance of such broader history to her consciousness. She describes her epiphany from the only Black male teacher and Black Studies (Karenga, 2003b) course in her high school as a sophomore in Waterloo, Iowa: "[He] navigated our class to the ancient Mali, Songhai, Nubian, and Ghana empires (it was he who taught me that 'from here to Timbuktu' referred to an African center of learning), surveying the cultures and knowledge and civilizations that existed among African peoples long before Europeans decided that millions of human beings ought to be forced across the ocean in the hulls of slave ships and then redefined as property" (2021, p. xviii).

Hence, Hannah-Jones (2021, p. xviii) also describes the problems addressed by her classroom in a way synchronous with Asantean dislocation theory: "We were not actors but acted upon. We were not contributors, just recipients. White people enslaved us, and white people freed us. Black people could choose either to take advantage of that freedom or to squander it, as our depictions in the media seemed to suggest so many of us were doing."

## AFROCENTRIC POLICY CONTRIBUTIONS

Critical Afrocentric gifts to public policy analysis include cultural and historical centering, Maaticity, and African Womanism (Hudson-Weems, 1993).

### Cultural and Historical Centering

Afrocentricity's significant contribution to public policy analysis centers on developing and equalizing history and culture (Asante, 2012b). Asante's Afrocentricity fills all cultural and historical analytical gaps of all three Western policy methods. He expressly describes these two constituent parts as integral to Afrocentricity, "a philosophical perspective associated with the discovery, location, and actualizing of African agency within the context of history and culture" (Asante, 1980, p. 3). Unlike continuing policies of exclusionary Euro-history and culture, from enslavement to present Black history and literacy negation, Native American reservation school bans on cultural language and clothing, colonial British coverture adaptations that denied women economic and legal rights, and the like—Afrocentricity is neither exclusionary of other-centered histories nor "an argument for any type of superiority based on biology" (Asante, 1980, p. 4).

Asante (1980, p. viii) instead asserts Afrocentricity as integral to moving society to a cultural revolution that increases equity. Conversely, the *Afrocentric Manifesto* notes, "the Afrocentric discovers as much as possible the authentic African understanding of the elements without imposing Eurocentric or non-African interpretations" (p. 43). Four decades after *Afrocentricity,* Asante and Dove (2021) further crystalized Afrocentricity's broad, complementary human elements of Afrocentricity in *Being Human Being.* Upholding Diop's primacy of historical culture, Asante and Dove established a process beginning with cultural identity through "components of history, language, psychology, and spirituality" (p. 36). Among these, they emphasize history as "the cultural glue that unifies a community with a sense of belonging ... historical continuity that is spiritually connected to the ancestors ... providing a consciousness that enables people to identify themselves as part of a population connected in ways that defined the traditional similarities in distinctions from other cultural groups" (p. 36). Asante and Dove further describe the culture in a fashion no less broad and ubiquitous than its public policy contexts. Culture, thus, acts as "a powerful purveyor of ideas, values, and beliefs ... aids in the shaping of human thoughts and behavior... provides a reservoir of information grounded in experiences that act as a foundation for making sense of life and how it may be lived ... affects decisions and actions in the methods employed to build social institutions like family, healthcare, education, politics, economies, entertainment, the arts, and spiritual systems" (p. 37, citing, Dove, 2015). Most importantly, they interpose knowledge/epistemology as generative of culture and, by implication, preceding the interaction of culture and policy. They, thus, describe knowledge as "gained through the historical, linguistic, psychological, and spiritual experiences of people ... affect(ing) the shaping of the mind (as) the mind affects the shaping of the knowledge and therefore culture" (p. 37).

*Afrocentric Manifesto* thus establishes in its project "a commitment to correct the dislocation in the history of Africa" (p. 41). Likewise, *Manifesto* squarely anchors the Afrocentric cultural foundation, describing the Afrocentric project variously as "an interest in psychological location ... commitment to finding the African subject place; (and) the defense of African cultural elements" (p. 43). Reinforcing his cultural thesis, Asante assesses that the Civil Rights Movement was deficient as "it offered no cultural program other than integration of Blacks into dominant white culture" (p. 19).

Maaticity

Asante well summarizes the various conceptions of Maat, a foundational ancient Egyptian or Kemetic philosophy: Whether one is looking at Bilolo's (1986, p. 7) philosophical notion of Maat as a knowledge ideal, a justice ideal or a metaphysical ideal or looking at Helck's concept of Maat as the foundation of human life, it is about the promotion of sanity, order, balance, harmony, peace, and justice among human beings (Asante, 2011, p. 50). Maatic balance also applies to the symmetry within this definition, for instance, including both harmonious and orderly peace on one hand and justice on the other. Merging both social values of correction and harmonious ease, Asante (p. 49) further points to Karenga's lexicon within the latter's seminal Maatic work: a "physical concept of straightness, evenness, and levelness."

What Ma'at recoils from, the Isfet of disorder, chaos, and evil (Asante, 2011, p. 54), then forms an adjoining theory of cultural contrast. "Afrocentric theory demands a discourse that privileges African reality from the perspective of humanity in civilization" (p. 20). The authors add, "[A]s Africologists, we establish the marker that we are human, and that is why we insist on the quality of difference and never on the ranking of humanity because of difference" (p. 208). They further relate the ancient Egyptian or Kemetic concept of Maat (Hilliard III, 1993). Maat constitutes the path to values relocation. "What is most human is the quest for Maaticity, that is, the attainment of truth, justice, righteousness, harmony, balance, order, and reciprocity. Therefore, we say *Being Human Being: Transforming the Race Discourse* agitates for an overturning of race in our language and the assertion of a language of seeking humanity, that is, Maaticity" (p. x).

Maaticity, Asante, and Dove describe it as "a philosophical posture emphasizing the optimum benefits of the ancient idea of Maat, ... truth, righteousness, justice, harmony, order, balance, and reciprocity serve as components of being human beings ... An active theory of ethics, knowledge, and metaphysics ... The process of becoming human in a relational sense, where we seek to relate to others, the environment, and the metaphysical world" (Asante & Dove p. 9). Vital to the family policy case insights below, they further establish Maatic and Afrocentric centrality to combating patriarchy. Maaticity's principles anchor in the female and male reciprocity of African matriarchy as "the theoretical framework for being" (p. 9). Ma'at becomes "the first spiritual idea ... (and) is fundamentally about unity, truth, justice, righteousness, order, harmony, balance, and reciprocity … the well-springs for other African societies" (p. 82). Hence, Afrocentric Maaticity provides a cultural and historical framework for critiquing and correcting codified familial public policies through the case studies that follow.

## African Womanism and Africana Womanism

The African ontological focus on gender-balanced and complementary harmony places such order as a defining characteristic and expression of African-descended cultures. It also signals the importance of infused, complementary African womanist (Dove, 2003) and Afrocentric (Asante, 1980) agency within any current sociocultural designs for African Americans. Consistent with Maaticity are Afrocentric humanity, African Womanism, and the Southern cradle. Afrocentrists appreciate their cooperative role in the shared project of the total human family. For example, African respect for the socialite of selfhood and connectedness of everyone and everything resonates in this pan-human spiritual morality. Moreover, to Africans, the land is not for dominion and exploitation. It was not a commodity for capitalists or Marxists to see in mere material terms but a shared spiritual space for shared stewardship and respect.

Thus, in Kemet, one would bury the placenta in the land and recognize the realm of the ancestors in the same (Nehusi, 2018). The conceptual framework of African and Africana womanism stems mainly from the works of Dove (2003) and Hudson-Weems (2003). Hudson-Weems's Africana womanist theory creates a bright line of separation from white feminist theory. This distinction is consistent with the importance she gives to race and then materiality before gender. She further developed a map of her conception. Dove pointedly expands these ideas to "emphasize the concept of culture as a tool of analysis for understanding the nature of African women's experiences." Notably, she includes in this scope broader global themes of cultural "resistance," motherhood, "defining a new world order," "liberate(ing) African people on a global scale," and behavior and values modification among African people. Hudson-Weems later further crystallized these ideas as "Global Africana Womanism," which brings "success, peace and amicability," and thereby benefits the entire world.

Thus, with Dove, Hudson-Weems provides an important starting place in her concept of global Africana womanism, a plea for all African women to embrace an African culture and family-first, a complementary Maatic paradigm. Importantly, Hudson-Weems implies that her framework indirectly promotes better global harmony as a further effect of African internal harmony. Yet, this chapter further asserts an international imperative for African women, which is not only centered on their own cultural and familial identity but operating in their center to influence other cultures and genders in functional African womanist cultural values. Pointedly, the world needs to embrace, indeed, and return to, the cultural values of African Womanism within Maatic culture. As noted, this reversal of the patriarchal global center of the last 500 years is a global existential necessity.

# THREE CASES

## Contesting Family

The three case studies that follow illustrate Afrocentric public policy attributes in each of the areas enumerated above: centering African history and culture within policies serving African-descended people; fostering Maatic harmony among diverse democratic cultural constituencies; and layering gender-complementary, anti-patriarchy within more comprehensive Afrocentric correctives rather than unipolar antiracist, antipoverty, and other siloed progressive policy frames. The cases revolve around the meaning of family for African-Caribbean, Afro-Latino, and African American people. Eurocentric policies penalized African cultural and historical family relationships concerning children, matriarchy, or ancestors. During my client interviews and resulting policy arguments, I came across Afrocentric elements more fully understood through further PhD study with Dr. Asante and reading of his works on Afrocentricity.

Upon reflection, each policy argument successfully centered on African historical and cultural research to repeal or overturn dislocated policies. The Bradshaw decision recognized broader nonnuclear kinship bonds for recognized caretakers of African and other children. The Moore decision redrafted benefit laws to remove a requirement of knowing and disclosing the noncustodial, generally male, biological parent—thereby valuing both complementary African matriarchy and the support of fictive kin. The Sanchez decision ultimately expands notions of family, not only to African constructions exceeding Euro nuclear, patriarchal, and consanguineous family but surpassing the physical realm to the metaphysical and ancestral.

Consistent with Asante, Karenga, Mbiti, Dove, Asante, and Mazama's works, the African family is not another manifestation of finite patriarchal ownership but an unabridged, sacred, complementary community of social selfhood.

## Case 1: In Re Bradshaw—The African Child, mtoto

*In re Bradshaw* culminated in the repeal of a state law that had barred my client from receiving benefits to care for the child of a drug-addicted and incarcerated distant cousin due to inadequate familial degree. Our new *Bradshaw* law supplanted the prior five-degree kinship requirement with an allowance of any demonstrable consanguinity, thereby recognizing nonnuclear African and Global South familial cultures and lifting a heavy burden on carceral and traumatized parents within extended families seeking to prevent family separation, foster care, and intergenerational recidivism. Where *Sanchez* and *Moore* highlighted African cultural values concerning ancestral veneration and African matriarchy, *Re Bradshaw* invokes cultural policy arguments drawn from expansive African village kinship bonds to children.

My client-initiated guardianship of her distant cousin's child to prevent the perils of foster care once her cousin required extensive drug rehabilitation. I argued to reform NJ's TANF or federal welfare law by expanding its scope of recognized caregiver families from those within five relational degrees, as the law then required, to all demonstrable degrees of relationship. While the primary arguments used to reverse these laws were based on legal doctrine and broader social policy, the emphasized cultural histories at their root reflect the source of their human dislocation and much of American public policy. This and each case illustrate the need for systemic cultural intervention before bills are enacted.

## Case 2: In Re Moore—The African Matriarch, mamamkuu

*In re Moore* repealed a prior state law's children's benefits bar to parents unable to name their noncustodial co-parent—a factual impossibility for my client who had conceived her child in a past life of prostitution. This case also illustrates an American policy ignorance of or contempt for African familial culture and history, specifically, a culture of communal child-rearing and complementary matriarchy. Historically, the irony rests in America's centuries of forcing children from their mothers in bondage. Douglass's narratives, thus, recount the wrenching complexity of his government-enforced estrangement with his mother through her dying day. So, too, Patrick Moynihan observed

American welfare law's decades of anti-African family policies (Wilson, 2009), and current observers of social welfare foster care document continuing anti-Black family patterns (Roberts, 2003). Culturally, too, the case cemented the state's triracial cultural policy disdain for poor, African womanhood as exemplified by a determined single Black mother rebounding from the oldest profession. The shame it ascribed to my client mirrored its projection:

My client's redlined homes and underfunded schools offered few pathways to economic agency compared with the plentiful jobs and contracts afforded mediocre white men in the state. By Maatic African contrast, "The woman is revered in her role as the mother who is the bringer of life, the conduit for the spiritual regeneration of the ancestors, the bearer of culture, and the center of social organization" (Dove, 1998). Likewise, the child is of the community and heir to the same, blameless for the moral mishaps of their parents. Her mother's resilience and transformation for her child reflected the best African womanist culture in history—from enslaved Harriet women freeing and building forbidden families, cultures, and communities to warrior Nzinga and Nanny queens, taking arms to repel western colonizers.

## Case 3: Sanchez v. DHS—The African Ancestor, mhenga

Finally, in *Sanchez v. Department of Human Services*, 314 *N.J. Super.* 11 (1998), my team, clients, and I successfully invalidated the statutory 1-year residency requirement for interstate migrating citizens needing federal welfare assistance. My legal argument successfully invoked the federal Constitutional Fourteenth Amendment Equal Protection Clause and the Right to Travel. *Sanchez* held NJ's residency statute and its bar on U.S. migrant citizen children's and families' benefits unconstitutional under both my assertions of the federal Equal Protection and Right to Travel. The historical migratory context for the case includes the Black familial fight for survival, from the Underground Railroad to the Great Migration and Caribbean migratory negotiation of U.S. hemispheric policy. As mentioned above, culturally, the prior policy ignored my lead client's Afro-Latin spiritual imperative to her Puerto Rican homeland to bury and honor her parental ancestor. As Afrocentricity is located and related to African history and culture,

Karenga's (2003a) shared orientation of veneration of one's ancestors constitutes a critical cultural concern within the Sanchez case.

In *Sanchez v. Department of Human Services*, our legal team represented 50 clients in challenging a state residency statute that had foreclosed vital children's benefits for citizen migrants to New Jersey from poorer states and territories. It directly impacted those migrating from Puerto Rico, Georgia, Mississippi, Southern states, and U.S. territories. My lead client, an Afro-Latina mother, had taken a month's leave from her area job to return to her childhood home in Puerto Rico to bury her deceased parent and tend to related family matters. Upon returning 1 month later, Ms. Sanchez lost her job and exceeded the period to receive unemployment compensation. Still grief-stricken and having worked all her adult life, she now had to act to prevent homelessness for herself and her child. She, therefore, applied for and received federal welfare benefits for her child as she sought a new job. Months later, the state reversed its decision and demanded she repay her benefits in full, just as she was to begin a new job. A similar scenario multiplied many times for each of our clients and the thousands of others they represented. Unfortunately, the law banned our clients and others similarly situated from benefits: Once someone has left the state for 1 month or longer, they must remain in New Jersey for at least 1 year before qualifying for state-level benefits. The law targeted those from poorer Southern states and territories, ostensibly discouraging them from migrating to the Northeast monetary "magnet" to access its meager but relatively higher benefit rates. This law's underlying migratory "magnet" theory had no basis in empirical data, as neither statistics nor case anecdotes supported its premise. Why would people experiencing poverty incur the added disruption and prohibitive costs of distant relocation in exchange for the supposed lure of an extra $100 to 200 of temporary monthly benefits?

Rather than Western universalist short-term cultural presumption, a fuller, rational cost-benefit analysis should have required weighing not only the higher benefits but the much higher net monetary cost and family-community disruption of moving North. Yet, the calculations that produced this and other laws emanated from somewhere far from holistic reason. As with anti-African state actions throughout history, no one had bothered to ask my clients, let alone their cultural collective or their ancestral historical record, why they had moved. Yet, centering their lives and "welfare" had no basis in American historical and cultural precedence upon which legal precedent could be founded. "Benefits" to their lives had never been the point of systems created, instead to extract from them and benefit others.

Conversely, from the historical perspective of policy-centered Eurocentric monetary culture, it did make sense to voyage afar for amoral, instant riches, as did a lost Columbus in 1492 and the British pirated enslavement vessel, the *White Lion*, in 1619. Had the lawmakers instead understood and centered Black migratory histories, they would have appreciated the relevant longitudinal data that such histories provide. These include, for example, the Underground Railroad to emancipation (Anadolu-Okur, 2017), the Great Migration from Jim Crow lynching northward hoping for *The Warmth of Other Suns* (Wilkerson, 2010), and the Caribbean-to-U.S. immigration of so many like my parents in the negotiation of decades of destabilizing U.S. hemispheric militarization and monetary policy (Foner, 2001). Like the most devastating Maafa migrations, including the Middle Passage and Trail of Tears, such displacements of African and global Southern cradle people emerged from brutal imposition and coercion, not casual greed.

What the law lacked in African American empirical data is, therefore, more than acquired in European American historical and cultural explanation. Its 17th-century British-adopted target was the "undeserving" poor (McIntosh, 2005), now extended from the Southern Black Belt and Puerto Rico. It found rich American historical precedents as well, dating back to post-emancipation vagrancy-convict leasing laws (Muller, 2018), and invoked pretextual 1970s Nixon-initiated Drug Wars, 1980s Reagan stereotypes of racialized welfare queens, and reprised 2000s Bush and Clinton welfare reform. The NJ State Appellate and Supreme Court ultimately rendered the law unconstitutional under the federal Equal Protection Clause and Right to Travel. Yet, the cultural policy arguments it illustrated are pertinent to this paper.

Like the simpler laws I would challenge and overturn without my team of lawyers, the residency statute directly projected the three central hierarchies or triarchies of Western culture: antiwoman, anti-poor, and anti-African. As importantly, it had ignored my lead client's Afro-Latin cultural imperative in returning to her Puerto Rican homeland to honor her decedent parent. The lawmakers had not thought to make an exception for intergenerational responsibilities such as the African value and shared orientations of elder honor through visitation and ancestral veneration through proper burial (Karenga, 2003a). They also remained oblivious to African land ideals such that in ancient Kemet (Egypt), one would bury a placenta in the land and recognize the realm of the ancestors (Nehusi, 2018).

Ms. Sanchez's cultural duties encompassed her roles as maternal-ancestral daughter and daughter to a motherland—neither of which the law recognized, nor did the prior law recognize the meticulous detail, time, and expense of honoring a revered communal matriarchal queen mother (Dove, 1998) and the responsibility expected of an only Afro-Latin-Caribbean child returning from mainland America in doing so. Asante (2009, p. 257) highlights in *Encyclopedia of African Religion*, "Often the African elder's only worry appears to be, 'Who shall ritualize me when I am deceased if I have no children." Therefore, the law disadvantaged my clients' class economically but dislocated it culturally. This sobering reality united my above career reflections on miseducation (Woodson, 1933), criminal injustice (Stevenson, 2019), and exploitative economic policies (Taylor, 2019). The more I analyzed laws and policies affecting every aspect of my clients' and students' lives, the more I observed the cultural basis undergirding them all. Thus, in seeding this project's merger of culture and policy, I sought to heed Asante's (2011) personal call to run toward Africa and Diop's (1989) guidance to unearth the profundity of her cultural unity.

## CONCLUSION

Rooted in the Afrocentric staples of location theory and agency reduction formation, critical Afrocentric gifts to public policy analysis include cultural and historical centering, Maaticity, and African Womanism. Asante and Dove set forth the Afrocentric cultural focus, "Culture will be used as the key to understand its powerful influence on human institutional development" (p. 35). "Culture … affects decisions and actions in the methods employed to build social institutions like family, healthcare, education, politics, economies, entertainment, the arts, and spiritual systems" (p. 37, citing Dove, 2015). The Bradshaw, Moore, and Sanchez case studies illustrate the integral role of Afrocentric analysis in recentering broadly deleterious laws that impact every aspect of African-descendant American citizens.

Other important Afrocentric concepts signal the way forward for Afrocentric public policy: suggesting more functional and policy-adaptable strategies within an aspirational multicultural democracy. Aaron X. Smith (bka) Jabali Adé's *beneficial extraction* thus suggests multidirectional African and Diasporan cultural cross-fertilization and mutually beneficial extractive exchanges. Malcolm X modeled this concept through his influence upon the African consciousness of Nigerian musical contemporary Fela Kuti. Consistently, the breadth of Maaticity properly embraces an expansive conception of African temporality, from African-human antiquity to its invocations of circular and multigenerational African futures. Vast is the tapestry from which Afrocentric policy may weave, yet Afrocentric principles will help wisely guide its creations and enable ethical futures.

# REFERENCES

Akbar, N. (2003). Africentric sciences for human liberation. In A. Mazama (Ed.), *The Afrocentric paradigm*. Africa World Press.

Akua, C. (2017, Fall). *The life of a policy: An Afrocentric case study policy analysis of Florida Statute 1003.42 (h)*. Georgia St. University Dissertation.

Anadolu-Okur, N. (2017). *Dismantling slavery: Frederick Douglass, William Lloyd Garrison, and formation of the abolitionist discourse 1841–1851*. University of Tennessee Press.

Anderson, C. (2015). *White rage: The unspoken truth of our racial divide*. Bloomsbury Publishing USA.

Ani, M. (1994). *Yurugu: An African-centered critique of European cultural thought and behavior*. Africa World Press.

Asante, M. K. (1980). *Afrocentricity: The theory of social change*. Amulefi Publishing Co.

Asante, M. K. (2003a). The quest for method. In A. Mazama (Ed.), *The Afrocentric paradigm*. Africa World Press.

Asante, M. K. (2003b). Locating the text: Implications of Afrocentric theory. In A. Mazama (Ed.), *The Afrocentric paradigm*. Africa World Press.

Asante, M. K. (2008). *An Afrocentric manifesto: Toward an African renaissance*. Polity.

Asante, M. K. (2009). *Encyclopedia of African religion*. Sage.

Asante, M. K. (2010). *Erasing racism: The survival of the American nation*. Prometheus Books.

Asante, M. K. (2012a). *As I run toward Africa: A memoir*. Paradigm.

Asante, M. K. (2012b). *The history of Africa*. Temple University Press.

Asante, M. K. (2011). *Maat and human communication: Supporting identity, culture, and history without global domination*. Temple University.

Asante, M. K. (2015). *As I run toward Africa*. Routledge.

Asante, M. K., & Dove, N. (2021). *Being human being: Transforming the race discourse*. Universal Write Publications.

Baldwin, J. (1993). *The fire next time (Vintage International)*. Vintage Books.

Blackmon, D. A. (2009). *Slavery by another name: The re-enslavement of Black Americans from the Civil War to World War II*. Anchor.

Bilolo, M. (1986). *Les cosmo-théologies philosophiques de l'Egypte antique: problématiques-prémisses herméneutiques-et-problèmes majeurs* (Vol. 1). menaibuc

Diop, C. A. (1974). *The African origin of civilization: Myth or reality*. L. Hill.

Diop, C. A. (1989). *The cultural unity of Black Africa: The domains of patriarchy and of matriarchy in classical antiquity*. Karnak House.

Dove, N. (1998). *Afrikan mothers: Bearers of culture, makers of social change*. State University of New York Press.

Dove, N. (2003). Defining African womanist theory. In A. Mazama (Ed.), *The Afrocentric paradigm*. Africa World Press.

Dove, N. (2015). African women, power of. In *The encyclopedia of African cultural heritage in North America* (Vol. 1, pp. 150–54). Sage Publishing.

Du Bois, W. E. B. (2014). *Black reconstruction in America*. Oxford University Press.

Foner, N. (Ed.). (2001). *Islands in the city: West Indian migration to New York*. University of California Press.

Hilliard III, A. (1993). *Bringing Maat, destroying Isfet: The African and African diasporan presence in the study of ancient KMT*.

Hudson-Weems, C. (1993). *Africana womanism: Reclaiming ourselves*.

Hudson-Weems, C. (2003). *Africana womanism*. In A. Mazama (Ed.), *The Afrocentric paradigm*. Africa World Press.

Karenga, M. (2003a). Afrocentricity and multicultural education: Concept, challenge and contribution. In A. Mazama (Ed.), *The Afrocentric paradigm*. Africa World Press.

Karenga, M. (2003b). *Introduction to black studies*. University of Sankore Press.

Kendi, I. X. (2016). *Stamped from the beginning: The definitive history of racist ideas in America*. Avalon Publishing Group.

Kerner Report. (1968). *Report of the National Advisory Commission on Civil Disorders*. Kerner Commission: U.S. G.P.O.

Kumah-Abiwu F. (2016). Beyond intellectual construct to policy ideas: The case of the Afrocentric paradigm. *Journal of Pan African Studies, 9*(2), 7–28.

Mazama, A. (Ed.). (2003). *The Afrocentric paradigm*. Africa World Press.

McIntosh, M. K. (2005). Poverty, charity, and coercion in Elizabethan England. *Journal of Interdisciplinary History, 35*(3), 457–479.

Moynihan, D. P. (1997). The Negro family: The case for national action (1965). *African American Male Research*, 1–35.

Muller, C. (2018). Freedom and convict leasing in the postbellum south. *American Journal of Sociology, 124*(2), 367–405.

Nehusi, K. (2018). *Land and identity in the Afrikan tradition* [Conference session]. 30th Annual Cheikh Anta Diop International Conference, DISA. The African American Museum, Philadelphia, 12 October.

Roberts, D. E. (2003). Child welfare and civil rights. *U. Ill. L. Rev.*, 171.

Tillotson, M. (2011). *Invisible Jim Crow: Contemporary ideological threats to the internal security of African Americans*. Africa World Press.

Wilkerson, I. (2010). The warmth of other suns: The epic story of America's great migration. *African Diaspora Archaeology Newsletter, 13*(4), 25.

Wilson, W. J. (2009). The Moynihan Report and research on the black community. *The Annals of the American Academy of Political and Social Science, 621*(1), 34–46.

Woodson, C. G. (1933) *The mis-education of the Negro*. The Associated Publishers.

# CHAPTER 4

## Dismantling the Racial Ladder: Toward an African Cultural Paradigm

### Taharka Adé, PhD

ABSTRACT

In this chapter, I investigate the Afrocentric theories presented in Asante and Dove's brilliant work, *Being Human Being*. In particular, I discuss the notions of "being human," the racial ladder, as well as Maaticity. In Asante and Dove's *Being Human Being*, they argue the existence of a racial ladder, which I find to be a useful metaphor. African people exist at the bottom rung of this ladder while all others ascend categorically upward. The authors introduce "the house of humanity" as an alternative to the paradigm of race, or "the house of race." It is a worthwhile alternative and leaves room for the identification of culture as paradigmatic centers for various ethnic groups as well as larger, transcontinental groupings of people once bound by the problematic boundaries of racial grouping (i.e., African, Asian, European).

Asante and Dove argue for the complete and utter destruction of the racial paradigm. I argue that the destruction of the racial paradigm would require the complete fall of the Western world and the development of the African world into a truly sovereign domain of power. Without such tremendous shifts in historical reality, the philosophical paradigm of *humanity*, being so dominated by Eurocentric universalism that any such paradigm will ultimately center Eurocentric ethos as long as the European world remains in power. While Africa may be the genetic home of humanity, the idea of a sociocultural humanity is a modern construction brought on by the events of war, colonialism, and domination that led to the shrinking of the world and the opening of borders, which exposed the world to a set of Eurocentric subjectivities that purports itself to be an objective and universal humanism.

Of course, we can speak of an African humanism, or rather a "house of humanity" based on African cultural foundations as paradigm, but within that exist the subjectivities of African people in determining for ourselves our ontological disposition. It is not the same as the humanism of Europeans and the Western world's past efforts at embracing such paradigms, or as de Souza Santos refers to as "the epistemologies of the south," have proven to be nothing more than exercises in intellectual thievery and the Eurocentric sanitation of cultural heritage.

Asante and Dove argue for "Maaticity," "where truth, righteousness, justice, harmony, order, balance, and reciprocity serve as components of being human beings." However, as the nature of the Western world's hegemonic power is one that continuously works against cultural pluralism without hierarchy, would then *Maaticity* simply become another epistemology swallowed up by the Eurocentric enterprise? While Asante and Dove's argument to dismantle the racial ladder as well as the utility of "the house of humanity" and *Maaticity* for the sake of a more pluralistic world is convincing, this chapter also explores avenues to advance these theories for the sake of posterity.

**Keywords:** Asantean, Racial Ladder, Marcus Garvey, Maaticity African World Antecedent Methodology (AWAM)

The contemporary notion of identity for people of African descent is often bound up in a collective identification through shared oppression under European terrorism. This typically provides the foundational ideology of unity through struggle within what we can call the race paradigm. Regarding African identities in the so-called new world, Paul Gilroy's theories have garnered much attention in the academy. In *The Black Atlantic*, Gilroy (1993) argues against notions of a cultural essence, mainly as those concepts are used to justify cultural nationalism. In his book, *After Empire*, Gilroy (2004) adopts Franz Fanon's "new humanism," terminology "where Black political thought was challenged to advance an interpretation of past and present sufferings with reference to the future."

Here, we have this fixation on suffering that historically roots the coming of Europeans to Africa as the bifurcating bases of past and present realities for African people. This is also theological (as matters involving temporal and spatial realities often are), for this creates a deified view of Europeans in history that bifurcates precolonial and postcolonial realities in a way.

Like Dionysius's and the Gregorian calendar's bifurcation of old and new world realities about the coming of Jesus, the coming of Europeans to Africa represents a point that is intellectualized as an intervention that sets the stage for a postmodern reality. In my estimation, Gilroy's phrase "with reference to the future" broadly alludes to this as discussions of the future in contemporary academic writing take on a postmodernist and poststructuralist framework. Conclusively, African temporal reality becomes maligned in such a way that African racial identity is defined by shared suffering, and African agency is thus inescapably bound to European providence. This poststructuralist take ignores the centuries of human history in Africa and the cultural processes that have led up to African present reality to assert that European intervention in Africa has upheaved that historical reality to such a degree that a bifurcation in temporal reality is necessary.

However, the Afrocentric analysis before you argue that European intervention in Africa, much like Arab intervention before it, is but a moment in the annals of African history. Continuing to use the racial paradigm to describe the collective identity of Africans is perilous because it inherently centers the narrative of African identity around oppression and the relationship between European colonization and racism. This paradigm confines African identity to a Eurocentric framework that emphasizes suffering and subjugation, thereby neglecting the rich, diverse, and dynamic cultural heritage of African peoples that predates and transcends colonial encounters. By focusing on race, the paradigm perpetuates a static and limiting view of African identity, reducing it to mere responses to oppression rather than celebrating and fostering the inherent cultural, social, and historical agency of African peoples (Gilroy, 2000). This diminishes the full spectrum of African experiences and contributions and hinders the development of an empowering and autonomous cultural paradigm that can better serve African communities.

Gilroy (2001) acknowledges the utility of racial identity for those who are racially oppressed. However, Gilroy's emphasis on the "racially oppressed" is primarily the crux of the issue. For African American historians and activists, *race* has held plenty of utility but has always been a borrowed term. To be clear, race is a term loaded with the conceptual inherency of superior and inferior subjects. Therefore, the term has always been limited in its application, mainly when it is meant to convey an Afrocentric analysis (Asante, 2015) of African descendants' historical and cultural agency of African descent. Even as W. E. B. Du Bois mulled over the notions of race in his early writings, such as in "The conservation of races," one can argue that what he described was the conservation, or protection, of cultural agency.

Du Bois (1897/2006) argues that the destiny of African Americans is not to be some emulation of Anglo-Saxons, being that African American culture is "not a servile imitation of Anglo-Saxon culture, but a stalwart originality which shall unswervingly follow Negro ideals." As Molefi Kete Asante and Nah Dove articulate in *Being Human Being*, we must "look outside the race construct and see in reality what we have been experiencing is a clash of cultures" (Asante, 2021). The concept of race has long been one without any clear scientific borders. Are races to be considered those of a particular nationality, such as how the French, German, and American "races" were described in the early 20th century? Or what do we think of the Phoenician Race, Ethiopian Race, and Persian race of the ancient past? Does one's race relate to the continent in which you originate, being one of either the African race, the Asian race, or the European race? Since the mid-19th century, it has been predominantly generalized as a description of people based on skin color and other such human aesthetics and thus broadened to represent large swaths of people who may or may not have any cultural relation to each other (Asante & Dove, 2021). Naturally, this has often produced erroneous concepts of supposed phenotypical racial types. In *The Negro*, Du Bois opens the chapter "The Negro problems" by stating, "It is impossible to separate the world accurately by race since there is no scientific criterion by which to divide races."

Du Bois (1897/2006) has had this view as early as "The conservation of races" as he states, "Color does not agree with the texture of hair, for many of the dark races have straight hair; nor does color agree with the breadth of the head, for the yellow Tartar has a broader head than the German." He also describes in "To the nations of the world" that the differences in race "show themselves chiefly in the color of the skin and the texture of the hair" (Du Bois et al., 2012). However, Du Bois himself still used this problematic type of classification even as late as the publication of his text *The World and Africa* in 1947. We can only assume this was simply due to the practical political applications of race by Du Bois (Adé, 2023) and many others. Nevertheless, Asante and Dove (2021) suggest that of racial classifications, "customs hardly mattered as long as the physical characteristics could be described in a certain way."

They then assert that culture is a much more viable method of categorization than race, with which I agree. The use of culture as a paradigm may be viewed as politically applicable as the racial paradigm—which makes the utilization of the need to fight against racial oppression more appealing for social and political movements. However, the power of race is just an illusion, a tool of European culture in which to oppress the world via the racial ladder. Race is a static and limiting paradigm, while culture leaves room for variation and dynamism. Race also maintains a certain essentialism based on color (West, 2018), while culture recognizes phenotype as a tenant but not the determining factor for group identity. To be sure, race has been most helpful in conversations on topics such as oppression, decoloniality, racial supremacy, and mental enslavement. However, all such concepts center on oppression, and, in the Western hemisphere, at the center of racial oppression are Europeans. Therefore, the racial paradigm often forces us to center Europeans in some form.

This is why I reject Gilroy's use of racial identity and advocate for an identity paradigm that focuses on cultural reality. However, the abandonment of the race paradigm will leave us with many questions regarding political organization that need to be answered. I submit that we must radically progress the cultural paradigm to answer these questions and serve African people in ways more effectively than the race paradigm ever could. Simultaneously, we should work to dismantle the racial ladder that has held us captive in the bottom rung of world society for centuries. Perhaps no one better articulated the utility of race for African people than Marcus Garvey. As Martin (1986) notes in *Race First*, "For Garvey, the Black man was universally oppressed on racial grounds, and any program of emancipation would have to be built around the question of race first. The race became a 'political entity' which would have to be redeemed." To be sure, Garvey acknowledged culture as a tool for liberation and was quite concerned with the political implications of culture as he did pay attention to the cultural activities of African Americans in his time. However, race as a paradigm was his primary concern, and the often centering of whites, or instead centering the need of Africans to break the shackles of white domination, was inescapable as Garvey feared that without the assured and protected autonomy of those of African descent in the United States, the continued educational and economic uplift of Black people would soon be put in competition with the white power structure and spell disaster for the Black race (Martin, 1986, pp. 24–27).

This, of course, is no slight on Garvey as his primary concern was indeed the upliftment of African people, but utilizing race as a political identity most often causes us to center the history and effects of our oppression at the hands of Europeans and not our cultural-historical connections to each other regardless of Europeans. Thinking hypothetically, if Europeans were to one day no longer exist, for what purpose would we have to unify racially? In *Race Matters* (West's (2001) racial definition of being Black is "being minimally subject to white supremacist abuse and being part of a rich culture and community that has struggled against such abuse. All people with black skin and African phenotype are subject to potential white supremacist abuse." It is telling that these two figures, Garvey and West, who house ideologically opposing views on race relations, share in their ideology that racial oppression by whites is foundational to defining Blackness.

While Garvey's notion of Blackness naturally includes substantial agency-affirming rhetoric, the racial paradigm ultimately constrains his philosophical stance on agency. This limitation is highlighted by Asante and Dove's concept of "the racial ladder," which positions African people at the bottom rung of a hierarchy dominated by European standards. By adhering to the racial paradigm, Garvey's framework inadvertently reinforces this hierarchical structure, centering the struggle for Black identity around combating oppression rather than celebrating and advancing African cultural and historical agency. This focus on racial struggle, while influential in mobilizing resistance, perpetuates the narrative of subjugation and fails to fully embrace the potential for cultural renaissance and self-determination inherent in an Afrocentric paradigm.

# THE RACIAL LADDER

Returning to Asante and Dove's *Being Human Being*, they argue the existence of a racial ladder, which I find a helpful metaphor. African people exist at the bottom rung of this ladder. In contrast, all others ascend categorically upward based on the skin color of the majority population within a particular racial group. I would submit that the beams of the racial ladder on either side symbolize the structural social immobility of race, and welded within it are the trampled rungs of humanity, with each rung being statically fixed into the beams and ranging phenotypically from darkest at the bottom to light or white at the top.

One could also argue that the histories of colonialism and imperialism symbolize each beam that frames the ladder. The combined histories inform the Western world how to remain on the top rung. Any group that dares trespass onto the top rung of whiteness, the Western world swiftly puts in its place. Moments in history have risked the structural integrity of the ladder, such as times of international conflict and uprising, and have made the structure easily prone to toppling. This has not however ever risked the destruction of the ladder.

It would be propped back up with everything in place. The only proper recourse is the complete and utter destruction of the frame, meaning those on the bottom rungs would have to gain power capable of overwhelming the Western power structures that keep the ladder steady. In anticipating the destruction of the racial ladder, Asante advances the idea of a world of pluralism without hierarchy. He and Dove mention the egalitarian visions of Charles Volney. I am skeptical of Volney's prophecies of the "union of all religions" and particularly suspicious of the real implications of us all "becoming human" (Asante & Dove, 2021). Humanism may seem a worthwhile alternative to the race paradigm, but the theory of *humanity* is laden with conceptual baggage. It is so dominated by Eurocentric universalism (frankly, Eurocentric subjectivity) that any such paradigm will ultimately center Eurocentric ethos.

While Africa may be the home of humanity, the idea of socioculture humanity is a modern construction brought on by the events of war, colonialism, and domination that led to the shrinking of the world and the opening of borders, which exposed the world to a set of Eurocentric subjectivities that purports itself to be an objective and universal human-ism. We can speak of African humanism, but within that exist the subjectivities of African people in determining for ourselves our onto-logical disposition. It is not the same as the humanism of Europeans. Asante and Dove are earnest in their search for solutions to ongoing racial oppression. Still, I do not think that we will come to an agreement on cultural pluralism without hierarchy anytime soon without African people first wielding power, which rivals all others. Then perhaps some-thing close could have been achieved. At the time, the European world willingly pursued *Maatic* principles rather than the usual *Isfetic* machina-tions they have been subjecting the world for the past few centuries.

## MAATICITY VERSUS ISFETICITY

Asante and Dove (2021) argue for a *Maaticity*, "where truth, righteous-ness, justice, harmony, order, balance, and reciprocity serve as components of being human beings." This term (and the seven principles) derives from our contemporary interpretations of the Kemetic term *Ma'at* (Asante, 2015), which existed for those ancient Africans as simultaneously a deity and a moral imperative. *Ma'at*'s counter is *Isfet*, the embodiment of chaos, and they are eternally entwined in a raging cosmic war of opposites and symbolize a complementary yet paradoxical dualism. Maaticity is an excellent Afrocentric theoretical enterprise, but I am suspicious of the implications of presenting Maaticity before what Boaventura de Sousa Santos (2014) describes in his *Epistemologies of the South: Justice Against Epistemicide* as the West's, "system of visible and invisible distinctions."

Would Maaticity become another epistemology swallowed up by the Eurocentric enterprise? Santos insists that the ethos of modern Western thinking is "abysmal thinking," as it creates and negates visible and invisi-ble distinctions to fuel its hegemonic machinations. Within this logical yet illogical dilemma, it is acceptable for Europe to, for example, pillage the epistemologies of other world cultures, as well as subjugate and hierarchi-cally categorize those cultures and their epistemologies as inferior to Europe while also creating a self-image (the visible line) of committing these atrocities in the name of world peace and justice. The invisible line of violence, plunder, and agency reduction is subsequently made invisible by hiding it in the shadow of this false self-image the West creates for itself and then disingenuously projects onto the world. Both lines are foundational, but one is negated to avoid internal conflicts (de Sousa Santos, 2014).

I argue that such chaotic ethos cannot cooperate with other cultural paradigms as it has created within itself an *Isfetic duality*. An Isfetic duality is an ethos that seeks to be void of internal moral conflict and feigns a sense of righteousness for the sake of order. In this circumstance, it is not informed by the complete set of seven principles, but a mere projection of such information informed by Isfet's cosmic tethering to Ma'at. Consequently, to use Maaticity as an example, the predominant brand of Eurocentric thinking projects an illusion of balance, harmony, justice, reciprocity, truth, and order.

The West, schizophrenically, will convince itself, or its populace, that it is submitting to the principles of Ma'at but simultaneously consciously operates on Isfetic tenants, which it negates the existence of in the face of internal moral conflict. Such Eurocentric narcissism would allow the United States, for example, to condemn the genocide in Rwanda in 1994, but yet had just 40 years prior, at the 1948 Genocide Convention, been involved in ratifying international law on genocide on the condition that the United States would be granted immunity from the charges of genocide, a charge presented before the U.N. Convention by delegates such as W. E. B. Du Bois (2006), Paul Robertson, and William Patterson (Horne, 1986). Perhaps this all underlines a metatheory of Asante and Dove's position. What is being proposed is a moral objective that Europe will never be able to accept or achieve and, therefore, will continue to expose its hypocrisy. Nevertheless, history has proven that dismantling the racial ladder for the sake of African agency can only be achieved by African people coming into their own, not by appealing to Isfetic powers for an "erection of a new human," as Dove and Asante suggest (2021).

Power will always determine the terms of reality, which has remained a truism in human history. Therefore, we must carefully promote our most sacred and ancient concepts as a universal human aim. Europe will use its present power to create a masquerade of the attempt to meet such goals, yet masked, as always, by its cultural subjectivities. Naturally, this exemplifies an unwillingness on my part to believe that Europe will ever relinquish the wheel of cultural domination. If it has power, it will continue to drive the world to the brink of utter catastrophe. In his later years, even Du Bois had long lost faith in Europe or, as he described it, this particular "pattern of human culture." While the notion of humanity may have remained an ideal for him, his increasing focus on the potentiality of Africa and Africans in his later years shows proof of where his faith resided.

This is not to say that Asante and Dove do not have ultimate faith in Africa, for in their own words, "Of course, *we* will have to accept African primacy in terms of humanity and human civilization so that *we* can then start from the fact of our common heritage..." (Asante & Dove, 2021). They also argue that African people must not relinquish the importance of our heritage in expressing our humanity but that the ethical paradigms of Africa should exist alongside and equal to the ethical paradigms of all world cultures, like an index of cultural wisdom that all of humanity can draw from. Such a beautiful idea of a utopian, sociocultural reality is nigh impossible as the lust for power and the propensity toward discrimination are some of humans' few naturally endemic traits. As previously stated, I believe that something remarkably close to it is achievable. However, I do not believe that such an achievement can occur by transforming this current world, as Europe's *Isfeticity* has clouded the world in so much darkness.

Unfortunately, it may have to completely consume us all and truly bring about the dark days of chaotic catastrophe before the light of *Ma'at* can be reborn in the womb of Nut's watery abyss (Asante & Mazama, 2009). I may here be courting the philosophy expounded in Frank Wildersson's *Afropessimism*. Wilderson speaks of an abyss that we may find ourselves peering into at the "end of the world." Wilderson's end of the world is a concept he borrows from Frantz Fanon in which to discuss a generative mechanism that provides what he argues is a libidinal relay in non-African groups to avoid "niggerization" (Wilderson, 2020). Dr. Frances Cress-Welsing (1991), referring primarily to Europeans in her seminal yet controversial text *The Isis Papers: The Keys to the Colors*, describes this as the fear of genetic annihilation.

Wilderson contextualizes this argument with an anecdotal story of his Palestinian friend Sameer, someone who he felt a kinship with as he, at the time, believed in the analogy of liberation struggles exhibited between his friend's revolutionary group, the Popular Front for the Liberation of

Palestine and Wilderson's beloved Black Liberation Army. However, Sameer betrayed Wilderson's (2020) trust in such solidarity when he confessed that "being frisked and molested by Black Jews was more humiliating and of a greater threat to the psychic life of Palestinians than being frisked and molested by White Jews."

Wilderson (2020) argues that destroying the generative mechanism that facilitates this thinking will end the world. This generative mechanism to which Wilderson is referring is consistent with Asante and Dove's racial ladder. One could say that Africans are at the bottom rung of a hierarchical ladder of racial life. As I mentioned earlier, the only recourse is the complete and utter destruction of the frame. Europeans in power may, as they have many times in the past, accuse such ideology of a type of reverse racism. They may also argue that to believe that there is no hope for the European world to right its wrongs on its own is, in a sense, dehumanizing them. This would be one of many ways they could use their power to turn Maaticity into a weapon. They would demand reciprocity from the African world while only giving the illusion of upholding their end of the bargain. Of course, the only reason is because they are unwilling to give up power.

Their only recourse at salvation is to relinquish power, but that is something we can never expect, so the only alternative is their power to be overcome. Not for the sake of dispelling them from this earth as so many of them fear. We should also not aim for power to recast the racial ladder with Africans at the top rung and Europeans at the bottom. The racial ladder must be destroyed for the sake of our freedom and, subsequently, the betterment of the world. Such an event will present us with the ending of the old world and the falling into an abyss of new possibilities—in a black hole that absorbs all current reality and, at least theoretically, reconstructs a new reality with the best of the old data. I am all for passing this event horizon and will do so with hopeful optimism. I am a believer in the Asantean philosophy of *victorious consciousness*; therefore, the creation of a new world can be brought about by Africans gaining for themselves social, cultural, political, and economic power.

The strength created by this Afrocentric optimism (Asante, 2007) is sufficient to assist the rest of the world in destroying the racial ladder. Until such a day comes into being, the focus should be on the victory of African people in reclaiming our African humanity or Africanity. To put it another way, I maintain a victorious consciousness set on reclaiming *ubuntu* as a paradigmatic reality for people of African descent (Asante, 2006). To accomplish this, we must eliminate *within ourselves* the race paradigm, which centers our oppression and our relationship to whiteness, and instead advance the African cultural paradigm, which focuses on our intracultural relationships with other Africans. The use of race as a tool of upliftment and struggle against oppression, as described above by Gilroy, Garvey, and West, certainly has, as Asante and Dove (2021) suggest, presented some very excellent and beneficial philosophies of survival and uplift. However, I am more inclined toward, for example, evolving the Du Boisian concept of *Pan-Africa* to utilize the cultural history of African (Provenzo & Abaka, 2019) people and maximize its possibilities to realize social, economic, and political autonomy and agency for African people (Adé, 2022). While the various Pan-African movements over the past few centuries have proven that race, with all its superficialities, can mobilize people for some time, it cannot sustain a movement on its own. I argue that for African people, only a cultural paradigm that informs the development of Pan-African ideals will prove the most successful. To that end, I have developed a methodology known as the Africa-World Antecedent Methodology, an apparatus within the Afrocentric paradigm to illuminate antecedents of culturally unifying phenomena throughout the African world (Adé, 2022).

## AFRICAN WORLD ANTECEDENT METHODOLOGY

The African World Antecedent Methodology (AWAM) provides a robust and functional framework for fostering Pan-African cultural unity by systematically uncovering, preserving, and celebrating shared cultural elements among African peoples. This methodology emphasizes the practical application of historical and cultural data, focusing on three primary concepts: Kanna (sameness), Fánna (similarity), and Naani (uniqueness). These concepts collectively offer a comprehensive understanding of African cultural phenomena, enabling a practical approach to enhancing Pan-African unity.

The methodological rigor of AWAM ensures that the identification and celebration of African cultural elements are not superficial but deeply rooted in historical and cultural analysis. It promotes a nuanced and authentic understanding of our cultural heritage, which is essential for genuine cultural justice. AWAM offers a transformative approach to dismantling the racial paradigm that positions the arrival of Europeans in Africa as the defining bifurcation of past and present realities for African people. By emphasizing cultural continuities and historical connections that predate colonial encounters, AWAM reclaims and recenters African agency and achievements spatially and temporally.

AWAM's focus on Kanna fundamentally consists of the same elements across different African cultural groups, such as traditional practices, spiritual beliefs, and social structures. This identification is not merely academic but carries significant practical implications. For example, African American musicians can utilize historical data on African musical patterns to deepen their understanding of past roots and incorporate new elements into contemporary genres like jazz, blues, and hip-hop. This direct lineage fosters a deeper appreciation of heritage and reinforces cultural continuity. Similarly, African American chefs can explore historical records of African culinary practices to uncover the origins of traditional African American (or "soul food") dishes, strengthening ties through a shared culinary heritage.

One example I mention in my book, *W. E. B. Du Bois' Africa*, is the connection between Jollof and Jambalaya (Adé, 2023). African diasporic spiritual leaders, for example, can use the Kanna approach to extrapolate historical data on African spiritual practices that remained persistent even in the Americas through the early 20th century to reincorporate or reinforce elements such as libation ceremonies and ancestor veneration into their religious observances, enriching spiritual practices and reinforcing cultural roots.

Fánna explores cultural similarities that suggest a shared heritage, even if the exact antecedents take time to be precise. This aspect of AWAM is exponentially functional in the diaspora, where diverse African-descended populations can find common ground in their shared cultural practices and historical experiences. For instance, educators can leverage historical data on African folklore to connect African American characters like Brer Rabbit and High John the Conqueror with their African counterparts, such as Anansi, the Spider. By identifying the Naani, uniqueness, and Fánna in these stories, they can illustrate how African narratives have been preserved and adapted within the African American experience. Integrating these stories into educational programs and community events reveals the enduring presence of African folklore in African American culture, fostering a sense of shared cultural heritage.

By highlighting these connections, AWAM encourages solidarity and mutual respect by practically understanding shared cultural narratives across the diaspora. Continuing the conversation on shared culinary traditions by examining the Fánna, or similarity, in ingredients and cooking techniques, such as the use of okra, rice, black-eyed peas, and yams, we can demonstrate connections to African culinary traditions. Hosting cooking classes or cultural events that highlight these culinary links can strengthen the community's understanding of the African roots of their culinary heritage, thereby enhancing cultural pride. Naani focuses on unique cultural phenomena, ensuring that the distinct identities of individual African communities are recognized and preserved. This recognition within the broader framework of cultural unity prevents the erasure of local traditions and practices, fostering a more inclusive and respectful approach to Pan-Africanism. By valuing commonalities and differences, AWAM encourages a pluralistic and dynamic understanding of African identity, which can be practically applied in community programs and educational initiatives.

There is also a functional aspect to AWAM. The emphasis on cultural antecedents provides a powerful counternarrative to Eurocentric historiographies that have long dominated the portrayal of African cultural histories and identities as either static, essentialist, or suffering from such overwhelming Eurocentric influence that cultural reclamation would prove elusive. Furthermore, by reclaiming and reasserting African cultural narratives, AWAM empowers African people to define themselves on their terms.

This functional reclamation of cultural agency is essential for fostering a sense of pride and solidarity among African communities. The functional application of AWAM can help guide the development of educational curricula, cultural programs, and community initiatives that celebrate African heritage. In essence, AWAM reveals the functional aspects of African cultural elements that are alive and well within African diasporic communities. This approach not only fosters a deeper understanding and appreciation of heritage but also strengthens the cultural bonds between Africa and its diaspora. By promoting a more accurate representation of African and African diasporic contributions to world civilization, AWAM is a crucial tool for promoting Pan-African cultural unity and advancing the cultural project of African peoples globally.

It can bridge gaps in historical data with contemporary practices, actively working to dismantle the remnants of the racial paradigm and creating a more culturally empowering future for people of African descent. For example, linguists, cultural organizations, and everyday people in the United States can use AWAM to explore linguistic connections between Ebonics and African languages. This linguistic exploration would not only reveal the deep African roots of Ebonics, enhancing the community's appreciation of their linguistic heritage but also serve as a data-gathering tool helpful in strengthening the already dynamic syntax and lexicon of Ebonics.

Further, understanding and embracing the African cultural elements extant within African diasporic culture through the AWAM is a *cultural justice* imperative for several compelling reasons. Primarily, it addresses the historical erasure and marginalization of African contributions to global culture, a legacy of colonialism and systemic racism that has long distorted our historical narratives. By highlighting the African roots of various cultural practices within our communities, AWAM restores rightful recognition and honors African people's rich heritage and achievements. This reclamation of our history and culture is crucial for correcting the false narratives that have dominated for centuries, providing a more exact and respectful representation of our contributions to world civilization.

Applying AWAM promotes a sense of pride and identity among the diasporas. It enables us to see our cultural practices not as mere remnants of a distant past but as vibrant, living traditions that continue to shape our lives and communities. This reconnection with our African roots empowers us, fostering a stronger sense of self-worth and belonging. Cultural empowerment is a form of justice, countering the psychological and social impacts of historical oppression by affirming the value and dignity of our African heritage. This is so dearly needed for many of us who suffer self-hatred regarding our cultural heritage due to Eurocentric social engineering, which, in the United States in particular, has historically socialized those of us of African descent to believe our cultural heritage to be inferior to that of Europeans. By emphasizing cultural continuity and shared heritage, AWAM fosters unity and solidarity within our communities and between the African diaspora and Africa. This unity is essential for international collective action and advocacy, enabling us to work together more effectively to address familiar challenges and pursue shared goals.

In this way, cultural justice extends beyond mere recognition to encompass the active empowerment and mobilization of African-descended peoples throughout the African world. The concept of cultural justice extends also into socioeconomic realms. Historically, African Americans have faced systemic denigration of their musical traditions, such as Jazz and Blues. Western music theorists often labeled these genres as inferior or "demonic" due to their use of tritones, augmented fourths, and diminished fifths, which were considered inharmonious and ungodly. Perhaps adding to the notion of a demonic basis in the Western imagination, these early songs often incorporated folk tales such as that of High John the Conqueror, Shine, Signifying Monkey, Legba, Stagger Lee, Anasi, and Brer Rabbit. All the names are known today as "trickster figures" who represent African Americans' abilities to outwit white Americans. These characters are represented in Black literature, movies, and music (Floyd, 1996). Despite this, the American music industry amassed significant wealth by exploiting African American pioneers of these genres.

This exploitation and marginalization were also a concern among Civil Rights leaders. On April 3, 1968, the night before his assassination, Martin Luther King, Jr. urged a crowd of African Americans in Memphis to support Black-owned businesses, highlighting growing economic disparity in the African American community despite the economic contributions those of African descent had made to American society. King's call to action was driven by observations of economic decline in Black establishments, such as the Ben Moore Hotel in Montgomery, AL, which had financially supported Civil Rights leaders during the Selma to Montgomery March but faced economic hardships after integration. By 1968, had African Americans retained more control over the wealth generated from entertainment alone, the community's economic standing could have been significantly different.

Consider iconic songs like "Smokestack Lightning" and "Mannish Boy" by Muddy Waters, which contain references to High John the Conqueror. Through the subsidiary label Chess Records, both songs are owned exclusively by the Dutch American multinational music corporation Universal Music Group and, along with a host of other African American created songs across several genres, continue to enrich the coffers of this cooperation. Additionally, films such as Disney's *Songs of the South*, which appropriated African American folklore, particularly the tales of Brer Rabbit, contributed substantially to Disney's wealth as this film continued to premiere in theaters for four decades. This pattern of cultural appropriation extends into early Hollywood, where movies like *White Zombie* and *I Walked with a Zombie* distorted Vodou traditions, fueling the burgeoning horror genre. Even earlier than that, authors like H. P. Lovecraft appropriated and misrepresented Vodou culture in their works, such as *The Call of Cthulhu*, which propagated the mistaken notion of Vodou as devil worship. At the same time, Cthulhu mythos has become a significant feature in many franchises. These cultural distortions and economic exploitations underscore the imperative for cultural justice, recognizing and rectifying the socioeconomic impacts of such historical injustices.

In sum, using AWAM to uncover and celebrate African cultural elements within our culture is a cultural justice imperative because it rectifies historical wrongs, empowers us as individuals and communities, fosters unity and solidarity, and promotes an authentic and respectful understanding of our African heritage. This multifaceted approach to cultural justice honors the past and builds a stronger, more inclusive future for African-descended peoples worldwide.

## CONCLUSION: ON BEING AFRICAN

The necessity of dismantling the racial ladder is evident as it perpetuates a hierarchical structure that has historically marginalized African people. The race paradigm, while providing a framework for solidarity and political mobilization, inherently centers on Europeans and oppression, limiting the scope of African agency. By shifting to a cultural paradigm, we can transcend the limitations of race and foster a more profound and holistic understanding of African identity and unity. Embracing a cultural paradigm allows us to reconnect with the rich and diverse heritage of African civilization that predates colonialism and slavery. This paradigm emphasizes the continuity and resilience of African cultural practices, beliefs, and values that have persisted *despite* centuries of oppression. It also dismantles the temporally bifurcating notion that African cultural history is bound by European intervention, ending the deification of European modernity, or *Euromodernity* (Ndlovu-Gatsheni, 2018).

As aforementioned, in the face of shared oppression during the late 19th and 20th centuries, people began to identify as African both on the continent and in the Americas. Thus, a Pan-African political and racial consciousness materialized that engendered African people to identify as Africans on a racial basis. However, a few figures emerged, such as Cheikh Anta Diop, John Henrik Clarke, Kwame Nkrumah, Kwame Ture, Carter G. Woodson, and W. E. B. Du Bois began, consciously or unconsciously, to emphasize the cultural unity of African people. Only one of them, Cheikh Anta Diop, wrote so deliberately on the cultural unity of African people in Africa and perhaps only one other spoke on the cultural unity of Africans throughout the diaspora in such an eloquent way as John Henrik Clarke, also known as the Dean of African American historians.

These intellectual giants helped develop the philosophy that subsequent generations of thinkers to advance what it means to be African. As a result of the influence of such scholars, Molefi Kete Asante would create the theory of Afrocentricity (Asante, 2003) and provide the African world with a theoretical paradigm for advancing African agency. We can now argue with great confidence for the promotion of a composite African identity based on cultural paradigms that predate the racial paradigm. Furthermore, the cultural paradigm aligns with the principles of Maaticity, advocating for a society grounded in truth, justice, harmony, and reciprocity. This Afrocentric vision rejects the *Isfeticity* of Eurocentric modernity, which perpetuates chaos under the guise of order and righteousness.

By centering African epistemologies and ethical frameworks (Asante, 1998), we can set an example for the world and provide a strong message of honoring the intrinsic value of all cultures and promoting genuine pluralism without hierarchy. As we move forward, we continue this intellectual and cultural reclamation. We must invest in education, research, and community initiatives that promote an Afrocentric worldview. Developing and applying methodologies like the AWAM are crucial for identifying and actualizing shared African cultural phenomena. This methodological approach allows us to draw from the deep well of African cultural knowledge and apply it in relevant and transformative ways for our present and future. Through this lens, we can promote cultural justice by redefining our political, economic, and social structures, ensuring they are rooted in African values and perspectives. By doing so, we honor our ancestors and empower future generations to build a world where African people are not merely surviving but thriving. The journey toward dismantling the racial ladder and embracing a cultural paradigm is undoubtedly challenging, but it is a necessary endeavor of significant historical and contemporary importance.

It requires an intentional shift from the Eurocentric conceptual baggage of race toward a more nuanced and empowering understanding of culture as the primary framework for African identity and unity. There must be a collective effort on the part of scholars, activists, and communities to challenge entrenched systems of oppression and envision *Sankofic* possibilities for African unity and empowerment. As we've explored, the notion of race has long been a borrowed term, laden with the implications of superiority and inferiority, thus limiting its efficacy in truly capturing the essence of African identity and agency.

By centering our cultural realities and embracing our shared heritage, we can dismantle the structures that have held us back and pave the way for a future rooted in African self-determination and autonomy. As we move forward, we must continue to challenge the remnants of the racial paradigm that persists in our thinking and organization. We must build a new framework that uplifts and empowers us based on our cultural strengths and historical truths. This process involves academic work and grassroots efforts to instill a sense of cultural pride and unity among African people everywhere. The transition from a racial to a cultural paradigm is not merely an academic proposition but a call to action. It requires a collective effort to reclaim and celebrate our African heritage, educate future generations, and build institutions and movements that reflect our cultural values and aspirations.

By doing so, we can create a future where African people are united not by our shared history of oppression but by a shared vision of empowerment, prosperity, and cultural integrity based on historical (and ancient) cultural foundations. For as I have attempted to elucidate in this chapter, being African transcends the racial constructs imposed upon us. The struggle to reframe and strengthen that identity is about embracing a cultural identity that is rich, dynamic, and resilient. It is about recognizing our interconnectedness and leveraging our collective strength to create a world that respects our agency and serves as an example that uplifts all of humanity. Together, we can dismantle the racial ladder and build a new paradigm that honors the true essence of African identity and unity.

# REFERENCES

Adé, T. (2022). Africological historiography: Primary considerations. *SAGE Open, 12*(1), 215824402210798. https://doi.org/10.1177/21582440221079881

Adé, T. (2023). *W. E. B. Du Bois' Africa: Scrambling for a New Africa*. Anthem Press.

Asante, M. K. (1998). *The Afrocentric idea*. Temple University Press.

Asante, M. K. (2003). *Afrocentricity: The theory of social change*. African American Images.

Asante, M. K. (2006). A discourse on black studies: Liberating the study of African people in the Western academy. *Journal of Black Studies, 36*(5), 646–662.

Asante, M. K., & Mazama, A. (Eds.). (2009). *Encyclopedia of African religion* (Vol. 1). Sage.

Asante, M. K., & Dove, N. (2021). *Being human being: Transforming the race discourse*. Universal Write Publications LLC.

Asante, M. K. (2015). *African pyramids of knowledge: Kemet, Afrocentricity and Africology*. Universal Write Press.

Asante, M. K. (2007). *An Afrocentric manifesto*. Polity Press.

de Sousa Santos, B. (2014). *Epistemologies of the South: Justice against epistemicide*. Routledge.

Du Bois, W. E. (2006). The conservation of races. *Raisons politiques, 21*(1), 117–130. (Original work published 1897).

Du Bois, W. E. B., Provenzo, E. F., & Abaka, E. (2012). *WEB Du Bois on Africa*. Routledge.

Floyd Jr., S. A. (1996). *The power of black music: Interpreting its history from Africa to the United States*. Oxford University Press.

Gilroy, P. (1993). *The Black Atlantic: Modernity and double consciousness.* Harvard University Press.

Gilroy, P. (2000). *Against race: Imagining political culture beyond the color line.* Harvard University Press.

Gilroy, P. (2004). *After empire* (Vol. 105). Routledge.

Horne, G. (1986). *Black and red: WEB Du Bois and the Afro-American response to the cold war, 1944-1963.* SUNY Press.

Martin, T. (1986). *Race first: The ideological and organizational struggles of Marcus Garvey and the Universal Negro Improvement Association* (No. 8). The Majority Press.

Ndlovu-Gatsheni, S. (2018). *Epistemic freedom in Africa: Deprovincialization and decolonization.* Routledge.

Provenzo Jr., E. F., & Abaka, E. (Eds.). (2019). *W. E. B. Du Bois on Africa.* Routledge.

Welsing, F. C. (1991). *The Isis (Yssis) papers.* Third World Press.

West, C. (2001). *Race matters.* Beacon Press.

West, C. (2018). Race matters. In J. Arthur & A. Shapiro (Eds.), *Color – class – identity* (pp. 169–178). Routledge.

Wilderson, F. (2020). *Afropessimism.* Liveright Publishing Corporation.

# CHAPTER 5

## *My Reflections Encountering Molefi Kete Asante: Notes on Afrocentricity, Decoloniality, and Decolonizing Knowledge in Africa*

Lehasa Moloi, PhD

### ABSTRACT

This chapter articulates my reflections on the encounter with Professor Molefi Kete Asante and the discourse surrounding Afrocentricity, analyzing the transformative impact this experience has had on my life during my doctoral studies, which I officially completed in 2021 and extending into subsequent years. Furthermore, I engage with Afrocentricity as a paradigm alongside concepts of decoloniality and the decolonization of knowledge within the African context, particularly about the expansive field of Development Studies. This chapter serves as a personal testament, illustrating that Afrocentricity transcends mere theoretical frameworks for academic advancement; it constitutes a profound, life-altering experience for individuals navigating the complexities of Eurocentric paradigms, facilitating a reconnection with one's African heritage as a restorative endeavor to reclaim dignity in the face of Eurocentric degeneration.

Professor Molefi Kete Asante (originally named Arthur Lee Smith Jr., born in 1942 in Valdosta, Georgia) stands as a pivotal figure among revolutionary Afrocentric Pan-Africanist philosophers, having endowed the African continent and diaspora with Afrocentricity as a liberatory metaparadigm. His influential contributions have been instrumental in reconstructing the African narrative, restoring African consciousness from the dislocation inflicted by violent colonial encounters that have left the continent in turmoil. Through his extensive writings and public discourses on Afrocentricity, Asante has catalyzed a renewed interest among scholars of African descent globally, prompting a reevaluation of humanity's narrative from an African viewpoint (Asante, 1990).

In this chapter, I focus on my reflections regarding Asante's scholarly contributions as a preeminent voice and thinker in the global advancement of Africology. I have organized my reflections into three main sections: First, I recount my journey of discovering Afrocentricity literature and my eventual personal meeting with its progenitor. This encounter profoundly altered the trajectory of my life. Second, I explore the interplay between Afrocentricity and Decoloniality, emphasizing the imperative of knowledge decolonization in the quest for African redevelopment and self-actualization. Lastly, I contemplate the significance of Molefi Kete Asante's scholarship in asserting African agency for future generations.

**Keywords:** Afrocentricity, Eurocentrism, Decoloniality, Development, Relocation

# INTRODUCTION

In the beginning, it is crucial to establish my identity as a continental African by birth, thus showing that my engagement with discussions on Afrocentricity is not from that perspective. Also, it is important to acknowledge my position as a university lecturer in the field of Development Studies as it informs my entry into these debates. Like many African children who were born and raised under a colonial education system, I received my elementary and tertiary education in South Africa during a period that encompassed both the apartheid colonial regime and the post-1994 transition to a democratic dispensation. Consequently, the education I received was historically and socially constructed to serve the political interests of the time.

After enrolling in 1995, I pursued political science and African politics at the University of South Africa. This decision was driven by a desire to understand my identity, history, culture, and the political environment I was raised in. From an early age, my education was infused with Christian ideology as a colonial subject, limiting my exposure to diverse perspectives in the realm of knowledge. The curriculum I encountered did not highlight the achievements of African people in history; instead, it focused on the perspectives of white people, portraying Africans primarily as enslaved people who needed to be mentally conditioned to view their reality through the lens of their violent encounters with whites, as perpetuated by the Bantu colonial education system.

Equally significant is that my entry into the academic scholarship program in the mid-1990s was still undergirded by the same ideologies that oriented Black students to understand the world through the lenses of European colonists. During my studies in African politics, I became acquainted with radical Black voices, which reshaped my comprehension of African conditions far beyond my experiences before tertiary education.

I enrolled in Development Studies as one of my major subjects, hoping to find solutions for Africa's redevelopment quest to overcome the gruesome colonial experiences. Within the context of this subject, I realized that the approach to African development discourse was informed by a racist modernization paradigm, which aimed to "redeem" African people from backward traditional ways of living. In my recently published book, *Developing Africa? New Horizons with Afrocentricity* (2024), I argue that "It became abundantly clear that development ideas and practices grounded in the modernization paradigm will not bring about the development that Africa wants but will continue to undermine African development initiatives and cement the Global North's domination agenda" (Moloi, 2024, p. 25). I do not intend to present my reflections on encountering Professor Molefi Asante and my notes on Afrocentricity, Decoloniality, and decolonizing knowledge in Africa in a defensive mode. Instead, I aim to offer candid reflections on my epistemic conversion journey from Eurocentrism to Afrocentricity as a Development Studies student and how that has reoriented my interpretation of the pursuit of knowledge decolonization in this field and my life.

In 2019, the University of South Africa awarded me a scholarship to pursue my PhD in Development Studies. Before this, I had been engaged in intense ideological debates with members of the African Decolonial Research Network (ADERN, 2019), led by my former supervisor, Professor Sabelo Ndlovu-Gatsheni. Professor Ndlovu-Gatsheni has been instrumental in sparking discussions at the University of South Africa on the need for knowledge decolonization in Africa and the global south. He argued that "we needed to shift the geography of knowledge and the biography of expertise." During the founding of ADERN, he explained, "At UNISA, just like in other universities located on the African continent, we were accustomed to consuming academic material from the West. There was little awareness of the rich local African scholarship and African knowledge production. As such, we needed to shift the geography and biography of knowledge. So, the first thing we needed to do was to establish who the decolonial scholars are in Africa and to recognize their contributions" (Ndlovu-Gatsheni, 2016).

Within this context of a search for decolonial knowledge, my interest in African literature and its offerings on knowledge decolonization was sparked. As I began exploring literature on African knowledge, I encountered the works of Professor Molefi Kete Asante, particularly his book *Afrocentricity: The Theory of Social Change*, initially published in 1980 and updated in 2003. This book offered illuminating insights into power, dominance, racism, and the need for African people to escape victimization. Asante's work emphasized the importance of viewing Africans as subjects rather than objects and how this philosophy, ethos, and worldview enable Africans to understand better and interpret issues affecting their communities and lived experiences. After reading this book, I recognized that I had found a liberating theory that would allow me to speak from an African perspective, not merely as a "global south" victim, but from my African identity as my locus of enunciation.

Shortly after, I met Professor Asante during his visit to the main University of South Africa campus. This encounter led to arrangements for me to visit Temple University, where he chaired the Africology department. From that point, my engagement with Afrocentricity deepened as I was introduced to the discourse by Professor Asante, a pivotal figure in the field. As I approached his office, I remembered that his first greeting was to address me by my clan name, Lehasa Moloi, rather than by my colonial name, Richard. He emphasized the importance of aligning oneself with one's cultural heritage and roots as a fundamental aspect of one's identity. This gesture was profoundly liberating for me, as I had predominantly used Richard as my given name, and this moment marked the beginning of my process of self-reorientation, prompting me to reconsider my identity and academic pursuits. When I left Temple University at the end of July 2019 after my visit, Professor Asante blessed me with books on Afrocentricity, reinforcing my determination to complete my studies later that year.

It is important to note that Afrocentricity became my ideological framework for pursuing my studies and evolved into my life philosophy. This philosophy compels one to question everything from the standpoint of African people, embodying the essence of personal liberation when a theory transforms you through the learning process. Molefi Asante (2007, p. 21) states in the *Afrocentric Manifesto* that "Afrocentricity is a way of interpreting reality and begins with the idea that it is teachable and accessible to anyone who cares to learn it. Just as we would not turn away an individual who wants to learn Marxist theory, methodology or capitalist theory, the Afrocentrists will teach anyone how to become a scholar who begins with studying African people as subjects rather than the objects of history." This perspective underscores the transformative potential of Afrocentricity, emphasizing its accessibility and the importance of viewing African people as active agents in their historical narratives.

According to Asante (2007, p. 2), Afrocentricity is "a paradigmatic intellectual perspective that privileges African agency within the context of history and culture trans-continentally and trans-generationally. This means that the quality of location is essential to any analysis. Afrocentricity demands a re-centering of African people in their own historical and cultural contexts, challenging dominant narratives and promoting a more accurate and empowering understanding of African experiences." Asante (2015, p. ix) further posits that "Afrocentricity, as an aspect of centrism, is a groundedness that allows the student of human culture investigating African phenomena to view the world from the standpoint of the African." This experience provided a foundational basis for connecting the inquiry and production of knowledge to questions of identity. Suppose we do not initially address who the knowledge is intended for and what goals we aim to achieve, we risk losing the critical context from the outset, thereby exemplifying the process of dislocation. This was not merely a basis for acquiring knowledge but a pivotal opportunity for transformative learning and personal growth.

# AFROCENTRICITY, DECOLONIALITY, AND KNOWLEDGE DECOLONIZATION IN AFRICA

Afrocentricity profoundly shaped the entirety of my doctoral research, functioning as my guiding philosophical framework, primarily focusing on the interrogation of modern development discourse in Africa based on three units of analysis, namely, African history, culture, and agency as the foundational aspects in reframing the reimagination. I also greatly benefited from reading decoloniality scholars' work, as advanced by many Latin American scholars in their analysis of the European modern world system frameworks and their critique of Eurocentrism. These theoretical perspectives provided essential ideological foundations for my critical assessment of the embeddedness of the discourse and practice of Development Studies within the Eurocentric paradigms, which further entrapped African people within what Anibal Quijano termed "the colonial matrices of power" (Mignolo, 2013).

The complementarity between these two ideologies lies in their scathing critique of Eurocentrism as a hegemonic ideological superstructure, which has contributed to the marginalization of alternative knowledge systems, notably African ways of knowing and sensing. At the core of my critical reflection was an analysis of how the colonial logic became the foundation for interpreting African conceptions of development, ultimately reducing it to an exogenous exercise that systematically excluded African thought and practice, thereby erasing African self-perception and agency from the developmental process. The foundational critique of Development Studies is rooted in the notion that the post-Enlightenment conception of development, culminating in Truman's 1999 inaugural address, positioned Europe and North America as the self-appointed custodians of development, tasked with shaping the global south, and Africa in particular, in their own image.

While scholars may not pinpoint an exact moment when this discourse emerged, many concur that Truman's inaugural speech marked a pivotal moment in the history of contemporary African development discourse. Truman (1999, p. 1) declared, "We must embark on a bold programme for making the benefits of our scientific advances and industrial progress available for the improvement and growth of underdeveloped areas." This framework exposes the colonial epistemological nature of

Development Studies, revealing a discourse conceptualized externally that marginalizes African voices and perspectives. This phenomenon exemplifies epistemic Eurocentric chauvinism, which perpetuates a form of knowledge racism wherein external entities dictate developmental trajectories for Africa while neglecting the viewpoints and agency of African people themselves.

This has made Ndlovu-Gatsheni (2018, p. 1) pose a critical question: "What does development signify for populations striving to emerge and liberate themselves from the deleterious legacies of enslavement, colonialism, imperialism, apartheid, neocolonialism, underdevelopment, and the imposition of the Washington Consensus and neoliberalism?" Therefore, it is crucial to examine the epistemological foundations underpinning the nature and structure of development discourse, particularly within the global south and, more specifically, in Africa. Consequently, the decolonization of knowledge remains an ongoing and unresolved endeavor that necessitates the active engagement of African scholars and intellectuals. They are called upon to undertake the substantial task of re-centering Africa in the production of knowledge to achieve intellectual coherence and rectify the dislocations imposed by colonial influences.

Asante (2017b, p. 24), challenging the hegemonizing European knowledge systems and voices, writes thus in his article titled "Adjusting the narrative lens": "I suspect that until we reset the social sciences, humanities, sciences, and arts more closely to our historical narratives, we will continue to assume the role of junior brother and sister to other world narratives as if our own experiences, that is, those of our ancestors, are less important than others." It has been over three decades since Professor Molefi Kete Asante (1980) published his book *Afrocentricity: The Theory of Social Change*. This monograph, and many others he wrote, laid a firm foundation for knowledge decolonization in how Africans must reinterpret their realities to oppose Eurocentrism as a colonizing perspective.

Afrocentricity as a theory of social change primarily addresses a detailed investigation and questioning of the Eurocentric canon in knowledge production. It seeks to avoid the personal and collective destruction of people of African descent and to reclaim an African cultural system as the coherent meeting point of every African cultural and historical past. Without Afrocentricity, African people willingly or unwillingly agree to become the footnote status in the European worldview. To use Molefi Asante's terms, we become spectators of a show that defines us from without. Thus, we continue to exist without our terms and rely on borrowed optical Eurocentric prism. The Afrocentric idea is essentially about location. Since Africans have been moved from their terms culturally, psychologically, economically, and historically, any assessment of the African condition in whatever study enterprise, be it political, social, cultural, or spiritual, must be made from an Afrocentric location (Asante & Karenga, 2005).

It is, therefore, vital to begin with the definition that Afrocentricity is a quality of thought, practice, and perspective that perceives Africans as subjects and agents of phenomena acting in their cultural image and human interest. Much of what has been studied in various fields, be it African history and culture, literature and linguistics, or politics and economics, has been orchestrated from the standpoint of Europe's interest. This has been the source of what constitutes dislocation and self-rejection among African people because of not operating on their terms in knowledge production about themselves. For this reason, Afrocentricity seeks radical reorientation of Africans toward their center as a position from which to engage with the world.

Eurocentrism, from the viewpoint of Afrocentricity, has resulted in the negation of African people under the system of white racial domination. This is not a mere marginalization but the brutal obliteration of the presence, meaning, activities, or images of the Africans. Within this racially driven ideology, Sabelo Ndlovu-Gatsheni (2013, p. 337) argues thus, "the African became suppressed and rearticulated by the Western opinion-makers as disabled being characterized by deficits." This articulation of African people has also been well captured by Ramon Grosfoguel (2007, p. 214) thus: "We went from the sixteenth-century characterization of 'people without writing' to the eighteenth and nineteenth-century characterization of people without history,' to the twentieth-century characterization of people without development' and more recently, to the early twenty-first century of 'people without democracy.'" For this reason, Asante (2007, p. 7) argues that "Afrocentricity, if anything, is a shout out for rationality amid confusion, order in the presence of chaos, and respect for cultures in a world that has trampled on both the rights and definitions of the rights of African people."

The challenge, therefore, given Afrocentricity is monumental; it rests on the ability of Africans to claim their agency to systematically detoxify and displace European modes of cognition, being, and feeling and to consciously replace them with ways that are culturally relevant to the African experience as an act of claiming power from decenteredness. Afrocentricity, therefore, discourages knowledge for the sake of knowing rather than active agency to reclaim the totality of our own lives as an act of resistance and self-affirmation to reject Eurocentric hegemonizing cultural ethos. Afrocentricity aims to strike a blow at the lack of consciousness among African people, not simply of consciousness of our oppression but also consciousness of what victories were possible. Within the context of such a clarion call after completing my doctoral studies, I embarked on a mission to publish my first academic monograph titled *Developing Africa? New Horizons with Afrocentricity* (2024), as my contribution within the scholarly fraternity of the centrists, seeks to debunk Eurocentrism in conceptualizing the African development ideal to contest knowledge production in this field of study (Moloi, 2024). Asante (1990) articulates fundamental principles underpinning any Afrocentric inquiry in Afrocentric knowledge production and the study of African phenomena. These principles have greatly aided me in my Afrocentric journey of self-discovery.

The first cardinal principle is the importance of considering the "psychological location" of the thinker. Any analysis of African subject matter is inextricably linked to the psychological location of the researcher, highlighting the need for Africans to reclaim their agency and centricity in knowledge production. As Asante argues, dislocation, perpetuated through Eurocentrism, relies on a European viewpoint that systematically denies African perspectives on various aspects, including politics, economics, social, spiritual, and cultural domains. Therefore, Africans must insist on "locatedness," rooted in their own African epistemological base. This emphasis on locatedness has significant implications for how African development should be conceptualized and pursued. It necessitates that development initiatives be grounded in the history and culture of African people, driven by their agency, and attentive to their unique experiences and perspectives. In this way, development becomes relevant to those it is intended for. The Truman imperial idea of development reveals that it is found within a foreign ideological base, leading to a misdevelopment from where African people stand.

The second cardinal principle is a commitment to finding a subject place for Africa. How do African people think about their own lives in the aftermath of violent colonial encounters? As an act of asserting their power for existence, they redefine and interpret their reality from their standpoint. Their culture and history should serve as the starting point, providing contextual relevance to understanding themselves and their lived experiences. As Archibald Mafeje (2000, p. 18) puts it, "Africans must think and do things for themselves to overcome domination by others." Any development initiative not grounded in the cultural context of the people it aims to serve leads to misdevelopment, disrupting their way of life. This is precisely what the European-inspired idea of development has done in Africa; it has further dislocated African people, reducing them to objects of European experimentation and stripping them of their agency. By prioritizing African perspectives and experiences, development can become a process of self-actualization rather than a continuation of external imposition.

The third cardinal principle is the defense of African cultural elements. Asante states, "One cannot assume an orientation to African agency without giving respect and place to the creative dimension of the African personality." Central to the dislocation experienced by Africans was the denial of their right to exist as themselves and to practice their own culture, which became demonized through Christianity. Colonialism not only dismembered the physical environment of Africa but also disrupted African culture, stripping Africans of the dignity of their way of life and imposing a Western way of life upon them. By defending and valuing African cultural elements, Africans can reclaim their identity and agency, restoring the cultural integrity disrupted by colonialism. Frantz Fanon, speaking from the revolutionary struggle in Algeria and the study of colonialism in Africa and the world, points out the dual physical and cultural context of domination.

He states that, in its very nature, colonialism is organized and suppressive; he further states that "Colonialism is not simply content to impose its rule upon the present and future of a dominated country. Nor is it satisfied merely with holding a people in its grip and emptying the native's brain of all form and content. By a kind of perverted logic, it turns to the past of the oppressed people and distorts, disfigures, and destroys it. Moreover, the colonial oppressor works to deny the culture of the oppressed" (Fanon, 1963, p. 41). Therefore, defending African culture is about reaffirming the humanity of African people and their right to freely express themselves without seeking permission from self-imposed European masters. This act of cultural defense is a reclaiming of their ontological density, which was denied through colonial subjugation. It signifies restoring their inherent dignity and reasserting their identity, allowing them to exist authentically and autonomously in their cultural context.

For this reason, Mbakogu (2004, p. 37) states that "[c]ulture plays an invisible role in determining our customs, values, morals, and growth in society, and that if we truly aspire for freedom from the shackles of under-development, there is an urgent need to break away from the confines of Western cultural systems and search for that which made us Africans before colonization." As a way to reclaim our power as African people, Maulana Karenga proposes the concept of Kawaida, grounded in classical African traditions for Cultural Revolution and to maintain sanity against the European oppressive culture. In his essay "Overturning ourselves," Karenga (1972, p. 8) explains Cultural Revolution in the following man-ner: "When we talk of Cultural Revolution, we are talking essentially about cultural reconversion, the conscious and programmatic restructur-ing of attitudes and relationships that aid us in our aspiration for national liberation. We are recognizing and responding to the fact that the first resistance in any social struggle is cultural resistance and that a critical component of struggle is to win the minds of our people, for if we lose this struggle, we cannot hope to win the political one." For this reason, there can be no reimagination of African development without African culture. Development is a process that must empower people; it must be culturally sensitive and relevant to their needs. The fourth cardinal is "a commit-ment to lexical refinement." The critical concern here is "Does the language used in a text treat or represent African people as subjects?" This is particularly important as it reveals the author's attitudes toward African people's interpretation of reality. Asante emphasizes that "the genuine Afrocentrist seeks to rid the language of negations of African beings as agents within the sphere of Africa's history" (Asante, 2017a, p. 5).

Colonial Western education became a tool of African negation. In almost every subject, there was a deliberate attempt to present Africans as objects that needed to be developed into the image of the European man and woman. Consequently, even within the context of Development

Studies, the modernization theory of the West was considered the grand theory that must guide the development of non-Western societies, including Africa. The main challenge facing Development Studies in Africa has been its foundation in Western epistemologies, which are informed by Western experiences and a Western agenda. Therefore, African scholars face the critical task of decolonizing development theory itself to ensure its contextual relevance. This involves creating development frameworks rooted in African cultural and historical contexts, enabling genuine progress that resonates with African realities and aspirations. By doing so, African scholars can foster development that is more effective but also more respectful of and aligned with African values and experiences.

The fifth cardinal is about "a commitment to a new narrative history of Africa." Asante (2017a, p. 5) argues that "African literature, history, behavior, and economics, the Eurocentric writers have always positioned Africa in the inferior place in every subject field." At the beginning of the 15th century, European scholars, thinkers, and policymakers advanced agendas which were intermingled with their supremacist Christian ideology about themselves as the chosen people by God to advance civilization. Asante (2014, p. 113) maintains that the emergence of the anti-African falsification has its origins in the rise of the European slave trade because, before the 15th century, Europeans had not yet formed the false logic of racial superiority and inferiority later used to justify negative ideas about Africa.

Monteiro-Ferreira (2014, p. 37) explains that in the 20th century, Africa's struggle for independence and self-determination came to embody a vast desire for liberation from oppressive colonial domination. This quest was more than political; it encompassed a call for economic, cultural, and social agency, as European modernity represented the face of oppression. African intellectuals, therefore, by insisting on the need for an Afrocentric historical orientation in the spirit of a search for an African Renaissance, opened doors long held shut by Eurocentric orientations to African phenomena. This approach aimed to reclaim and celebrate African identity, culture, and history, challenging the dominant narratives imposed by colonialism and striving to establish a more authentic and empowering understanding of the African experience.

Decoloniality, on the other hand, is an epistemological and political movement in the 21st century that seeks to deepen and widen decolonization movements in those spaces that experienced the effects of the slave trade, imperialism, colonialism, apartheid, neocolonialism, and underdevelopment. This is because the domains of culture, the psyche, mind, language, aesthetics, religion, and many others have remained colonized even after the official dismantlement of white colonial administration (Ndlovu-Gatsheni, 2015, p. 13). According to Nelson Maldonado-Torres, "the decoloniality does not refer to a single theoretical school of thought, but rather it points to the family of diverse positions that share a view of coloniality as the fundamental problem in the modern (as well as postmodern and information age), and decolonization or decoloniality as a necessary task that remains unfinished." Torres (2011, p. 2) argues that decoloniality is based on the premise that colonization was an inherently oppressive process that imposed itself on various levels within affected societies and did not cease entirely with the departure of the colonizing forces.

Colonial powers employed military force, torture, and other forms of violence to subjugate and control populations. Moreover, decoloniality calls on intellectuals from imperialist countries to undertake a de-imperialization movement by reexamining their imperialist histories and the harmful impact of those histories on the world (Ndlovu-Gatsheni, 2015, p. 490). To advance its mission, decoloniality is framed around three vital analytical units, namely, coloniality of power, coloniality of knowledge, and coloniality of being, as the markers to unmask the Eurocentric hegemonic cosmology. The concept of coloniality of power assists in examining how the existing global political system was formed, established, and organized as a structure of power that is racially hierarchized, Euro-American-centric, Christian-centric, patriarchal, capitalist, heteronormative, hegemonic, asymmetrical, and modern.

The idea of coloniality of power allows for a deeper exploration of how the world was divided into the "Zone of Being" (the realm of those controlling global power systems and reaping the benefits of modernity) and the "Zone of None-Being" (the fabricated world that produced enslaved people and suffered from imperialism, colonialism, and apartheid). Most importantly, the coloniality of power speaks to how the colonial matrices of power continue to shape the global south and entrap it within the colonial paradigms. The coloniality of knowledge serves as the second unit of analysis in decoloniality. This idea helps us understand how endogenous and indigenous knowledge has been marginalized to the boundaries of society, often seen as "barbarian." Today, it is saturated with useless colonial knowledge that hinders Africa's progress. For this reason, the demand for knowledge decolonization remains a legitimate clarion call in pursuit of cognitive justice. The third unit of analysis is that of coloniality of being, which signals the pertinent questions of the making of modern subjectivities and into issues of human ontology (Ndlovu-Gatsheni, 2015).

During my reflections with Professor Molefi Kete Asante, his critical argument he made was while decoloniality tries to challenge Eurocentrism as a mixed theoretical viewpoint emerging from the global south, its scope and focus is not exclusively African. Asante argues thus: "Decoloniality remains a theoretical parasite that lives on the bark of the Eurocentric tree. It is derived from the same source as other Eurocentric popular terms of the moment." There is a long history of discovery rooted in the quest to find ways to extend the life of a system that has poisoned the waters of the human community. The values are often wrong because the decoloniality scholars have not started with the ancient African systems. Their chronology is wrong; they still think that Homer's *Iliad* and *Odyssey* are the starting points of civilization. Afrocentrists must interrogate all forms and concepts that "seem" to explain what Europe imposed on the world.

Without seeing Africa as the source, the earliest stages of the continent as teachers, and Europe as a latecomer in culture and civilization, the only thing that the decolonial experts can do is to reframe their previous accounts of the colonial experience by reorientating toward Africa as a base in the aftermath of the *Homo sapiens* (Moloi, 2025). Thus, Afrocentricity focuses primarily on the substance of African history and culture, as well as an insistence on the centrality of African experiences as a base from which to decolonize and build an African awakening. This is preeminently in line with three facts. First, *Homo sapiens* emerged on the African continent. Second, human civilization emerged in Africa.

Third, *Homo sapiens* spent three-fourths of the time that humans have been on earth as a species in Africa before they ever ventured out of Africa. For Afrocentrists, interrogating African culture and history implies returning to human history. Therefore, European childishness is expressed in how Europe centers the whole history of the world around Europe when it is but the child of Africa. Thus, Europe is guilty of distorting the human record by employing an individualistic, selfish, and imperialistic *Geist* (Moloi, 2024, p. xv). Knowledge decolonization, therefore, from an Afrocentric perspective, should not merely be about the critique of Eurocentrism while falling within its very trap of colonial logic. Instead, it should be about rewriting the human civilization account from the African base as the starting point, letting critique Eurocentrism with its logic. We, therefore, need to step out of the European moment and start elsewhere, which is the Nile Valley Civilization as the focal point.

## THE SIGNIFICANCE OF MOLEFI KETE ASANTE'S SCHOLARSHIP AND THE ASSERTION OF AFRICAN AGENCY

It is without a doubt that Professor Asante has contributed immensely, and continues to do so, to the project of African reclamation of agency unapologetically. His very life and attitude toward his work are proof of someone who is an active agent for Afrocentric revivalism. With over a hundred books and more than 600 articles against his name, the latest among his books being *Africa's Gifts of the Spirit* (2024), he has proved his durability and consistency as a committed activist scholar. As one among thousands of the students he has revolutionized, I also bear testimony to his selflessness and enduring commitment to educating with passion and humility. This, for me, is a marker of greatness and servant leadership in honor of African ancestors till the Afrocentric kingdom is established in our minds for self-liberating experience. In part one of a conversation between Professor Toyin Falola and Professor Molefi Kete Asante, Professor Toyin Falola (2021) says: "I have listened to his lectures. I have served on committees with him. I have read his books. I have adopted many of his ideas and reworked them into Black liberationist thoughts. He has taught me as much as I have taught his works and ideas in classes for over forty years. I have reviewed his books. I have evaluated his manuscripts for publishers. I have gone to Temple University on multiple occasions to give a lecture on 'the construction of words' to his graduate class. I have been asked to endorse using his name for two significant prizes named after him." This bears testimony to the Afrocentric prowess expressed through the works of Asante as a dedicated scholar.

Indeed, Afrocentricity is about advancing an Afrocentric agency as a measure of self-liberation for the human spirit determined to advance revolution in knowledge contestation for the functional purpose of African liberation. The future of Africa can only be attained when Africans act in their best interests. Therefore, Africans must think, plan, implement, and be the beneficiaries of their ideas as a position of resistance against imposed dislocation through Eurocentrism. In this way, Africans will not only be reduced to puppets of the European games of conquest but will also take charge of their lives and map out their futures (Moloi, 2025, p. 105).

It is important to note that the advent of modernity, which began in the late 15th century, ushered in European domination over Africa, which reached its apex during the Berlin scramble from 1884 to 1885 and sought to dislocate Africans from their historical and cultural patterns of life and converted Africans into European subjects. The domination of Africans from that time set in motion the processes for Africa's dismemberment and loss of African agency. According to Asante in *Afrocentric Manifesto*, "an agent means a human being who can act independently in his or her own best interest." Agency refers to the ability to provide the psychological and cultural resources necessary to advance human freedom (Asante, 2007, p. 40). Asante further argues that "when agency does not exist or is disempowered, we have the condition of marginality, and the worst form of marginality is to be marginal in our own story."

Thus, white racial domination implies more than marginalization: It also means the obliteration of the presence, meaning, activities, or image of the African people (Asante, 2007, p. 41). Africans must, therefore, relocate to their own cultural and historical terms of reference as an expression of a standpoint from which they can engage with the world as free agents. The redevelopment of African societies requires Africans to take charge of their own lives, shaking off domination, and map out their development path within the ideal of an Afrocentric Pan-Africanism to challenge the bias toward neoliberalism. Asante warns in his paper titled "Afrocentricity's Afrofuturism and the countdown to the future" that "Africans cannot enter their imaginary future on the wagons of victimhood, hounded by the dogs of marginality, with their minds centered only on their colonial past."

The idea of African development future not informed by African history, culture, and agency only serves to sustain the perpetuity of the colonial culture of domination and African marginalization (Asante, 2018, p. 10). Our challenge is, therefore, monumental in the sense that we have a task to claim our power to resist any system that has relied on our dehumanization for its survival. We must break free from the chains of our enslavement, beginning with decolonizing from misinformation created through the colonial education system, which reduced us to objects waiting to be developed. Thus, Afrocentricity is our *djed* and *stasis* to undergird our demand for freedom.

## CONCLUSION

It is my submission that if African people realign themselves with their terms of reference—namely, their history, culture, and agency, as articulated through Afrocentric theory—then the process of reclaiming their power can commence. In these brief reflections, I have sought to convey my experiences engaging with Professor Asante, the discourse of Afrocentricity, and how these experiences have influenced my entry into Africological analysis. This critical reflection on the trajectory of African development underscores the opportunity for Africans globally to interrogate the body of colonial knowledge that has contributed to their dehumanization. It also offers the opportunity to rethink knowledge production, liberate African people from the chains of colonialism and neocolonialism, and reassert their agency for advancement.

## REFERENCES

African Decolonial Research Network (ADERN). (2019). Retrieved July 13, 2024, from https://din.today/sabelo-j-ndlovu-gatsheni-we-needed-to-shift-the-geography-of-knowledge-as-well-as-the-biography-of-knowledge/

Asante, M. K. (1980). *Afrocentricity: The theory of social change.* Amolefi Publishing Company.

Asante, M. K. (1990). African elements in African-American English. In J. E. Holloway (Ed.), *Africanisms in American culture* (pp. 19–33). Indiana University Press.

Asante, M. K. (2007). *An Afrocentric manifesto.* Polity Press.

Asante, M. K. (2017a). Afrocentricity: Notes on a disciplinary position. In J. Conyers (Eds.), *Afrocentric traditions* (pp. 1–14). Routledge.

Asante, M. K. (2017b). Afrocentricity and knowledge: Adjusting the narrative lens. *The Thinker*, 74.

Asante, M. K. (2014). *Facing south to Africa: Toward an Afrocentric critical orientation.* Lexington Books.

Asante, M. K. (2015). *African pyramids of knowledge: Kemet, Afrocentricity and Africology.* Universal Write Press.

Asante, M. K. (2018). *The history of Africa: The quest for eternal harmony.* Routledge.

Asante, M. K. (2024). Afrocentricity's Afrofuturism and the count up to the future. In A. X. Smith (Eds.), *Afrocentricity in Afrofuturism* (pp. 165–184). University Press of Mississippi.

Asante, M. K., & Karenga, M. (2005). *Handbook of Black studies.* Sage Publications.

Falola, T. (2021). *A conversation with Molefi Asante.* Retrieved August 7, 2024, from https://www.thecable.ng/a-conversation-with-molefi-asante-part-one/

Fanon, F. (1963). The wretched of the earth. *Grove Weidenfeld.*

Grosfoguel, R. (2007). The epistemic decolonial turn: Beyond political-economy paradigms. *Cultural Studies*, 21(2–3), 211–223.

Karenga, R. (1972). Overturning ourselves: From mystification to meaningful struggle. *The Black Scholar*, 4(2), 6–14.

Mafeje, A. (2000). Africanity: A combative ontology. *Codesria Bulletin*, 1(1), 66–71.

Mbakogu, I. A. (2004). Is there really a relationship between culture and development? *The Anthropologist*, 6(1), 37–43.

Mazama, A. (2001). The Afrocentric paradigm: Contours and definitions. *Journal of Black Studies*, 31(4), 387–405.

Mignolo, W. D. (2013). Introduction: Coloniality of power and de-colonial thinking. In *Globalization and the decolonial option* (pp. 1–21). Routledge.

Moloi, L. (2024). *Developing Africa? New horizons with Afrocentricity.* Anthem Press.

Moloi, L. (2025). *Unpublished conversations between Lehasa Moloi and Molefi Kete Asante.*

Monteiro-Ferreira, A. (2014). *The demise of the inhuman: Afrocentricity, modernism, and postmodernism.* SUNY Press.

Ndlovu-Gatsheni, S. J. (2013). The entrapment of Africa within the global colonial matrices of power: Eurocentrism, coloniality, and deimperialization in the twenty-first century. *Journal of Developing Societies*, 29(4), 331–353.

Ndlovu-Gatsheni, S. J. (2015). Decoloniality as the future of Africa. *History Compass*, *13*(10), 485–496.

Ndlovu-Gatsheni, S. J. (2018). The African idea of development. In T. Binns, K. Lynch, & E. Nel (Eds.), *Handbook of African development* (pp. 19–33). Routledge.

Ndlovu-Gatsheni, S. J. (2016, October). Decolonizing the university and the problematic grammars of change in South Africa. In *Keynote address delivered at the 5th annual students conference on decolonizing the humanities and social sciences in South Africa/Africa* (pp. 6–7). University of KwaZulu-Natal.

Ndlovu-Gatsheni, S. J. (2021). The cognitive empire, politics of knowledge and African intellectual productions: Reflections on struggles for epistemic freedom and resurgence of decolonisation in the twenty-first century. *Third World Quarterly*, *42*(5), 882–901.

Torres, N. M. (2011). Thinking through the decolonial turn: Post-continental interventions in theory, philosophy, and critique: An introduction. *Transmodernity*, *1*(2), 1–15.

Truman, H. S. (1999). *Inaugural address: Thursday, January 20, 1949* (p. 12). Western Standard Publishing Company.

# CHAPTER 6

## What Asante Said: A Philosophical Engagement With Asante and His Theory of Social Change

Bongani Mkhonza, PhD

### ABSTRACT

This chapter postulates the imperative emergence of a philosophy of Afrocentricity as rooted in an African-centric zone of thought and being. It contends that being human is to emerge from the deceptive Eurocentric ontology of being. This contribution is a study and meditates on what Molefi Kete Asante says in his prolific writings on Afrocentricity as the theory of social change. The chapter employs Afrocentricity as a combative force to debunk the myth of Eurocentrism imagination which places it as an absolute being. It starts by borrowing from the ideas deployed by Lewis Gordon when he elaborated that such a self-imposed absolute being has always stood in the way of a human being or a human way of being. The chapter explores how Eurocentrism dehumanized the African people by imposing rigid bipolarities, which positioned Europe and its colonizers in the zone of being human and placing the African-colonized subjects in the zone of nonbeing. Afrocentricity as a theory of social change challenges Eurocentric culture, history, and narratives and works to restore the centrality of the African people's dignity and pride. As a contribution, the chapter achieves this by proposing that being human is not only a physical experience. However, it is also a conscious project of stepping into a zone where African voices, narratives, experiences, aesthetics, histories, and innovations are recognized and celebrated. The ontology of this zone is African based, but it goes beyond the geographical boundaries. Asante's theory of social change promulgates that African aspirations, visions, and concepts drive the project of Afrocentricity. Asante acknowledges that Afrocentricity builds upon intellectual foundations such as Garveyism, Kawaida, and Negritude, compelling the African people to reclaim their humanity and assert their right to fully exist authentically. Thus, the chapter concludes by reflecting on what philosophers observe or speculate on Asante's philosophy of Afrocentricity.

Keywords: Afrocentricity, Social Change, Molefi Kete Asante, Zone of Humanity

## LOCATION AND KNOWLEDGE

Molefi Asante created a movement with the publishing of *Afrocentricity: The Theory of Social Change* (Asante, 2003b). The seminal book became the tower of hope and inspiration for the liberation of African people from colonial and Eurocentric forces of domination. The book ushered a unique "coherent intellectual enterprise" (Stewart, 1984, p. 297) in African and Black Studies today (2024); after a revised version (2003), the book graces university libraries worldwide. The book is a philosophical study of African peoples from an African-centered prism. I prefer to begin by introducing the author. This gives a framework for thinking and context of the things I engage in. I am an artist, a lecturer in art history, and an art curator from KwaZulu-Natal, South Africa (Azania). I was born near Lebombo, the same region where the Lebombo Bone, known as the oldest mathematical artifact, was discovered. I grew up in the same province where Bhambatha kaMancinza rebelled against the English colonizers. I was trained in Eurocentric Western conceptions of fine arts and art history. Even after the postcolonialism movements in art, the story of fine arts and art history worldwide has been a story of Europe told by Europeans and Americans. In Andrew McNamara's (2015, p. 67) review of a book titled *Western Art and the Wider World* by Paul Wood, who is a well-known author about art history, Woods appears to confirm this affinity at many points in his argument. For instance, he notes that "all stories of modern art have been told by Europeans and Americans about Europe and America" (Wood, 2013, p. 101). The discourse of art history was not only located in the Eurocentric paradigm of thought but also highly informed by white upper-class elitism and church doctrines. So, there are fundamental questions about how relevant this type of history, thinking, and practice might be to the people of African descent globally. However, specifically, it means being a Black African Zulu person. The body of this chapter reads from Asante's quality of thought and his pronouncement on employing Afrocentricity as a theoretical lens of engagement. Further, it is to probe into the evolution of Asante as a person and his ideas. Asante's identity testifies as a compass of his evolution and influences as a philosopher of Afrocentricity.

In asking the fundamental question of agency, Asante's identity, his actions, and Afrocentricity are intertwined. There is harmony in the interactions between Asante, the philosopher, and Asante, the active participant in the practice of emancipation of African-colonized subjects. According to Dastile (2013, p. 95), "centredness implies an emergence of new knowledge, and a new reality on the subject which transforms an African subject from a state of victimhood, servitude, powerlessness to a state of victory, participant and an agent." Thus, the agency looks to answer the following questions: "How do we break open the psychological and intellectual prison that holds humans in mental bondage? How do you bring about justice in situations where there is only injustice? How do you create conditions of freedom when the ruling powers deny people the resources for life?" (Asante, 2007, p. 49). In response to these questions, Afrocentricity demands that the displaced humans in mental bondage embark on a journey of conscious victory by seeking to reclaim Africa as their center. Notably, one of the strategies adopted by Asante was to change his name and adopt an African name.

The name "Asante" is an act of reclaiming his life and his lost heritage. It reflects his search for his family's ethnic descent (Asante, 2008). Frantz Fanon describes this type of cultural reclamation as the moment of blackness when a Black person realizes his Black condition. Asante's name change was in line with many of the Pan-African movements' ideological ammunitions for emancipation against colonial white supremacy. As an emancipatory posture of conscious victory from the history of enslavement, for many African American revolutionaries, the acquisition of African names was necessary. In mapping this point about the pursuit of self-determination toward the Pan-African and Afrocentric conscious victory, I trace the following examples of name-shedding around the 1960s and 1970s. At the beginning of 1964, a prominent religious figure—Elijah Muhammad, shocked America and the world by announcing the changing of the name of a famous boxer from Cassius Marcellus Clay to Muhammad Ali. To Cassius Clay, the name change was a critical move that released him from the psychological bondage of bearing the identity of his family's enslavers. So, as for many, changing his name was a step toward reclaiming his African heritage (Onaci, 2016). A decade before Muhammad Ali, Elijah Muhammad had initiated the conscious victory of Black power by influencing one of the most known name changes in the history of Black power movements. In 1952, Malcolm Little recognized the history of anti-Black violence embedded in his surname, so he dropped the name of his ancestors' enslavers in exchange for an "X." The letter represented his ignorance of his family's original name (Onaci, 2016). As the patron saint of the Black Power movement, Malcolm's name journey acted as a road map for many of those who carried on his work following his murder. They embraced the idea that the "lost tribe of Shabazz" needed to undo the shackles of slavery that, according to Malcolm, cut these Black people off from all knowledge of their kind and cutoff from any understanding of their language, religion, and past culture, until the Black man in America was the earth's only race of people who did not know their true identity (Onaci, 2016). Pan-African movements are part of the Afrocentric paradigm of thought. As Asante contends, "Pan-Africanism itself is a political perspective and a political ideology as well as a social theory, the one does not negate the other." Afrocentricity is a broad paradigmatic intellectual perspective that privileges African agency within the context of African history and culture transcontinentally and transgenerationally (Asante, 2003b).

Asante demonstrates intellectual conceptualization of Afrocentricity by asserting that:

> Before Du Bois' Pan-African Congress in Paris, the movement for Black intellectual understanding, that is, the framing of proper political questions for Africans had been accorded only a small space in our history. Since that time we have incorporated the best thinking of Du Bois, Kwame Nkrumah, Malcolm X, Frantz Fanon, George Padmore, and Marcus Garvey to fuel the philosophical discussions of Africology.

As discussed in this section, Asante employs Afrocentricity as a location of thinking about the world around us, the knowledge of oneself. Asante (2007, p. 2) further elaborates this by affirming that Afrocentricity "allows for a trans-continental, trans-generational explanation of phenomena…, thus, the new thinking, therefore, leads to a reconceptualization of the social and historical reality of African people." Afrocentricity is a victorious epistemic journey back to the source of the great heritage of the ancestors. It is not a reactive anti-Eurocentrism force.

## ASANTE AND A THEORY OF SOCIAL CHANGE

Asante centralizes Afrocentricity as the critical theory for social change. The change is a move away from Eurocentrism, "the colonial enterprise [which] disrupted the progress that Africa was making towards its amalgamation and the attainment of a form of progress defined by African standards and experience" (Moloi, 2024, pp. 92–93). Afrocentricity is not Afrocentrism, and it does not preoccupy itself with reversing Eurocentrism. However, it is a quality of thought, practice, and perspective that perceives Africans as subjects and agents of phenomena acting in their own cultural image and human interests (Karenga, 1982). In Asante's (2017, p. 231) words,

> Afrocentricity refers to the intellectual work of a group of African philosophers, historians, and sociologists during the late twentieth century with varying degrees of attachment to the central idea that the key crisis in the African world is the profoundly disturbing decentering of African people from a subject position within their own narrative. In Afrocentricity, the opening consciousness is assumed to be an awareness of the off centeredness of Africans as a result of Arab and European and military, cultural, and social intrusions that have dislocated African people.

Thus, Asante's list of proponents illuminates that Afrocentricity has undergone several stages of ideological critique of the Eurocentric frame of Africa and African people. The section meditates on critical aspects of Asante's Afrocentricity as a theory of social change. It is based on my reading of what Asante said in this seminal book, *Afrocentricity: The Theory of Social Change*, which was first published in 1980 and revised

and expanded in 2003 as a positive ideology of Afrocentric consciousness. It also considers my encounters with Molefi Asante's theory of
Afrocentricity and its influences on my daily practice as a lecturer of Art
History in South Africa. This is what Asante considers as a move from
theory to practice. Within the Eurocentric paradigm, the ideas around art
and history are employed to negate African people's existence as human
beings. Western epistemologies are taught in universities as universal evidence that African people have no history and have no contribution to
art, science, medicine, engineering, and literature. Asante (2003b, p. 56)
refutes this narrative and says, "In art, science, medicine, engineering, we
[African people] are the vanguards for humanism and sensitivity because
we use our history to teach us how to approach relationships of people
and concepts. There is no greater teacher than our own history." Thus, to
challenge this logic by employing Afrocentricity to read my experiences
is encouraged by Asante. It is my truth, and "even though it may not be
their truth…, this singularity of purpose is close to Afrocentricity because
it does not ignore logic and emotions" (Asante, 2003b, p. 56).

Self-determination and liberty are determined through the antagonistic
struggle between imposed universal Eurocentrism and the relocation to
Afrocentric conscious victory. As a concept, the theory of social change is
a paradigm of thought that seeks to bring about the social revolution. In
the context of this contribution, the theory of social change is rooted in the
notion that throughout modernity, the conceptions of Africa and African
subjects remain a contested terrain that has endured numerous forms of
misrepresentation as intellectual and ideological terrains. The change is an
undertaking to debunk the narrative of the white superiority complex, a
"racial mythology" based on the "rather strange belief on the parts of
whites that they are superior to Africans, that they have a right to establish
and maintain a hierarchy over Blacks by force of arms or customs or laws
or habits" (Asante, 2007, p. 136). For this reason, the theory of social
change demands a total overhaul of the colonial conceptions containing
distorted knowledge systems and epistemologies imported from the
Western perceptions about Africa and African subjectivity. Afrocentricity
orders a call for the relocation of the frame of mind for Africans by
Africans. The relocation is not just a response to years of colonialism,
enslavement, and the fallacy of white supremacy. It is a revolutionary

theory of social change and victory for Africans and Black people. Confronted by such various forms of dehumanization of African people, Asante's theory offers a possibility for African renaissance. The rebirth of greatness will come "with the constant nurturing of African intellectuals and artists," a sentiment that was inspired and echoed by the proponents of the *Negritude* movement, such as Aime Cesaire, Leon Damas, Leopold Senghor, and Jacques Rabemananjara (Asante, 2003b, p. 91). Asante (2003c, p.1) raises the consciousness of victory by affirming that "an African renaissance is only possible if there is an African ideology, distinct from a Eurocentric ideology, that allows African agency, that is, a sense of self-actualizing based upon the best interests of African people."

## ON REASON AND REHUMANIZATION

The dehumanization of Africans in South Africa was based on two dreadful states of affairs. "Africans have been negated in the system of white racial domination. This is not mere marginalization but the obliteration of the presence, meaning, activities, or images of the Africans. This is negated reality, destruction of the spiritual and material personality of the African person" (Asante, 1998, p. 41). The second one emanated from the Western "Hegelian negation of Africa from history and civilization" (Adegbindin, 2015).

From this Hegelian perspective, "Africa is said to be unhistorical; undeveloped spirit—still involved in the conditions of mere nature; devoid of morality, religions, and political constitution. Hence, he holds that there is a justification for Europe's enslavement and colonization of Africa" (Adegbindin, 2015, p. 20). In an interview with Sayan Dey and Shankhadeep Chattopadhyay (published in 2023), I highlighted this plight of African negation regarding art history in South Africa. In the interview, I drew attention to the historiography of art periods as they are primarily illustrated in art history books in South Africa. In my critique and analysis, I follow the tenets of Afrocentricity, based on the following questions: Does it place Africans in the center? Is it in the best interest of African peoples? (Asante, 2003c, p. 57). These questions are based on the existential question of being African in a world that is anti-Black and has proven to be anti-African. This explains Karenga's profound assertion that our

Africanity is our ultimate reality. In the following passages, I stencil my analysis of art history on Afrocentricity as a theory of social change.

In most art history books, the chapters start with rock art painted by the San and Batwa people around the Drakensberg mountains, spanning over 400 years. The art history of San Rock art was recorded and interpreted by white academics such as J. D. Lewis-Williams, David Pearce, Pieter Jolly, and Thomas Dowson, and it is highly ethnographic. Sometimes, historians use derogatory words such as "Bushman art." The conception and depiction of San and Batwa people's art was "consolidated a racial stereotype of the Bushmen as simple, childlike people" (Dowson, 1994, p. 332). This logic aligns with modern European philosophers such as Hegel, who believed Black Africa was primitive and childlike. Such diffusionist ways of thinking gave way to the violation and dehumanization of African people. Such history continues to be taught in schools and universities in South Africa. As a result, "the subtext of the discourse on Africa continues to remain essentially Hegelian because Africa is still perceived through the prism of essential otherness" (Tibebu, 2011, p. 174). In an ongoing existential situation, Mazama (2014) explains that what educational institutions, schools, or universities functioning within the Eurocentric premises deliver is not proper education. Asante (2007, p. 82) asserts that it is "Eurocentric triumphalist propaganda, a racist education, that is, a white supremacist education."

After the San Rock art, the history moves to the so-called colonial art with an anthropological format. It covers mainly art produced by white South African male artists portraying landscapes and wild animals they encountered while traveling through colonies. It is a documentation of non-European flora, fauna, people, and landscapes by artists of European descent. Scholars have referenced a standard division of African history into precolonial and colonial which attests to this Eurocentric historiography. Within these two epochs, the European disruption of African societies is assigned a principal place in "African" history. Trevor-Ropper (1973, p. 9) confirms this Eurocentric superiority complex when he asserts that "there is only the history of the Europeans in Africa." So, in line with it, the following chapters are typically mapped from the formation of the 1910 Union of South Africa to the apartheid era. Most artworks of this era depicted empty landscapes and farmlands. It is now recognized that such depictions were predominantly done by Dutch-born painters such as J. H. Pierneer, who nourished what was later conceived as Afrikaner nationalist ideology. There is no presence of Black South Africans in those artworks. Asante (2007, p. 35) contends that through centuries of cultural erase, degradation, and dehumanization, problems persist, "lost sense of their cultural ground and often live in a state of mental and cultural exile."

Later, around the 1930s, the transformation of subject matter emerged. Most Afrikaner artists were influenced by African traditional and cultural objects, forms, and San-Batwa artifacts. It is vital to note the total absence of contributions from other Indigenous groups and races from these historical records. Many cultures thrived long before the English/Dutch settlers arrived in South Africa. Although they practiced art and produced artifacts, there was a concerted effort to erase their existence and contributions from art history books. However, this conforms to the colonial narrative, which claims that former colonies had no history, education, or civilization. This colonial logic serves as an essential measure of human development. It is premised on propping up European imperialism as a colonial gift to the colonized subject. At the heart of these predominantly Eurocentric aesthetics and cultural discourse are often toxic, exclusionary cultural assumptions. Consequently, the logic seeks to justify the transmission of imperial cultures, art, religion, languages, norms, and ways of existence to the "new worlds" as development and progress. It is only later that art history books admit the existence of what they term "emerging" Black artists. The selection and categorization of this group of artists also raise several compelling philosophical questions. Asante (2003b), p. 79) deploys Afrocentric and Africology ideology to reject such kinds of categorizations and negations of African people and their art history. Asante (2003b), p. 79) declares that "no longer will our art mimic white art and be separate from the people; it will retouch the essence of our souls and be spirit and body force and energy, shape and sound."

So, Asante's stance on Afrocentricity should be considered a revolutionary location of thought rather than a reactionary philosophy. Afrocentricity is grounded on the agency to rehumanize Africans by empowering them and making them masters of their fate. Asante (2006, p. 649) reminds us to be free from the notions of white supremacy and white hegemony which privileges whiteness to experience true liberation if you are African. This concept places freedom as the central tenet of Asante's philosophy. Just like Jean-Paul Satre's (1985) and Sartre's (2007) assertion that humans are "condemned to be free," Asante places the freedom of African people around the world as the fundamental principle.

## REFLECTIONS ON ASANTE AND AFROCENTRICITY

This last section of the chapter aimed to describe the impact of Asante's (2003b) book, *Afrocentricity: The Theory for Social Change*, and what other Afrocentric Black thinkers say about Asante's contribution to the liberatory studies of framing the ideas about African people. The reflections are peer reviews on the main ideas of Asante (2003b, p. 56) to prove that "Afrocentricity can stand its ground among any ideology or religion: Marxism, Islam, Christianity, Buddhism, or Judaism."

Mazama (2001, p. 387) frames the mammoth impact of the book *Afrocentricity: The Theory for Social Change* (2003b) by making an exposition that ever since its release, it "has become a formidable Pan-African force that must be reckoned with…, the reason for its appeal lies both in the disturbing conditions of African people and the remedy that Afrocentricity suggests." Furthermore, the power of Afrocentricity as a theory of social change that guides Africans to liberation. As a significant emancipatory paradigm of thought linked to Black Studies, Karenga (1988, p. 404) further describes Afrocentricity as "essentially a quality of perspective or approach rooted in the cultural image and human interest of African people." This perspective is at the center of the definition of Afrocentricity. As a revolutionary humanistic theory, "The Afrocentric idea rests on the assertion of the importance of the African experience for African people. It aims to give us our African, victorious consciousness back … in the process, it also means viewing the European voice as just one among many and not necessarily the wisest one" (Mazama, 2001, p. 388). Mazama (p. 387) even suggests that "Afrocentricity contends that our main problem as African people is our usually unconscious adoption of the Western worldview and perspective and their attendant conceptual frameworks. The list of those ideas and theories that have invaded our lives as normal, natural, or even worse, the ideal is infinite." The Western worldview has demonstrated beyond a point of imagination that it is anti-Black and anti-African. It places Africa and Africans at an inferior level of being. The Western worldview is inspired by the notions of supremacy.

Hence when referencing Hegel's theses on the *Philosophy of History*, Adegbind (2015, p. 20) notes: "In Negro life, the characteristic point is that consciousness has not yet attained to the realization of any substantial objective existence—for example, God, or Law—in which the interest of man's volition is involved and in which he realizes his being. This distinction between himself as an individual and the universality of his essential being, the African in the uniform, undeveloped oneness of his existence has not yet [been] attained; so that the knowledge of an absolute Being, an Other and a Higher than his self, is entirely wanting. The Negro, as already observed, exhibits the natural man in his completely wild and untamed state."

This kind of arrogant supremacist position can be perceived in connection with the ideology of apartheid in South Africa. Mazama's stated problem of African people unconsciously adopting the Western worldview and perspective can be perceived as what Steven Bantu Biko meditated about when challenging the apartheid system in South Africa with the philosophy of Black consciousness. Just like Asante and Afrocentrists, Biko and "Fanon [are] greatly preoccupied with and deeply distressed by one major legacy of colonialism and imperialism, the paralyzing inferiority complex of Blacks and their abject idolization of whites as their role models" (Ranuga, 1986, p. 182). Biko (1978) in his book *I Write What I Like* brings to a fore "the psychology, the frame of mind of Afrikaners as they sought to justify the notion of their superiority over the Africans…, he concluded that the Afrikaner community was a community of people who enjoyed a privileged position that they did not deserve" (Mungazi, 2000, p. 128). In countries such as South Africa, "where they [were] now in undisputed control, white racist settlers [had] constructed formidable environments of fear and terror for Blacks to maintain their privileged status within the systems" (Ranuga, 1986, p. 183). "However, out of his braveness and fearlessness, Biko demonstrated to the Afrikaners that because of their false notions of supremacy and privilege, their Afrikaner psychic was so badly damaged that were unable to think rationally" (Biko, 1978, p. 59). Thus, in addressing this settler colonialist unconscious reason, Lewis Gordon (2005, p. 2) then asked: "What should we [Black people] make, then, of racist rationality?" In addressing this question, Gordon (p. 3), inspired by the words of Fanon (1952), *Black Skin White Masks*, announces the following:

> The Black is marked by the dehumanizing bridge between individual and structure posed by antiblack racism; the Black is, in the end, "anonymous," which enables "the Black" to collapse into "Blacks." Whereas "Blacks" is not a proper name, antiblack racism makes it function as such, as a name of familiarity that closes off the need for further knowledge. Each Black is, thus, ironically nameless by virtue of being named "Black." So, Blacks find themselves, Fanon announces at the outset, not structurally regarded as human beings. They are problematic beings, beings locked in what he calls "a zone of nonbeing."

The zone of nonbeing is a state of being confronted with a Western worldview that is anti-Black. In this way, Afrocentricity is inspired by Fanon's (1952) existential work and draws on the lived experiences of African people to be uncompromising in pursuit of anti/decolonization. The idea of victorious consciousness insists that being human is not only a physical experience based on European power structures. However, it is also a conscious project of stepping into a zone where African voices, narratives, experiences, aesthetics, histories, and innovations are recognized and celebrated. This change is further established as Mazama (2001, p. 388) reasserts, the "Afrocentric idea is a powerful on..., [it] rests on the assertion of the importance of the African experience for African people..., it aims to give us our African, victorious consciousness back." As informed by African experiences, African scholars should develop paradigmatic discourses rooted in the consciousness of existential conditions (Asante, 2007; Mazama, 1998). Accordingly, it also means viewing the European voice as among many and not necessarily the wisest one (Mazama, 2001). Fanon (1967, p. 173) agrees, as he forces us into action: The "oppressed Africans cannot afford to entrust their total liberation to the good graces or faith of their colonial masters."

## SUMMARY AND CONCLUSION

In conclusion, the discussions began with the presentations of the imperative emergence of a philosophy of Afrocentricity rooted in an African-centric zone of thought and being. The chapter deliberates on what Molefi Kete Asante says in his book *Afrocentricity: The Theory of Social Change*. The chapter defines and employs Afrocentricity as a combative force to debunk the myth of Eurocentrism imagination, which places it as an absolute being. The ideas that Lewis Gordon has about Afrocentricity are discussed. Gordon borrows from Fanon and elaborates that a self-imposed absolute being has always stood in the way of a human being or a human way. The chapter then explores how Eurocentrism dehumanized the African people by imposing a rigid supremacy complex that suspends all the faculties of human reason. This Hegelian universalist notion of thought positions Europe and its colonizers in the zone of being human while placing the African-colonized subjects in the zone of nonbeing. Afrocentricity as a theory of social change challenges Eurocentric culture, history, and narratives and works to restore the African people's central-ity, dignity, and pride. The ontology of this ideology is African based, but it should be conceived and adopted beyond the geographical boundaries. In his 1979 essay titled "African American historians and the reclaiming of African history," Clarke (1979, p. 29) claims: "The Afro-American con-nection with Africa is not new. In perspective, this connection was never completely broken. 'Africa-consciousness', in varying degrees, good and bad, has always been a part of the psyche of the African people, in forced exile in South America, the Caribbean Islands and in the United States." Asante recognized the Afro-American connection with Africa and used the Kemet African civilizations as his locus of enunciation.

Molefi Asante said that Afrocentricity promulgates that African aspira-tions, visions, and concepts drive the project of Afrocentricity. The chapter concludes by reviewing the connections between Asante's Afrocentricity and what other Afrocentric, decoloniality and thinkers from Black Studies expressed or considered Asante's philosophy of Afrocentricity to be (Asante, 2003a).

## REFERENCES

Adegbindin, O. (2015). Critical notes on Hegel's treatment of Africa. *Ogirisi: A New Journal of African Studies, 11*, 20–43.

Asante, M. (1998). *The Afrocentric idea revised*. Temple University Press.

Asante, M. (2003a). Locating a text: Implications of the Afrocentric theory. In A. Mazama (Ed.), *The Afrocentric paradigm* (pp. 235–244). Africa World Press.

Asante, M. (2003b). *Afrocentricity: The theory of social change.* African American Images.

Asante, M. (2003c). African American studies: The future of the discipline. In A. Mazama (Ed.), *The Afrocentric paradigm* (pp. 97–108) Africa World Press.

Asante, M. (2006). A discourse on Black Studies: Liberating the study of African people in the western academy. *Journal of Black Studies, 36*(5), 646–662.

Asante, M. (2007). *An Afrocentric manifesto. Toward an African renaissance.* Polity Press.

Asante, M. (2008). Dubois and Africa: The convergence of consciousness. *UMBCtube Lecture*, 12 November 2008. https://www.youtube.com/watch?v=DcwD_3Y_DxM

Asante, M. K. (2017). Afrocentricity: Notes on a disciplinary position. In J. L. Conyers (Ed.), *Afrocentric traditions* (pp. 1–14). Routledge.

Biko, S. (1978). What is Black consciousness? In *I write what I like: A selection of his writings* (p. 104). Harper & Row.

Clarke, J. (1979). African American historians and the reclaiming of African history. In *Présence Africaine, 2e TRIMESTRE*, Nouvelle série, No. 110 (pp. 29–48). Présence Africaine Editions.

Dastile, N. (2013). Beyond Euro-Western dominance: An African-centred decolonial paradigm. *Africanus, 43*(2), 93–104.

Dowson, T. (1994). Reading art, writing history: Rock art and social change in Southern Africa. *World Archaeology, 25*(3), 332–345.

Fanon, F. (1952 [2008]). *Peau noire, masques blancs, Seuil.* Translated as Black Skin, White Masks (R. Philcox, Trans.). Grove Books.

Fanon, F. (1967). *Towards the African revolution.* Grove Press.

Gordon, L. (2005). Through the zone of nonbeing: A reading of black skin, white masks in celebration of Fanon's Eightieth birthday. *The CLR James Journal, 11*(1), 1–43. Special Issue: Frantz Fanon's 80th Birthday. Philosophy Documentation Center.

Karenga, M. (1988). Black Studies and the problematic of paradigm: The philosophical dimension. *Journals of Black Studies, 18*, 395–414.

Karenga, M. (1982). *Introduction to Black studies.* Kawaida Publications.

Mazama, A. (1998). The Eurocentric discourse in writing: An exercise in self-glorification. *Journal of Black Studies, 29*(1), 3–16.

Mazama, A. (2001). The Afrocentric paradigm: Contours and definitions. *Journal of Black Studies, 31*(4), 387–405.

Mazama, A. (2014). *Afrocentricity and the critical question of African agency.* Afrocentricity International. Retrieved August 5, 2024, from https://dyabukam.

com/index.php/en/knowledge/philosophy/item/136-afrocentricity-and-the-critical-question-of-african-agency

McNamara, A. (2015). Review: Critical reckonings: Global art and art history after the west and Eurocentrism. Reviewed Work: Western Art and the Wider World by Paul Wood. *Art Journal, 74*(3), 67–69.

Moloi, L. (2024). *Developing Africa? New Horizons with Afrocentricity*. Anthem Press.

Mungazi, D. (2000). *In the footsteps of the masters: Desmond M. Tutu and Abel T. Muzorewa*. Bloomsbury Publishing USA.

Onaci, E. (2016). Black power, name choices, and self-determination. *Black Perspectives*. Retrieved August 5, 2024, from https://www.aaihs.org/black-power-name-choices-and-self-determination/

Ranuga, T. (1986). Frantz Fanon and Black consciousness in Azania (South Africa). *Phylon, 47*(3), 182–191.

Sartre, J. (2007). *Existentialism is humanism*. Yale University Press.

Satre, P. J. (1985). *George Rochberg's complete works for solo piano: Their style and the culture they reflect*. American Conservatory of Music.

Stewart, J. (1984). The legacy of W. E. B. DuBois for contemporary Black Studies. *The Journal of Negro Education, 53*(3), 296–311.

Trevor-Roper, H. (1973). Re-inventing Hitler. *Sunday Times*, 18.

Tibebu, S. (2011). Population, family planning and long-term development goals: "Predicting an unpredictable future." In C. Teller & A. Hailemeriam (Eds) *The demographic transition and development in Africa: The unique case of Ethiopia* (pp. 285–301). Springer.

Wood, P. (2013). *Western art and the wider world* (p. 314). Wiley.

# CHAPTER 7

## Asante's Afrocentric Decolonization of Education: From Kindergarten to Institutions of Higher Learning

### Simphiwe Sesanti, PhD

## ABSTRACT

The year 2025 marks 30 years since, in 1995, the Witwatersrand (Wits) University's Deputy Vice-Chancellor for Academic Affairs, Malegapuru Makgoba, called for a shift from Eurocentric Higher Education to Afrocentric Higher Education. The year 2025 also marks 10 years since, in 2015, the University of Cape Town's Rhodes Must Fall movement's students demanded a decolonized and Afrocentric education. Hostile opponents demanded, and curious bystanders enquired, how this was to be done, *practically*, especially in relation to Science, Technology, Education, and Mathematics Education (STEM), in the false belief that both the concept "University" and STEM are European, not African concepts. In this chapter, I examine how the leading Afrocentric philosopher and historian, Molefi Kete Asante, has addressed these questions both *theoretically* and *practically*.

## INTRODUCTION

I became aware of Molefi Kete Asante's theory, Afrocentricity, around 2003/2004. In 2007, I chose Afrocentricity as one of my theoretical frameworks when I embarked on a PhD in Journalism Studies at Stellenbosch University. I was interested in Asante not only as an academic but also, in his linking Afrocentricity to Pan-Africanism—a political ideology advancing Africans' unity and liberation both on the home continent and in the diaspora (Rabaka, 2020, p. 8). In line with Pan-Africanism, Asante (2003, p. 64) defines "Afrocentric awareness" as "the total commitment to African liberation anywhere and everywhere by a consistent determined effort to repair any psychic, economic, physical, or cultural damage done to Africans." The foregoing definition also brings out another reason for my interest in Asante, namely, his commitment to the African Renaissance. Linking the African Renaissance to Afrocentricity, Asante (2003, p. 134) notes that "the Afrocentric cultural project is a holistic plan to reconstruct and develop every dimension of the African world from the standpoint of Africa as subject rather than object." Such means having Afrocentric "movie theaters [...] a museum, book store, a documentary center [...] the creation of schools, factories, laboratories, institutes" (Asante, 2003, p. 69). Commitment to the African Renaissance inspired the writing of Asante's (2003, p. 1) book, *Afrocentricity: The Theory of Social Change*, "with the idea that an African renaissance is possible if there is an African ideology, distinct from a Eurocentric ideology, that allows African agency, that is, a sense of self-actualizing based upon the best interests of African people."

But, even among Pan-Africanists, there are differences. As Rabaka (2020, p. 9) notes, while it is true that "many Pan-Africanists have been influenced by Marxism, among other European theories," there is a "tendency to privilege Eurocentric theories over the myriad theories arising out of the Africana intellectual tradition that influenced Pan-Africanism before and after the emergence of Pan-Africanism":

> It is as if Marxism intellectually eclipses all of the Africana theories that provided Pan-Africanism with its philosophical foundations, social visions, and political pragmatism.

Aware of, and sensitive to these differences, Asante (2021, pp. xiii–xiv) holds the view that

> If Pan Africanism is an objective of conscious Africans, then the mechanism that we must employ to bring us to that objective is Afrocentricity [...] To be Afrocentric is to believe in the agency of African people, the ability of Africans to be self-determining, and to see ourselves in the center of our own historical experiences [...] My path in Afrocentric Pan Africanism, for one can have the dream of Pan Africanism, and not be Afrocentric, has been consistent since the 1970s [...].

Saying such is not the same as elevating and prioritizing Afrocentricity above Pan-Africanism. Instead, Asante (2003, pp. 78–79) locates Afrocentricity within the ideology of Pan-Africanism by stating that "Africology"—a study of African people using the Afrocentric method—"is primarily pan-Africanist in its treatment of the creative, political, and geographic dimensions of our collective will to liberty." In line with the foregoing, Afrocentricity is defined as a "philosophical perspective associated with the discovery, location, and actualizing of African agency within the context of history and culture," the reference to "agency" being "an attitude toward action originating in African experiences" (Asante, 2003, p. 3). Emphasis on history in Afrocentricity is cognizant of Diop's (1987, p. ix) observation that "[f]or a long time many of our compatriots have thought they could get by without any deep knowledge of African society and Africa in all aspects: history, languages, ethnicities, energy potentials, raw materials, and the like" (Diop, 1987). As a result of ignoring these factors, Diop (1987) continues, the conclusions reached have often been "abysmally banal, when not plain and simply wrong." In these false assumptions was the false thinking that "they could make up for the lack of ideas, breath, and revolutionary perspectives by the use of the offensive, excessive, and murky vocabulary," forgetting that "the truly revolutionary quality of language is its demonstrative clarity based on the objective use of facts and their dialectical relationships, which results in irresistibly convincing the intelligent reader" (Diop, 1987).

Reference to "culture" means the "totalization of the historical, artistic, economic, and spiritual aspects of a people's lifestyle" (Asante, 2003, p. 134). Culture "is not a narrow term" but, broadly, "includes science, music, engineering, architecture, dance, art, philosophy, and economics" (Asante, 2003, pp. 64, 134). With this understanding, Asante (2003, p. 15) argues that "Economic freedom must always be connected to political and cultural freedom else freedom does not truly exist."

Interested in how Asante applied Afrocentricity, *practically*, both within, and outside of the academy, in 2012, I requested to meet him in Philadelphia, USA, and the journey made possible by a grant I had received from Stellenbosch University for my PhD studies. When I stepped out of the airport building in Philadelphia, my eye quickly caught Asante as he stood there, alone, carrying a placard with my name on it, a deeply touching gesture from this giant, internationally renowned

Afrocentric scholar, humbling himself by coming, personally, to welcome a person he did not even know. I had acquired his email address from Mathatha Tsedu, a fellow Pan-Africanist, and, at the time, the editor of a South African weekly newspaper, the *City Press*.

Since my first meeting with Asante, I have traveled with him, together with his kind wife, Ana Yenenga, and met him more than 10 times in Egypt (twice), in different South African universities and provinces of South Africa (Eastern Cape, Gauteng, Kwa-Zulu Natal, Limpopo, Mpumalanga, Western Cape), and, again, when he invited me to an international Afrocentric conference in Philadelphia, advancing Afrocentric academic projects. In the second visit to Philadelphia, he extended the same gesture of welcoming me at Newark Airport, accompanied by another leading Afrocentric scholar, Nah Dove. This exercise is a reflection on *selected historic moments* with Asante, in the context of our Afrocentric engagements, since our first meeting. Space constraints did not allow accommodation of other historic moments. I begin with the Philadelphia moment, followed by the Limpopo moment, followed by the University of South Africa (UNISA) moments, followed by the Wits moment and then, concluding remarks.

## THE PHILADELPHIA MOMENT

Since the mid to the late 1990s, and in 2015, when Afrocentric scholars and students, called for Afrocentric Africanization of higher education, in South Africa, the calls were met with skepticism and cynicism from opponents. The opponents charged that the concept "Africanization" lacked "clarity, coherence and detail" as far as what its definition and implications entailed (Seepe, 1998, p. 63). Issues that emerged with "alarming monotony whenever the concept of Africanisation [was] raised" included questions about the "relevance to the learning and teaching of science and mathematics" of African culture since the advocates of Africanization were insisting that African culture(s) should be reflected in the curricula of institutions of higher learning. How decolonization and Africanization would address STEM was not just a concern for the opponents of Afrocentric education but also one independently appreciated by African scholars committed to decolonization of education, the recognition being that such would have to entail "deconstructing Western epistemological hegemony and building vibrant knowledge systems [...] in all branches of knowledge, however configured," such including "the natural sciences, social sciences and the humanities and the professional disciplines [...] raising the global presence of African knowledges" (Zeleza, 2024, p. 31). Underlining the importance and urgency of decolonizing scholars to address STEM education, Zeleza (2024, p. 51) warns that "Populist injunctions for decolonisation [...] are inadequate to the task, however satisfying they might be as radical gestures," adding that certainly "little will be achieved by social sciences and humanities scholars talking to themselves, failing to actively engage with colleagues in STEM [...] and confronting the complex and concrete questions of what it takes to maintain viable higher education institutions." Such a practical engagement with STEM by Afrocentric scholars took place in Philadelphia, in 1998, with the establishment of Imhotep Institute Charter High School, whose mission statement reveals that it is an "African-Centered science, mathematics, and technology learning-center whose mission is to provide a standards driven, high quality educational program for urban learners grounded in the Afrikan principles of Ma'at and the Seven Principles of the Nguzo Saba" (imhotephighschool.com). The school's "underlying philosophy is that a rigorous, integrative, constructivist curriculum, combined with the historical and cultural richness of our cultural heritage, will result in well-rounded and productive citizens" (imhotephighschool.com).

The naming of the school after Imhotep, ancient Egypt's man of many talents (to be discussed below), was an Afrocentric move of African Americans' reclamation of, and identification with their African heritage. It was, in a way, a response to the Senegalese versatile scholar, Cheikh Anta Diop's (1974, p. xiv) clarion call:

> Ancient Egypt was a Negro civilization. The history of Black Africa will remain suspended in air and cannot be written correctly until African historians dare connect it with the history of Egypt [...] The African historian who evades the problem of Egypt is neither modest nor objective, nor unruffled; he is ignorant, cowardly, and neurotic. Imagine, if you can, the uncomfortable position of a western historian who was to write the history of Europe without referring to Greco-Latin Antiquity and try to pass that off as a scientific approach.

Imhotep was ancient Egyptian king Djoser's "vizier" around 2650 BC, a "Chief of the Observers or Chief of the Astronomers," and a "high priest" of Heliopolis (Bauval & Brophy, 2013, pp. xv, xvi, 1). A "vizier" in ancient Egypt served as a "prime minister, responsible for public order" and "the supreme legal authority in the land of Pharaoh and the Minister of Justice" (Yoyotte, 1990, p. 84). The main function of the Chief of Astronomers was to observe the sky and the motion of the stars (Bauval & Brophy, 2013, p. 1). Imhotep was also an architect who is credited with conceiving the "world's very first architectural complex" known as the Step Pyramid Complex that stands in Cairo (Bauval & Brophy, 2013, pp. xv). Imhotep could be a combination of all these professions in one because of the education acquired by people called "priests" in ancient Egypt who were trained as a "judge[s] and interpreter[s] of the law," and whose education "*consisted also in the specialization in secret systems of language and mathematical symbolism*" (James, 2001, pp. 132, 133). As a result of their education, "Priests of Egypt were also Lawyers, Judges, officials of government, Business Men and Sailors and Captains. Hence, they must have been trained in Economics, Civics, Law, Government, Statistics, [...] navigation, ship building, military science [...]" (James, 2001, p. 136). In the field of medicine, ancient Egypt's priests "discovered [...] drugs of such a nature that they are harmless as daily food, yet in their effects are so beneficial that all men agree that the Egyptians are the healthiest and most long of life among men" (Isocrates et al., 1944, p. 115). When performing mummification (the preservation of dead bodies through chemicals) "surgically-trained priests who specialized in the preparation of cadavers," made "an incision in the left side. Through the wound the priest broke through the diaphragm and eviscerated the corpse" (Grimal, 1994, p. 130). It is in this context that Imhotep was celebrated not only by the ancient Egyptians, but, also by the ancient Greeks such that the Greeks celebrated Imhotep as the "Father of Medicine" (Bauval & Brophy, 2013, p. 2). The ancient Greeks had deep respect for Imhotep because Hippocrates "had access to the library of the Imhotep temple at Memphis," and also because "other Greek physicians later followed his example" (El Nadoury, 1990, p. 111).

The Greek philosopher, Aristotle (2004, p. 6), in his book, *The Metaphysics*, acknowledges that "it was in Egypt that the mathematical sciences were first developed." In *The Odyssey*, Homer (1991, p. 47) notes that "in medical knowledge Egyptians are supreme among men." Appreciating the high level and quality of teaching and learning of mathematics in ancient Egypt, Plato (2004, p. 267) urged Greek gentlemen to "study each of these subjects to at least the same level as very many children in Egypt, who acquire such knowledge at the same time as they learn to read and write." It is no small significance that Plato urges Greek adults (gentlemen) to strive for the level of mathematical comprehension displayed by Egyptian children. Plato knew these details because he had "travelled extensively in Egypt [...] a country in which intelligent Greeks took much interest" (Armstrong, 1981, pp. 34, 64). Plutarch (1960, p. 45) notes that "Plato paid for the expenses of his stay in Egypt by selling oil."

That ancient Egyptians' leadership is acknowledged in little or not at all, and thus little known by some, or not known at all, not only in hard sciences such as mathematics and natural sciences but also in humanities and social sciences such as philosophy, is not an accident of history but a deliberate falsification by Eurocentric scholars. Peck (2010, p. xx) observes that the "history of Egypt traditionally taught in the west has, for the most part, been written by western scholars who followed on the footsteps on their armies," and I add, "colonial armies serving colonial aims." Along these lines, Russell (2004, p. 15) claims that the Greeks "invented mathematics and science and philosophy" adding that the Greeks "wrote history as opposed to mere annals." In support of his claim that the Greeks invented mathematics, science and philosophy, Russell (2004) adds that

> Philosophy begins with Thales, who, fortunately, can be dated by the fact that he predicted an eclipse which, according to the astronomers, occurred in the year 585 B.C. Philosophy and science—which were not originally separate—were therefore born together at the beginning of the sixth century.

Having associated the invention of mathematics with Greece, and the beginning of philosophy with Thales, the Greek, in a footnote, Russell (ibid) acknowledges that while "Arithmetic and some geometry existed among the Egyptians and Babylonians," such was "mainly in the form of rules of thumb," insisting that "Deductive reasoning from general premises was a Greek innovation." Justifying his point, Russell (2004, p. 34) goes on to note that

Thales is said to have travelled in Egypt, and to have thence brought to the Greeks the science of geometry. What the Egyptians knew of geometry was mainly rules of thumb, and there is no reason to believe that Thales arrived at deductive proofs, such as later Greeks discovered.

Russell's claims that ancient Egyptians' "geometry was mainly rules of thumb," meaning "inexact," have not gone unchallenged. El Nadoury (1990, pp. 112–113) points out that

Mathematics is an important field of science in which the Ancient Egyptians worked. The accurate measurements of their enormous architectural and sculptural monuments are worthy proof of their preoccupation with precision [...]

Even as Russell makes the claims, which contradict statements by the Greeks themselves to whom he attributes inventions attributed to ancient Egyptians, he makes an observation that exposes uneasiness on his part. Russell (2004, p. 15), notes that "In all history, nothing is so surprising or so difficult to account for as the sudden rise of civilization in Greece," adding that much of what makes civilization had "already existed for thousands of years in Egypt and in Mesopotamia, and had spread thence to neighbouring countries." While, on the one hand, Russell (2004) acknowledges that the "art of writing was invented in Egypt about the year 4000 B.C., and in Mesopotamia not much later," on the other hand he argues that "certain elements had been lacking until the Greeks supplied them." This falsification was and continues to be entrenched by the fact that that "[i]n every history of philosophy for students, the first thing mentioned is that philosophy began with Thales," a Greek (Russell, 2004, p. 33). As if responding directly to Russell, Dunn (2010, p. 5) points out that the "cultural assumptions that are disturbed most by the idea of an advanced Egyptian race in prehistory lie in the libraries and halls of Western countries and the belief system that has been generated by generations of Western scholars [...] It is our own culture's chauvinistic view of Egypt that threads throughout our own history books." Eurocentric hostile scholarship to ancient Egyptians has "become so effective at convincing the world that the Egyptian civilization was not as technically advanced as the Greeks or Romans, and certainly not the West, that many modern Egyptians themselves believe [the] story and are loath to accept any other" (Dunn, 2010, p. 39).

Conscious of, and sensitive to Eurocentric scholars' monopolization of the writing of history in general, and that of philosophy, in particular, Asante contested the space by writing and publishing *The Egyptian Philosophers: Ancient African Voices from Imhotep to Akhenaten*. In the book, Asante (2000) demonstrates that ancient Egyptians delved in philosophy long before the Greeks did, identifying them by their individual names. Individual identification of ancient Egypt's philosophers enables scholars and students of philosophy not only to appreciate ancient Egypt's collective philosophy called *Maat* but also to interrogate individual philosophers' engagements with *Maat* from *an ancient period*.

It is intervention, not only advocated but also practiced by Diop, Asante, and other Afrocentric scholars, such as reclaiming ancient Egypt as an African heritage, that has enabled visionaries who brought about Imhotep Institute Charter High School so that "All Africans, be they on the mother continent or in the West among the diaspora of African Americans and Afro-Europeans, should be proud of such an illustrious ancestor [Imhotep]—one known to the ages as He Who Comes in Peace" (Bauval & Brophy, 2013, p. 201). Such a daring move, however, comes at a high price, as Diop came to realize. Diop's bold move (Van Sertima, 2007, p. 8) took him "straight in the mouth of the guns." The "guns" that Van Sertima (2007) refers to is the jury of the University of Paris, which roundly rejected Diop's thesis, labeling it "unfounded." Diop's thesis was rejected three times before it was finally accepted in 1960—9 years after he had submitted in 1951 (Carew, 2007, p. 26). What this indicates about Diop is that he was prepared to suffer, unlike many African intellectuals who, "in their frantic bid to deny their heritage and to win acclaim from their white mentors," literally tear themselves to pieces psychologically (Carew, 2007, p. 25).

In 1967, when Professor Emeritus of Hunter College, in the USA, John Henrik Clarke (1991, p. xv) attended the second meeting of the International Congress of Africanness, which was convened at the University of Dakar, he was surprised to learn that Diop's office was located on the campus of the university, less than 300 yards from the assembly hall where the Congress was being held. Yet, Diop was not one of the participants at the conference and "[n]either his name nor his work was mentioned at the conference" (Clarke, 1991). The reason for Diop's exclusion was that, Clarke (1991) notes, the "sponsoring organization, the African Studies Association, was then dominated by white scholars, and to this day it has not recognized the scholarship of Cheikh Anta Diop and his contribution to a new concept of African history."

In 1980, 23 years after this incident, a similar one took place when Asante visited Diop (Asante, 2007, pp. xv–xvi). Asante (2007, p. xvi) was in Senegal attending a meeting hosted by Pathe Diagne, discussing the possibility of organizing a Festival of the African World subsequent to the one that was held in Lagos, Nigeria, in 1977:

> There were many scholars at this meeting. I was stunned to find as we assembled that Diop was not among the people who had been brought to the University. He was still considered an outsider to those in the elite groups of Senegal. (Clarke, 1991)

The foregoing observations may come across as African scholars' protection of a fellow African scholar on the basis of color. Even if that were to be the case, there is nothing wrong, and there is everything right in African solidarity against racist white supremacy. But these observations are *more* about Diop's scholarship than his color, and these observations have not only been waged by fellow Black or African scholars, but White ones too. Among such works are *Black Genesis: The Prehistoric Origins of Ancient Egypt* and *Imhotep: The African Architect of the Cosmos*, both books authored by Robert Bauval and Thomas Brophy. In their introduction to *Black Genesis*, Bauval and Brophy (2011, p. 1) note that their "book is the product of a deep and strong desire to use the best of our intellect, knowledge, and abilities to put right an issue that has long beleaguered historians and prehistorians alike: the vexed question of the Black African origins of the ancient Egyptians." Bauval and Brophy (2011) further note that "In spite of many clues that have been in place in the past few decades, which strongly favour a Black African origin for the pharaohs, many scholars and especially Egyptologists have either ignored them, confused them, or worst of all, derided those who entertained them." Bauval and Brophy (2011) "first came across this inherent bias and prejudice against African origins of the Egyptian civilization in the debate—more of an auto-da-fé really—against the Black African professor Cheikh Anta Diop."

> Anta Diop was both an eminent anthropologist and a highly respected physicist, and as such, he was armed with an arsenal of cutting-edge science as well as the use of the latest technology in radiocarbon dating and biochemistry to determine the skin color of ancient mummies and corpses by analysing their content of melanin, a natural polymer that regulates pigmentation in humans. (Bauval & Brophy, 2011, pp. 1–2)

Exposing a strong prejudice by powerful forces, including those in government of Egypt, Bauval and Brophy (2011, p. 2) point out that "in spite of his careful scientific approach, the Egyptian authorities refused to provide Anta Diop with skin samples of royal mummies, even though only minute quantities were required, and they pilloried and shunned him at a landmark symposium in Cairo in 1974 on the origins of ancient Egyptians." However, even after his passing in 1986, the battle did not die. As Bauval and Brophy (2011) point out,

> the debate on African origins was quickly taken up by Professor Martin Bernal, who, in 1987, published a three-volume opus, *Black Athena*, that flared even further the already-heated debate. Bernal, a professor emeritus of Near Eastern studies at Cornell University, was the grandson of the eminent Egyptologist Sir Alan Gardiner, yet this did not prevent Egyptologists from attacking him with even more vehemence than they had his Black African predecessor Anta Diop.

A further examination of ancient Egypt's history enables Afrocentric scholars to demonstrate how, in *practice*, African culture historically contributed, and can contribute to the decolonization of STEM education. We learn that in the "Egyptian Pharaonic civilization of historical times two main currents can be discovered," the first being the "material legacy" and the second being the "abstract cultural legacy" which are "interrelated and together comprise the Egyptian cultural phenomenon" (El Nadoury, 1990, p. 104). The "material legacy" includes crafts and science (geometry, astronomy, chemistry), applied mathematics, and medicine and surgery (El Nadoury, 1990). The "abstract cultural legacy" includes religion,

literature, and philosophy (El Nadoury, 1990) Cognizant that both legacies are "interrelated," we learn that the ancient Egyptians' practice of
mummification—the preservation of dead bodies—which exhibited their
"mastery of a number of sciences including physics, chemistry, medicine
and surgery" was a "practical fulfilment of their demands of their belief
in the after-life" (El Nadoury, 1990, p. 109). In explicit words, the ancient
Egyptians sought, *scientifically*, to give meaning, to their *cultural* belief
in life after death. Aware in their ancient time that what has been "analyzed in modern times," that the compounds of natron are a mixture of
sodium, carbonate, sodium, bicarbonate, salt and sodium sulfate, ancient
Egyptians, in the process of mummification, "soaked the body in natron
for seventy days [...] drew the brain out through the nostrils and [...] also
removed the intestines through an incision made in the side of the body.
Such operations as these necessitated an accurate knowledge of anatomy,
and the good state of preservation of the mummies illustrates this intimate
knowledge" (El Nadoury, 1990).

It was not just the naming of the school after Imhotep that fascinated me
when I visited the school with Asante and meeting the school's founder,
Christine Wiggins, Asante's mentee, who had consulted her mentor to assist
her to conceptualize her school. Seeing the pupils wearing African dashikis,
and hearing that it was a school uniform swept me off my feet and took my
breath away! This is because the wearing of an African dress code is a very
powerful, revolutionary, and Afrocentric cultural statement, taking into
cognizance that among the most powerful colonial cultural instruments
employed to erase African cultural identity was the forced abandonment of
African names by Africans and at the same time the imposition of European
names, the forced abandonment of African languages, and at the same time
the imposition of European languages, and the forced abandonment of
Africans' dress codes, and the imposition of European dress codes! On this
score, having noted that after European colonialists in South Africa had
made Christianity a "central culture" which brought with it "new styles of
clothing," and forcing Africans to cast away their "indigenous clothing,"
Biko (2004, p. 60) further notes that the difference in clothing between
African Christian converts and those who resisted Christianity, "made what
otherwise could have been merely a religious difference actually become at
times internecine warfare," among Africans, resulting in Africans becoming

"a playground for colonialists"! Afrocentric visionaries who conceptual-ized Imhotep Institute Charter High School were not prepared to subject their children to being "a playground for colonialists"! On the other hand, in spite of Africa regaining "independence" or "freedom" since the late 1950s from their colonial masters, to date, children in Africa, continue to wear school uniforms imposed by their European oppressors!

In his personal capacity, Asante (2011, pp. 165–166) had, in 1973, made his own African Renaissance statement by dropping his birth name, Arthur Lee Smith Jr., henceforth becoming Molefi Kete Asante:

> I wanted to be anonymous in neither Christian nor Islamic circles; I wanted to claim my African heritage and legacy, and the place to start was my name [...] I did what the African American women had done during the 1960s, when they revolted by wearing their hair in its natural state. Changing my name was a relief, a celebration of my Africanity, and an honor to my ancestors because whenever someone called my name, they would be remembering the ancestors' name.

For Asante (2011, p. 2) carrying "the surnames of those who enslaved" Africans was a "constant reminder of a lack of self-determination, a badge of conquest." Asante (2011) "hated these names" because they meant nothing to his history but "oppression, shame, domination, defeat, and depres-sion." His reference to his refusal to be "anonymous in neither Christian nor Islamic circles" was to his rejection not only of European Christian slave names, but also Arabic names adopted by African American Muslims who had rejected European Christian names and adopted Arabic Muslim names: "Why choose an Arabic name instead of an English name and think you have arrived at freedom?" (Asante, 2011, p. 3). However, name-changing was not the only African Renaissance statement that Asante made. The other, among others, was to replace the imposed European dress code with the "practice of wearing something made by the hands of Africans," in other words, the African dress code (Asante, 2011, p. 241). This example shone the light for Imhotep Institute Charter High School.

Until 2018, when Asante was invited as a keynote speaker at the at the University of Limpopo's Faculty of Humanities whose theme was *Calling for Transgressive and Constructionist Dialogues on Africanisation and Decoloniality*, from September 4 to 6, Asante enthusiastically told me that he had never seen such a large number of students, all at once, pursuing their studies using the theory of Afrocentricity!

## THE UNIVERSITY OF LIMPOPO MOMENT

The students we met were between were about 30 or so and were studying toward their Honors' degree in Psychology. It was a great moment of joy and a historic occasion for Asante and Afrocentricity! His joy can best be captured in his (Asante, 2003, p. v) own words captured 15 years earlier in his book, *Afrocentricity: The Theory of Social Change (Revised and Expanded)*:

> Over the years I have received numerous recognitions and awards for the work that I have done in Afrocentric education but the proudest moments have been those where African people, in the United States and other countries, have embraced Afrocentricity as a positive ideology of consciousness.

The occasion was historic for other reasons, as well, which had a direct link to Afrocentricity. The University of Limpopo was a site where the Black Consciousness-inspired South African Students Organisation (SASO) was inaugurated, in July 1969, with Bantu Steve Biko elected as the organization's first president (Gerhart, 1979, p. 261; Karis & Gerhart, 2013, p. 97). The formal launch followed a consultative meeting at Marianhill in December 1968, which approved the name of the organization and the draft constitution (Gerhart, 1979; Karis & Gerhart, 2013).

In his book, *As I Run Toward Africa: A Memoir*, Asante (2011, p. 305) leaves no one in doubt about his deep appreciation and admiration for Biko:

> Biko was the first South African to have had a visceral effect on me. I have read the classic critiques, reviewed the liberation magazines, kept up with the Pan-Africanist Congress and the African National Congress, and considered myself knowledgeable about all aspects of South Africa until I began to read a few of the words, unsanctioned and courageous, of Steve Biko. I found myself lifted to a level of antiracism sentiment that had not been tapped before. I think this was because Biko's words echoed not only the South African story but also my own Georgian story as well.

When, in 2004, Asante (2011, pp. 304–305) was invited to South Africa by Mafube Publishing, to give the main speech on the celebration of the tenth anniversary of South Africa's democracy, he expressed a desire to see where Biko was born and buried, a request that was granted. Subsequent to laying wreaths on Biko's grave. Asante (2011, p. 305) was invited for lunch by Biko's wife, Ntsiki Biko, to whom Asante refers as "one of the saints of liberation" because of her "eternal sacrifice." Recognizing that Africans "can never repay her or her children's loss," when he was invited by the *City Press*' newspaper's political journalist, Jimmy Seepe, to write a column in Biko's spirit, Asante "donated the small fee to Biko's wife" as a token of appreciation (ibid). In a "dispute" with the newspaper's management, later, Asante (2011) discontinued the column "because the paper had ceased to give the fee to Ntsike (*sic*) Biko."

Afrocentric articulations on education are in line with Biko's (2004, p. 57):

> We are aware of the terrible role played by our education and religion in creating amongst us a false understanding of ourselves. We must therefore work out schemes not only to correct this, but further to be our own authorities rather than wait to be interpreted by others.

It was also at the University of Limpopo—formerly known as the University of the North—where Onkgopotse Abram Tiro, a member of SASO, and the Student Representative Council president, who, on April 29, 1971, at a graduation ceremony, in his speech on behalf of the graduates, "shocked the assembled dignitaries by attacking the segregated university system," a speech that earned him an expulsion from the university while doing a post-graduate diploma course (Karis & Gerhart, 2013, p. 128). It was not just the attack on racism that was historic in Tiro's (2013, p. 510) speech, but the content of his speech, which articulated a Pan-Africanist and Afrocentric philosophy of education:

> Of what use will be your education if you can't help your country in her hour of need? If your education is not linked with the entire continent of Africa it is meaningless.

In February, 1974, Tiro was parcel-bombed and martyred by the racist South African government in Botswana where he was exiled (Gerhart, 1979, p. 298). The University of Limpopo was not the only African institution of higher learning, which embraced Asante. The UNISA did, too.

# THE UNISA MOMENTS

In 2019, while still working for UNISA's Institute for African Renaissance Studies, and editing the International Journal of African Renaissance Studies (IJARS), I was invited by the then College of Graduate Studies' Dean, Prof Lindiwe Zungu, to coordinate the Principal and Vice-Chancellor, Prof Mandla Makhanya's African Intellectual Project (AIP; Sesanti, 2020, p. 2). My task was to identify and invite African scholars, on the home continent and abroad, to address ills confronting Africa and offer possible solutions. We wanted the best of the best among Africa's intellectual daughters and sons. At the top of my list was Asante. We invited him and he came. Most of the presentations were selected and published in *IJARS*' Special Edition whose focus was the AIP.

When Zungu read Asante's profile, she pointed out that it would not be enough for him to give a keynote address, but that it would be essential that Asante to visit all UNISA's colleges so that Asante would be able to indicate how Afrocentricity could practically inform mathematics, natural sciences, commerce, communication, history, anthropology and language education. In other words, Zungu understood that informing and underlining all disciplines in education is, or should be, *philosophy*. Asante agreed and delivered.

Subsequent to his lecture tour, on December 4, 2019, UNISA's Council met, deliberated, and decided to confer an honorary doctorate to Asante to be conferred on December 4, 2020. In a letter signed by UNISA's registrar, Prof MS Mothata (2020), UNISA stated that the award was in recognition of his

- commitment to the liberation struggle and equality of life in a democratic South Africa;
- leadership qualities;
- contribution to the struggle of Black people in South Africa;
- contribution to the education of the masses; and
- pioneer in intellectuals project (AIP).

Asante's nomination was informed by the nominators' appreciation of Asante's (2011, p. 14) commitment to the liberation struggle informed by his Pan-Africanist outlook, which drove him to be preoccupied with the "cause of liberation at home and abroad, the possibility of fighting in the military wing of the African National Congress [the ANC of South Africa], and resisting that anti-Africanisms [he] saw in American society." Asante did not just dream of these possibilities but accomplished some. His participation in student politics saw him joining and becoming the president of the Student Nonviolent Coordinating Committee (SNCC) at the University of California and Los Angeles (UCLA) from 1966 to 1968 (Asante, 2011, pp. 145, 177). As a member and leader of the SNCC, he got together with his peers "to discuss the role students had to play in the liberation struggle" (Asante, 2011, p. 178). He participated in campaigns to support the liberation struggle of Zimbabwe by attending support committees of the Zimbabwe African National Union (ZANU), a liberation struggle movement that ultimately became Zimbabwe's ruling party after the country regained independence in 1980 (Asante, 2011, p. 206). While he was lecturing and writing on Afrocentricity, Asante (2011, p. 160)

> was working with the anti-Rhodesian forces and the anti-apartheid forces to bring about freedom in southern Africa. A small group of committed intellectuals and activists gathered around the Center for Positive Thought to provide money, materials, and medicines to the resistance forces, advancing the liberation of Zimbabwe and South Africa.

Not to be left out in institutions of higher learning in honoring Asante was Wits University.

## THE UNIVERSITY OF WITS MOMENT

On July, 19, 2022, a silent, but significant, revolutionary occasion took place at Wits University, in South Africa. An Honorary Doctorate was awarded to Asante by the institution's Vice-Chancellor, Zeblon Vilakazi. It was an historic occasion and a victory for Afrocentricity because 27 years earlier, in 1995, the institution's then Deputy Vice-Chancellor for Academic Affairs, Malegapuru William Makgoba, was subjected to a relentless vilification campaign by his colleagues including the questioning of his Curriculum Vitae (CV; Makgoba, 1997, p. 54). The irony was that Makgoba was "invited and head-hunted for this position" (Makgoba, 1997, pp. 51, 58). Recalling the dramatic events that surrounded him, Makgoba (1997) notes that the cause of these attacks would be my views and thoughts on the nature of an African university. My views threatened the very foundation of the university and all teaching at the institution; for all these were steeped in Eurocentrism, seen by its proponents as mutually exclusive of Africanism and of lower standards. Within nine months of my arrival at Wits, twelve of the university's dons, including eight deans and one registrar, had signed a petition that challenged my curriculum vitae. The 13th person was an African American.

Makgoba's (1997, p. 74) problems started a few months after his arrival at Wits on October 1, 1995, when, through the media, he started articulating his views about the future of Wits University. Makgoba (1997) believed that Wits needed to prioritize transformation, affirmative action, access and a "cultural revolution," the latter drawing "more attention or sensation" because, he pointed out,

> liberals do not want to dwell on values and culture systems in their debates on programmes for transformation. Culture is too threatening and too close to home to debate. It goes right to the heart of the identity issue, something all liberal philosophies throughout the world have tried consciously or unconsciously to avoid.

Makgoba (1997, p. 86) emphasized that "the transformation process at the university was not fundamental enough if it did not address the issue of the curriculum, the culture of the people whom this transformation is really about." This meant, in clearer terms, that "[t]he curricula have to change as the university comes to terms with the reality that it is educating all South Africans in South Africa" (Makgoba, 1997, p. 82).

Holding the view that institutions of higher education in South Africa were driven by "a Eurocentric philosophy," Makgoba (1997, pp. 180, 203) called for their "Africanization" by which he meant the "process or vehicle for defining, interpreting, promoting and transmitting African thought, philosophy, identity and culture." Opposed to the Eurocentric character of institutions of higher education in South Africa, Makgoba (1997, p. 209) argued that

> Central to transforming higher education in South Africa is the elimination of the present racist, dominant Eurocentric education and its total replacement by a non-racial, equitable Afrocentric education.

The conferment of an honorary doctorate to Asante by Wits University was a vindication of the correctness of Makgoba's call for Afrocentric higher education.

## CONCLUDING REMARKS

When on December 20, 1980, Asante (2014, pp. 48, 51) met Diop in Senegal and expressed a desire to dedicate his life on a mission to "defend Africa," Diop told Asante that "African history and Africa needed no defense; it only had to be advanced." Asante's Afrocentric scholarship has been focused on that sole mission, his major thrust, in line with the definition of Afrocentricity, being history, philosophy, and culture. With reference to history, Asante has published a seminal text, *The History of Africa: The Quest for Eternal Harmony*, which is now in its 4th edition. His Afrocentric thrust in writing this book comes out clearly as Asante (2024, p. xi) states that "[t]oo much of African historiography has been about writing Africa for Europe without writing Africa for itself, as itself, from its own perspectives." In opposition to this Eurocentric approach, his Afrocentric approach in writing this book is to see to it that "all historical subjects and phenomena [...] must be revisited in light of African agency." In doing this, Asante is responding Biko's (2004, p. 105) statement, namely, that "a lot of attention has to be paid to our history if we as Blacks want to aid each other in our coming into consciousness." In putting emphasis on "African agency," Asante endorses Biko's (2004) argument that Africans "would be too naïve to expect our conquerors to write unbiased histories about us." In pointing in this direction, Biko was not daydreaming. To the contrary, Biko (2004) recognized that this task calls for "intense research to provide some sorely-needed missing links." Rising to Biko's challenge, Asante (2024, p. 1) points out that in the 4th edition of his *The History of Africa*, he has "added insights and ideas from more ordinary women and men whose accomplishments may have been missed by more grandiose narratives in the past." The foregoing observation gives a clear indication that he is conscious of, and against, the tendency where in the past historiography has given attention to society's "prominent" people, ignoring the significant contribution made by "ordinary" people, and rejects the tendency of past historiography of giving attention to "heroes" and ignoring significant contribution made by "sheroes." Hammering the need to give due attention to the deserving, but marginalized people, Asante (2024, p. 3) emphasizes that there can be no "comprehensive history of Africa without engaging the numerous smaller linguistic and ethnic groups that people the interstices between large families of people." Small groups of people "matter, and they make history since each achievement of a people, each inventive moment, and all aspects of culture aggregate in a cohesive manner that provides context and reality to our overall narrative" (Asante, 2024). Asante further points out that by concentrating on larger ethnic groups, scholars "often miss important aspects of culture that stitch together economic or political fabrics of nationality." The future tasks of Afrocentric historians, therefore, Asante (2024) concludes, is to "explore the smaller linguistic and ethnic groups to discover cultural convergences and historical relationships." The point made by Asante is that it is through studying small ethnic groups that we can establish what Diop (1989, pp. 1–2) did, through his book, *The Cultural Unity of Black Africa: The Domains of Matriarchy & of Patriarchy in Classical Antiquity*, namely, "to bring out the profound cultural unity still alive beneath the deceptive appearance of cultural heterogeneity" and to "bring to view the common denominator in African culture." This African cultural unity can be explained by the fact that Africans, having a common geographical origin, spread, as a result of migration, throughout the continent (Diop, 1987, p. 3).

Intimately linked and central to these efforts is the need to have African philosophy as they basis of African education because philosophy raises and answers the question that all of educators must confront: For what purposes are we educating? To prepare some to be slaves of some masters or to create a humane world, through Ubuntu/Botho philosophy, where there is truth, justice, order, and balance as advanced by ancient Egyptians' Maat philosophy? In *practical terms*, to build an "African university" means, as Asante (2014, p. 65) points out in his chapter, "The Philosophical Bases for an African University" in his book, *Facing South to Africa: Toward an Afrocentric Critical Orientation*, that African intellectuals must "build a curriculum on what the ancestors have left behind." Asante's call makes sense to those who appreciate that from an African philosophical perspective, the "ancestors" are an integral part of the family since reference to family in African culture is to the living, the ancestors (living dead) and children yet to born (Mbiti, 1990, pp. 104–105; wa Thiong'o, 1997, p. 138). In the divine African link between the ancestors, the living, and the yet-to-be-born, the ancestors are regarded as "the source of inspiration," the living as actors in the "arena of perspiration," and the yet-to-be-born are a "collective aspiration" (wa Thiong'o, 1997, p. 139).

In appreciation of the ancestors as inspiration, Kunene (1982, pp. xii–xiii) observes that

> Our perspectives are therefore philosophically deeply anchored in the past, which is the sine qua non of our present. It is thus unthinkable to view the Ancestors as primitive, uncivilized, backward, since their actions achieved their intended purpose despite all the odds against them. We also assume that since their primary intent was to satisfy not only their needs but those of the next generations, their actions supersede all the selfish motivations that otherwise dominate society.

If, as Kunene points out, the ancestors' commitment "was to satisfy not only their needs but those of the next generations," such means that they were *not* driven by *selfishness* and were *futuristic—not primitive*—in their orientation and conduct. Maintenance of the link between the living, the ancestors, and those yet to be born means upholding a spirit of *selflessness* and sacrifice to the point of being willing to lay down one's life for the preservation of the community—a revolutionary performance. Dying for others to live was "The High Law of Life" among "The Laws of the Bantu," which is recorded as follows:

> Man, know that your life is not your own. You live merely to link your ancestors with your descendants. Your duty is to beget children even while you keep the Spirits of your Ancestors alive through regular sacrifices. When your Ancestors command you to die, do so with no regrets. (Mutwa, 1998, p. 625)

From an African philosophical perspective, therefore,

> Reverence for the ancestors is actually a reverence for life; for continuity and change [...] It means learning from them. Learning from our past. And that means learning from the strengths and the weaknesses of the past experience. When a people forget or are made to forget their history, to

forget that is, their collective experience of the past, they are actually being put in a position where they are unable to draw any lessons from their past. (wa Thiong'o, 1997, p. 139)

Summarizing of all of the above, Asante (2014, p. 65) observes that

This is where the ancestors are meaningful to us [...] ancestors give us a good reason for sacrifice, our readiness and willingness to die for the future of the society, goes in tow with the caring for the young [...] When a college is dedicated to the ancestors, the dead, then information is laid aside for the future generations.

Association of education with the philosophy of the ancestors is an ancient African tradition. Illustrating this, Kunene (1982, p. xi) points out that

Few societies have projected the past with such philosophic and creative intensity as the African. Where other societies describe social and material progress in identical terms of growth from lower levels to higher levels, African society separates the two, depicting the ethical element and the technological aspects as often capable of moving in opposing directions [...] Thus, a highly ethically advanced society need not necessarily be technically advanced; equally a technologically advanced society does not automatically possess a high ethical level. Indeed more often than not technological advancement tends to barbarize society, since by its very nature it implies a high degree of competitiveness for resources.

In line with Kunene's observation, Hilliard (2003, p. 271) observes that "given [...] many [...] examples of high level technical developments in Egypt, what is important is not so much the level of technical development as the 'philosophical orientation of the users of the technology.'" The philosophical orientation of ancient Egypt toward technology was that it was aimed at enabling human beings to develop a greater understanding of humankind's relationship with, and place in nature (Hilliard, 2003). Asante's association of education with the wisdom (philosophy) of the ancestors is traceable to the writings of ancient Egyptian philosophy, one of them being *The Instruction Addressed to King Merikare* (Lichtheim, 1975, p. 99):

Justice comes to him distilled,

Shaped in the sayings of the ancestors.

Copy your father, your ancestors,

See, their words endure in books,

Open, read them, copy their knowledge,

He who is taught becomes skilled.

Cognizant that our ancestors' philosophy was the basis of everything, including politics, economics, and education, Afrocentricity, therefore stands for a type of education—from kindergarten to higher education—that is based on African philosophy.

# REFERENCES

Aristotle. (2004). *The Metaphysics* (translated with an introduction by Hugh Lawson-Tancred). Penguin Books.

Armstrong, A. H. (1981). *An introduction to ancient philosophy*. Rowman & Allanheld.

Asante, M. K. (2000). *The Egyptian philosophers: Ancient African voices from Imhotep to Akhenaten*. African American Images.

Asante, M. K. (2003). *Afrocentricity: The theory of social change (Revised and Expanded)*. African American Images.

Asante, M. K. (2007). *Cheikh Anta Diop: An intellectual portrait*. University of Sankore Press.

Asante, M. K. (2011). *As I run toward Africa: A memoir*. Paradigm Publishers.

Asante, M. K. (2014). *Facing South to Africa: Toward an Afrocentric critical orientation*. Lexington Books.

Asante, M. K. (2021). *An Afrocentric Pan-Africanist vision: Afrocentric essays*. Lexington Books.

Asante, M. K. (2024). *The history of Africa: The quest for eternal harmony*. Routledge.

Bauval, R., & Brophy, T. (2011). *Black genesis: The prehistoric origins of ancient Egypt*. Bear & Company.

Bauval, R., & Brophy, T. (2013). *Imhotep the African: Architect of the cosmos*. Disinformation Books.

Biko, S. (2004). *I Write What I Like*. Picador Africa.

Carew, J. (2007). Conversations with Diop and Tsegaye: The Nile Valley revisited. In I. Van Sertima and L. O. Williams (Eds.), *Great African Thinkers: Cheikh Anta Diop* (pp. 19–27). Transaction Books.

Clarke, J. H. (1991). Foreword. In C. A. Diop (Eds.), *Civilization or Barbarism: An authentic anthropology* (translated from the French by Yaa-Lengi Meema

Ngemi, edited by Harold J. Salemson and Marjolijn de Jager; pp. xiii–xxi). Lawrence Hill Books.

Diop, C. A. (1974). *The African origin of civilization: Myth or reality* (edited and translated by Mercer Cook). Lawrence Hill Books.

Diop, C. A. (1987). *Black Africa: The Economic and Cultural Basis for a Federated State* (Exp., ed., Trans. H. J. Salemson). Lawrence Hill Books and Africa World Press.

Diop, C. A. (1989). *The cultural unity of Black Africa: The domains of matriarchy & of patriarchy in classical antiquity.* Karnak House.

El Nadoury, R. (1990). The legacy of Pharaonic Egypt. In G. Mokhtar (Ed.), *General history of Africa II: Ancient civilizations of Africa* (pp. 103–118). UNESCO, James Currey, University of California Press.

Gerhart, G. M. (1979). *Black power in South Africa: The evolution of an ideology.* University of California Press.

Grimal, N. (1994). *A history of Ancient Egypt.* Blackwell Publishers.

Hilliard, A. (2003). Pedagogy in Kemet. In A. Mazama (Ed.), *The Afrocentric paradigm* (pp. 265–281). Africa World Press, Inc.

Homer. (1991). *The Odyssey* (Trans. E.V. Rieu). Penguin Books.

Imhotephighschool.com. Retrieved March 5, 2025, from https://www.imhotep highschool.com/apps/pages/index.jsp?uREC_ID=1456939&type=d&pREC_ ID=1615370.

Isocrates, Norlin, G., & Van Hook, L. (1944). *Isocrates, With an English Translation by George Norlin… in Three Volumes.* The Loeb Classical Library.

James, G. G. M. (2001). *Stolen Legacy: Greek Philosophy is Stolen Egyptian Philosophy.* African American Images.

Karis, T. G., & Gerhart, G. M. (1972). *From Protest to Challenge—A Documentary History of African Politics in South Africa, 1882–1990: Nadir and Resurgence, 1964–1979* (Vol. 5, revised and updated by Gail M. Gerhart). Jacana.

Kunene, M. (1982). *The Ancestors & the Sacred Mountain.* Heinemann Educational Books.

Lichtheim, M. (1975). *Ancient Egyptian Literature: The Old and Middle Kingdoms* (Vol. I). University of California Press.

Makgoba, M. W. (1997). *Mokoko: The Makgoba Affair: A Reflection on Transformation.* Florida Hills: Vivlia Publishers and Booksellers.

Mbiti, J. S. (1990). *African Religions and Philosophy* (2nd ed.). Johannesburg: Heinemann.

Mothata, M. S. (2020, October 30). *Degree of Doctor of Literature and Philosophy (Honoris Causa).*

Mutwa, C. (1998). *Indaba, My children: African Tribal history, legends, customs and religious beliefs*. Edinburgh: Payback Press.

Peck, J. C. (2010). Recognizing the brilliance of ancient manufacturing. In: C. Dunn (Eds.), *Lost technologies of ancient Egypt* (pp. xvi–xxi). Bear & Company.

Plato. (2004). *The laws*. Translated by Trevor J. Saunders. Rosebank: Penguin Books.

Plutarch. (1960). The rise and fall of Athens: Nine Greek lives (translated by Ian Scott-Kilvert). Penguin Books.

Rabaka, R. (2020). Introduction: On the intellectual elasticity and political plurality of Pan-Africanism. In R. Rabaka (Ed.), *Routledge Handbook of Pan-Africanism* (pp. 1–32). Routledge.

Russell, B. (2004). *History of western philosophy*. Routledge Classics.

Seepe, S. (1998). Towards an Afrocentric understanding. In S. Seepe (Ed.), *Black perspective(s) on tertiary institutional transformation* (pp. 63–68). Vivlia Publishers & Booksellers (Pty) Ltd.

Sesanti S (2020). The African intellectuals' project. *International Journal of African Renaissance Studies, 15*(1), 1–24.

Tiro, O. R. (2013). Graduation speech by O.R. Tiro at the University of the North, Turfloop, April 29, 1972. In T. G. Karis and G. M. Gerhart (Eds.), *From protest to challenge—A documentary history of African Politics in South Africa, 1882–1990: Nadir and Resurgence, 1964–1979* (Vol. 5, pp. 508–510). Revised and updated by Gail M. Gerhart. Jacana.

Wa Thiong'o, N. (1997). *Writers in politics: A re-engagement with issues of literature & society* (revised & enlarged edition). James Currey, EAEP, Heinemann.

Yoyotte, J. (1990). Pharaonic Egypt: Society, economy and culture. In Mokhtar, G. (Ed), *General history of Africa II: Ancient civilizations of Africa* (pp. 79–89). UNESCO, James Currey, University of California Press.

Zeleza, P. T. (2024). *Re-envisioning the African and American Academies*. Codesria.

# CHAPTER 8

## From Orientalism to Afrocentricity: Navigating the Postcolonial Pedagogical Crisis in Light of Asante and Said

Abu Noman, PhD

There are no post-modern gray lines here; you either stand with the oppressed and against the oppressor, or you stand with the oppressor against liberation.

(Asante, 2007, p. 164)

Molefi Kete Asante in a talk given at Howard University (Asante, 2013) makes an illuminating statement that directly inspired this research. Asante states, "The African American student who sits in a classroom at a college and or high school in this country, normally sits inside the classroom but [s/he] is outside of the content of information. There is little organic relationship between the subject [being taught] and that student's historical experiences. The educational experience in America presumes that there is very little connection between mathematics and politics and African people, or psychology and African people, except as objects but not as subjects, not as agents, not as creators or actors. What is the relationship between African people and literature and arts? Our students are rarely given ownership of ideas: they become renters of white information." Building on Asante's observations, this research demonstrates that not only the content of education but the very theories used to investigate and explain these contents are predominantly European. Learners from the decolonized parts of the world are in the position of receivership of Eurocentric knowledge and theories on issues entirely Asian and African.

Ngugi wa Thiong'o's 1972 essay, "On the Abolition of the English Department" forced most of the Europeanized academic scholars to "reconceptualize" the curriculum by incorporating some native texts in English first under the title "Common Wealth Literature in English," then "Third World Literature (Prasad, 1997) in English," and finally "Postcolonial Literature" (Nayar, 2008) in the early 1980s. Undoubtedly, it simultaneously marked a profound change and significant triumph for the "ex-colonized" writers: being included in the curriculum of a department historically rooted in the values of empire and imperialism. Postcolonial literature, thus, initially represented an emancipatory and, to some extent, inclusionary zeal hitherto unseen in the decolonized academia.

Unfortunately, the postcolonialism of Frantz Fanon et al. (1963), Aimé Césaire (2023), Amilcar Cabral (2016), and Ngugi wa Thiong'o (1998) has been replaced with another postcolonialism dominated by Western and Westernized Asian and African scholars at the helm. Molefi Kete Asante's development of the first doctoral program in African American Studies in the 1980s resulted from his vision to decolonize academia. This vision found its finest articulation in the theory of Afrocentricity through which Asante advocated for a depoliticized pedagogy in higher education.

Afrocentricity maintains its radical stance amidst all this academic parochialism and reinforces its core philosophy of liberation through scholarly advancements. Afrocentricity as a critical theory has the potential to address cross-disciplinary issues related to oppression and suggest viable ways of emancipation. My objective here is to demonstrate the applicability of Afrocentricity as a critical theory in addressing the epistemological and pedagogical discrepancies in postcolonial studies.

To demonstrate the wide applicability of Afrocentricity, I examine the subtle ways postcolonial theorization rebrands previous patterns of epistemological oppression and pedagogically reproduces the idea of European superiority through the works of Europeanized Asians and Africans (Goldberg, 2006). Through a comparison between Afrocentricity and Orientalism, I will trace the development of postcolonialism as a radical movement and its subsequent neutralization through its institutionalization in Western academia and demonstrate why postcolonialism (Loomba, 2022) is incapable of helping a learner to emancipate himself from the age-old continuation of Eurocentric epistemology. As an effective remedy to this epistemological crisis, Afrocentricity can function as a transformative pedagogical tool and help the learners reclaim their agency in the production of knowledge on their culture and history, reconstruct their identity from European misrepresentations, and reassert their contributions to the development of human civilization.

Afrocentricity, defined as a worldview by Molefi Asante, is not limited to the African American studies discipline: Afrocentricity strongly advocates a transformative pedagogy, and it can be effectively applied in challenging and changing any misrepresentations, be it Eurocentric or not, of African and Asian people in the name of postcolonial and postmodern approaches to literature, culture, and history. English as a discipline in the Indian subcontinent (Sheorey, 2006) came into existence long before it did in the United Kingdom, and its mission was to manufacture bureaucrats who perpetuated the colonial regime through the cultural transformations of the colonized people. This mission was a part of the British education policy in India proposed by Thomas Babington Macaulay in his "Minutes on Indian Education" (Macaulay, 1835, pp. 237–251). Macaulay's plan was to "form ... a class of persons Indian in blood and color, but English in tastes, in opinions, in morals and in intellect" (Ashcroft, 2024, p. 8).

The central force contributing to the development of state policies in the colonized nations had been the imposition of the colonizers' language, here English, through formal education systems. The intention of that imposition was not only to establish English as a dominant medium of discourse but also to inject and perpetuate hegemonic ideologies and Western system of values, reducing indigenous people and culture to the OTHER—inferior, exotic, uncultured. Gauri Vishwanathan in her groundbreaking study of the institution and ideology of English studies in India under the British Raj—*Masks of Conquest*—rightly notes that long before English literature as an academic subject was institutionalized in England, English as the study of literature and the study of culture "appeared as a subject in the curriculum of the colonies" as early as the 1820s (Vishwanathan, 1989, p. 3). Manipulating the education system of the colonized people through systematic inclusion of European authors and texts had been the most effective strategy to strengthen and maintain colonial control: Deployment of the military works best for invasion, and it does not guarantee colonialism's complete success.

Applying external force thus brings temporary success in controlling the masses: Rebellion and resistance are the immediate effects of such efforts. But, if a change in temperament and attitude, a transformation in the subject's worldview, and his sense of agency comes from within the subject himself in favor of his oppressor, nothing more is needed to perpetuate the domination. He and his successors will then willingly conscript themselves as the obliged followers of the dominant oppressors (Gottlieb, 1976) values as his own, because they are taught and made to believe these values as the only legitimate ones that could enrich them. This is the core of British colonial policy (Egerton, 2018) that Macaulay (1835) proposed to the British Parliament a long time ago.

This is what the colonial administrators in India successfully implemented through the changes in the education system. Indians were made to discard their pride in their age-old culture and rich heritage that dates to antiquity and develop a gradual love for the "modern" European ones: Michael Madhusudan Dutt (Paranjape & Paranjape, 2012) is the exemplary representative of the Indians who rejected their ties to India only to embrace it later. However, very few could relocate themselves as Dutt did. Of course, colonialism's ultimate purpose had been economic exploitation through the manipulation of the colonized peoples' resources. When political control alone became inadequate, cultural domination became inevitable for assisting the colonizers in their pursuits. Thus, civilizing missions (Prasad, 2005) in the form of dispersing enlightenment, humanism, and ethics strategically maneuvered the educational institutions and instilled a Western system of values by replacing the Indian ones.

No doubt, the objective of the colonial education system was to Europeanize the non-Europeans by inculcating Eurocentric values in them (Alexiadou, 2005). The uncritical and spontaneous devouring of Romantic poets strolling in the Lake District and singing the beauty of the daffodils not only furthers the native's gap with his own culture but also dislocates him from the very soil that nourishes his creative potential. In the process, he suffers from a kind of artificial sensibility that has nothing to do with creativity: As the Caribbean poet Roger Mais states, our minds "stopped growing with school syllabus"—reading Chaucer (Patterson, 1991), Shakespeare, and Milton among other stuff—leaving us "stagnant" or mimicked, which has hampered the growth of the creation of vibrant and immediate local literature.

The effects of such education are humorously reflected by the Caribbean poet The Mighty Sparrow (Slinger Francisco) in his pidgin poem "Dan is the Man":

> According to the education you get when you small
>
> You'll grow up with true ambition and respect from one and all
>
> But in days in school they teach me like a fool
>
> The things they teach me I should be a block-headed mule.
>
> Donnell (1996, p.131)

Ironically, from the contexts of the ex-colonies, the task of the English departments is nothing but to produce "block-headed mule." Despite the inclusion of some "native" writers in the syllabus first under the title "Commonwealth Literature" (Tiffin, 1983) and then "Third World Literature in English," the departments failed to exorcise them from the ghosts of Shakespeare, Forster, or Conrad (wa Thiong'o, 1972). As has been asked by the "imperial" poet Rudyard Kipling, the department humbly shouldered "The White Man's Burden" (Kipling, 1899) to educate and civilize the "sullen peoples,/ Half-devil and half-child" through the "canonized" texts.

Amidst the daily Shakespearean tragedies (Harrison, 2013) and Conradian horrors (Conrad, 1901), postcolonial literature represents a fresh change, a renewed hope, and a sense of identity for Asian and African students. Reading writers like Ngugi wa Thiong'o, Chinua Achebe (1958), Wole Soyinka (Gibbs, 1986), Ben Okri (Golding, 2012), Derek Walcott (1974), and Salman Rushdie (2000) was celebratory: Doing postcolonial literature was thus a way out of the colonial bondage that the English department has been perpetuating since its inception during the old colonial times. Unfortunately, the recipes most palatable to students are mostly borrowed from Europe and America, and this is where Afrocentric intervention becomes effective in the reclamation of agency.

"From what base did the African peoples look at the world? Eurocentrism or Afrocentrism?" (wa Thiong'o, 1993, p.8) is the question that should challenge postcolonial perception of the concepts of agency and location. Being so much enamored with the tenacity of Okonkwo's resistance against the colonial intruders in Igboland (*Things Fall Apart*; Achebe, 1959) or genuinely shocked by the horrors that came under the guise of independence to the people of Ilmorog (*Petals of Blood*; wa Thiong'o, 2005) learners from the ex-colonies discover with awe what writers from our own territory have got to say: The first shock comes with Naipaul who refers to the people of Port of Spain as "monkeys pleading for evolution, each claiming to be better than the other, Indians and Negroes appeal to the unacknowledged white audience to see how much they despise each other" (*The Middle Passage*, p. 84).

Our ideas on postcolonial identity and agency arrive at a critical venture when we encounter Salman Rushdie preaching "the consequences of embracing those [Western] ideas and practices and turning away from [the Indian] ones that came with us" (Rushdie, 1983, p. 81) and justifying his so-called double-consciousness through his confession that "we are Muslims who eat pork [and that] our identity is at once plural and partial" (Rushdie, 1991, p. 15). The initial hope that postcolonialism brought with the African writers ends up in utter frustration with Rushdie who, "Having been borne across the world, [he is now] a translated man [and believes that, though] something always gets lost in translation ... something can also be gained" (Rushdie, 1983, p. 17). Hope turns into utter frustration when we discover in Edward Said the "oriental subject" forever silenced and in Gayatri Spivak "the subaltern" eternally speechless.

Frustration finds a rather comic relief in Homi Bhabha who prescribes that our only way to redefine our identity is to mimic our oppressor and hybridize ourselves. The question arises, who do these Indian postcolonial writers speak for? From what standpoint? To whom? Why?

The Afrocentric propositions, namely, a new historiography, an authentic subject position with a clear sense of location, and a bold rejection of anything biased or false said by others that concern the subject, place the postcolonial concepts of mimicry, ambivalence, and hybridity in conversation. The Afrocentric location theory (Archie, 2009) not only exposes the bankruptcy of postcolonialism but also the ideological corruption of its theorists primarily based in Western universities. African American Studies, because of its solidified radical stance against oppression, both symbolic and material, does not enjoy the benefits of institutionalization, which postcolonialism receives from the English departments. Postcolonialism's reactionary and revisionist projects are already reduced to typical textual interpretations: Subversive postcolonialism has been contained by the West.

Tracing the emergence of postcolonialism in Edward Said's (1977) much acclaimed book *Orientalism* and comparing Said's "orientalism project" with Molefi Kete Asante's "Afrocentricity," I will demonstrate that "orientalism," despite its objective of representing the "oriental subjects," reproduces the same pattern of misrepresentations it questions. The objective is to examine why postcolonialism as a school of thought is incapable of addressing the problems related to the identity and agency of the formerly colonized African and Asian people as well as to show with evidence that the Afrocentric approach grounded in Africology is more suitable both as an academic framework and as a transformative philosophy in the resistance against oppression. Molefi Kete Asante's Afrocentric theory is an effective tool in emancipating the disadvantaged and disempowered "oriental subject" that Edward Said traces in hegemonic European discourses.

Said's formidable scholarship in locating African and Asian people as voiceless objects in their history written from a European perspective does not necessarily help them rescue and reconstruct their agency. Asante's systematic methodology grounded in an African worldview, compared with that of Said's highly criticized one based on the postmodern idea of anti-humanism that he borrowed from Michel Foucault, provides a strong platform to the victims of oppression to emerge with a victorious consciousness from their subjugated positions. Through an Afrocentric analysis of Saidian "orientalism," one can identify the inconsistencies of Said's so-called radical opposition to Western epistemology, the same radicalism that inspired early contributors to postcolonial studies in developing the field as a valid discourse of difference.

Afrocentric reading of "orientalism" constitutes a valuable and necessary intervention into postcolonial studies as no interaction between scholarship on Edward Said and Molefi Kete Asante has taken place, despite Said's contradictory views on Afrocentricity. Said's claim that "Afrocentrism is as flawed as Eurocentrism" (Hindle, 1996, pp. 3–6) contradicts his earlier recognition of its potential to "provoke[ing] and challeng[ing] the fundamentally static notion of identity that has been the core of cultural thought during the era of imperialism" (Said, 2012, pp. xx–xxv). Said's interchanging deployment of Afrocentrism and Afrocentricity results in a complete misunderstanding of the "centric" ideology behind Asante's theory of Afrocentricity, which is "not the reverse of Eurocentrism; neither it is counter Eurocentrism" (Asante, 2007, p. 6). Said's reference to Afrocentricity, so it seems, is his postmodern technique of responding to the bitter criticism he invited through his version of orientalism. Moreover, this analysis will demonstrate that the epistemological crises in postcolonial studies, which is the primary focus here, originate from some postcolonial theorists' reappropriation of Saidian ambivalence through sophisticated poststructuralist jargon.

Edward Said's contribution to postcolonial studies is so influential that Gayatri Spivak (1998) and San Juan (1998) rightly identified his *Orientalism* as the sourcebook of the field. *Orientalism* exposed the long tradition of misrepresentation of Asian and African people and the falsification of their history and culture by European discourses. Following the footsteps of Aimé Césaire and Frantz Fanon, Said in *Orientalism* traces the "racism, cultural stereotypes, political imperialism, dehumanizing ideology" that resulted in "[t]he nexus of knowledge and power creating the oriental" (Said, 1977, p. 27). "Written with several audiences in mind," *Orientalism* was Said's scholarly effort to "criticize the often-unquestioned assumptions on which" European misrepresentations of Asian and African people depend, as well as to remind the "readers in the so-called Third World of the strength of Western cultural discourse" (Said, 1977, p. 25).

Said's "deconstruction of Western representation of the non-Western world," as he states in *Culture and Imperialism*, was triggered by the "alleged universalism of fields such as historiography, anthropology, and sociology," which he found to be "Eurocentric in the extreme, as if other literatures and societies had either an inferior or a transcended value" (Said, 1993, p. 44). Said's oppositional stance against the textual misrepresentation of Asian and African people can easily convince the victims of European imperialism to recognize in him the continuation of the emancipatory spirit one finds in the anti-colonial struggles initiated by Aimé Césaire's *Discourse on Colonialism* (Cesaire, 2023). Said's (1977,

p. 25) self-representation as "the oriental subject" on the one hand, and his self-identification as a philologist Inspired by the ideas of Giambattista Vico (1916), Goethe (2014), Von Humboldt (1999), Dilthey et al. (2018), Nietzsche (2000), Gadamer (1977), and Erich Auerbach (Auerbach & Porter, 2021) put him in a precarious position, which is ironic and ambivalent. The Western-educated oriental subject that Said detects in himself embraces a Western cultural apparatus in *Orientalism* to investigate how the West "orientalized" the East.

This investigation, which he claims to accomplish through a "contrapuntal reading" (Said, 2012) that "must take account of both processes, that of imperialism and resistance to it (Said, 1993, p. 66), surprisingly focus mostly on European representations of Asia and Africa: Said reproduces the same orientalist discourse that he sets out to dismantle. Even before the publication of *Orientalism* in 1978, Molefi Kete Asante has been speaking of the necessity of "an Afrocentric orientation to data," that is the systematic reevaluation of the production and dissemination of knowledge that concern exploited humanity in general and African people in particular. With the publication of *Afrocentricity: The Theory of Social Change*, Asante (2003) developed a systematic framework to carry out such reevaluations, this structure has been instrumental in challenging and significantly changing the racist pedagogical practices in the United States.

Jerome Schiele's (1994) critical analysis of the Afrocentric intervention in integrating "Afrocentric content in primary and secondary schools" with the objective of improving African American children's academic performance by exposing them to "the past accomplishments of their ancestors" can help one compare Afrocentricity with Said's Orientalism. The purpose of such a comparison is not to compel one to disregard Said's formidable scholarship over his topic but to explain why Said's effort ends up in further deterioration of the wounds he wants to heal. Unlike Said, Asante does not invest his scholarship in exploring the misrepresentation of the orientalized Other in European discourses as he is already aware of the hypocrisies of European imperialism in its naked form, that is, the enslavement of his ancestors here in the United States, as well as of the shameless state-endorsed discriminations against African Americans and other minority groups after emancipation.

Asante targets the victims of imperialism as his readers and sets out not to inform them about the strength of their oppressors but to rescue and

reconstruct the glorious past of their ancestors, a past rich with contributions to mankind, a past remarkable for artistic, philosophical, and
scientific achievements. Whereas Said locates the oriental self at the beginning of imperialism, as if the oriental Other did not exist before contact
with the occident, Asante begins with the civilizations in Kemet and Nubia,
the two ancient Egyptian cities ruled by Black kings and queens. Asante
locates himself in the genealogy of scholars like Diop (1991), Obenga
(2004), Ben-Jochannan (1991), Garvey and Garvey (2022), Melville
Herskovits (Jackson & Herskovitz, 1986), and Du Bois (Smith & Asante,
2025) and goes beyond them in formulating the first theoretical and philosophical platform that reinstates the oppressed as agents in the
reconstruction of their history and culture. The necessity behind developing another theoretical framework amidst so many in the liberal arts and
humanities is justified when we hear Edward Said claim:

> Frankfurt School critical theory, despite its seminal insights into the rela-
> tionships between domination, modern society, and the opportunities for
> redemption through art as critique, is stunningly silent on racist theory,
> anti-imperialist resistance, and oppositional practice in the empire. Much
> the same thing can be said of most Anglo-Saxon cultural theory ...

> European theory and Western Marxism as cultural coefficients of libera-
> tion haven't in the main proved themselves to be reliable allies in the
> resistance to imperialism-on the contrary, one may suspect that they are
> part of the same invidious "universalism" that connected culture with
> imperialism for centuries—how has the liberationist anti-imperialism tried
> to break this shackling unity? (Said, 1993, pp. 278–279)

"Contrapuntal orientation in history," "emancipatory theory," and "invest-
ment in nomadic, migratory, and anti-narrative energy" are the ways, as
Said claims, anti-imperialist scholars fought European hegemony. Asante's
approach to history might not be called contrapuntal as it completely
negates the European version of history, but it is exclusively emancipatory and transformative in the sense that it prioritizes the position of
Africans as subjects/agents in their history. The emancipatory philosophy
of Afrocentricity is manifested in the victorious consciousness that Asante
identifies as one of the foremost requirements to be an Afrocentrist who is
aware of the textual anarchy that he/she must encounter the moment he/she

reclaims his/her position in the production of knowledge that directly or indirectly relates to him/her. Said's concern related to the politicized nature of critical theories has already been voiced by Professor Wade Nobles who uses the phrase "conceptually incarcerated" to describe scholars operating from an alien theoretical framework. As Nobles (1978) states:

> The worldview, normative assumptions, and referential frame upon which the paradigm is based must, like the science they serve, be consistent with the culture and cultural substance of the people. When the paradigm is inconsistent with the cultural definition of the phenomena, the people who use it to assess and/or evaluate that phenomena become essentially conceptually incarcerated.

The "conceptually incarcerated" scholar, because of his training in that alien framework and methodology, often fails to understand his trapped condition which Asante (2003) describes as dislocation. Disorientation is the logical consequence of dislocation, noticed in someone who is suffering from not being centered in their history and culture.

In the disoriented state, the "conceptually incarcerated' scholar consistently changes his ideological positions and reinterprets his statements only to provide a different meaning from the one he initially intended to convey. Said demonstrates all the classic symptoms of disorientation through his numerous efforts in explaining orientalism, his realignment with the agents of imperialism he so passionately criticizes, and his reluctance to disclose his cultural and ideological location. A self-identified "oriental subject" misrepresented by hegemonic European imperialism, a displaced Arab living in exile, an Arab American under the surveillance of a Zionist-influenced Pentagon (Petras, 2010), a third-world intellectual living in the first world, and finally a humanist trained in the European philological tradition, Said is the perfect example of someone who defies homogeneity. Perhaps this is why he claims that

> No one today is purely *one* thing. Labels like Indian, or woman, or Muslim, or American are not more than starting points, which if followed into actual experience for only a moment are quickly left behind. Imperialism consolidated the mixture of cultures and identities on a global scale. But its worst and most paradoxical gift was to allow people to believe that they were only, mainly, exclusively, white, or Black, or

Western, or Oriental. (Said, 1993, p. 336)

Said is right in articulating the heterogeneity of human identity and that imperialism dissolves these diversified identities and essentializes the East and the West. As Benita Parry points out, Said himself creates another homogeneity in *Orientalism* in which, exactly as in the European discourses, the Orient is stripped of its agency (Parry, 2023). Said's view of the oriental subject premises on the European notions that the orient is mute, that there has never been any resistance to imperialism, and that the misrepresentations of the orient always go unchallenged.

This was possible for Said (1993, p. xxvi) mostly because he belonged to two "worlds, without being completely of either one or the other." Said talks about this predicament in "Between Worlds," a predicament best expressed by Joseph Conrad. In Said's (1998, p. 3) words "No one could represent the fate of lostness, and disorientation better than Conrad did, and no one was more ironic about the effort of trying to replace that condition with arrangements and accommodations." Said's lifelong effort to understand this predicament through the eyes of his oppressors started with his first book *Joseph Conrad and the Fiction of Autobiography* (Said, 2008). An Afrocentric reading of Said's latter works like "Orientalism Reconsidered" and "A Window on the World," and to some extent, *Culture and Imperialism* make it clear that Said mostly, if not completely, focuses on the aesthetic aspects of European writers instead of exposing their misrepresentations of the orient. It is no surprise that Said (1993, pp. xx–xxi) rediscovers the great artist in Kipling, as he states:

> What a sobering and inspiring thing it is therefore not just to read one's own side, as it were, but also to grasp how a great artist like Kipling (few more imperialist and reactionary than he) rendered India with such skill, and how in doing so his novel *Kim* not only depended on a long history of Anglo-Indian perspective.

The radical Said of *Orientalism*, who drew worldwide attention to his uncompromising critique of imperialism, pivots analytically, describing imperialism as a positive force that "brought the world closer together," it is a world where "the history of imperialism and its culture can now be studied as neither monolithic nor reductively compartmentalized, separate, distinct" (Said, 1993, pp. xx–xxi). Labeling the emergence of Afrocentricity as "a disturbing eruption of separatist and chauvinist discourse," Said (1993, p. xxi) ambivalently claims that "far from invalidating the struggle to be free from empire, these reductions of cultural discourse prove the validity of a fundamental liberationist energy that animates the wish to be independent, to speak freely and without the burden of unfair domination." Said identifies an energy in this emergence which, in his view, needs to be understood historically. He fears that this emancipatory zeal will make the world a chaotic place, because:

> ... if everyone were to insist on the radical purity or priority of one's own voice, all we would have would be the awful din of unending strife, and a bloody political mess, the true horror of which is beginning to be perceptible here and there in the reemergence of racist politics in Europe, the cacophony of debates over political correctness and identity politics in the United States. (Ibid, pp. xx–xxi)

Said here directly reverberates Foucault's idea of resistance, which receives relatively less importance compared with the theory of power and knowledge that Said so generously used in developing his method. Foucault's theories on the formation of subjects and the production of knowledge by deploying power often bypass the fact that such knowledge or power do not go uncontested. This gap in Foucault's discourse on power and systems of domination reappears in Said's discourse on Orientalism and the domination of the oriental subjects, a gap that Said (2012, p. xii) confesses in the sequel to *Orientalism*:

> What I left out of Orientalism was the response to Western dominance which culminated in the great movements of decolonization all across the Third World ... Never was it the case that the imperial encounter pitted an active Western intruder against a supine or inert non-Western native; there was always some form of active resistance, and in the overwhelming majority of cases the resistance finally won out

Had Said developed a methodology prioritizing the oriental subjects as agents in critiquing their misrepresentations by Europe, he certainly would have incorporated the rich tradition of resistance to colonization that he understood later. Said's failure to see imperialism from the perspectives of the orientalized is the direct result of his dependence on the Foucauldian notion of resistance as an integral part of power: Foucault sees resistance as a required condition for power to operate, not as a reaction or consequence to it. For Foucault:

> there are no relations of power without resistances; the latter are all the more real and effective because [resistances] *are formed right at the point where relations of power are exercised*; resistance to power does not have to come from elsewhere to be real, nor is it inexorably frustrated through being the compatriot of power. *It exists all the more by being in the same place as power*; hence, like power, resistance is multiple and can be integrated in global strategies. (Foucault, 1980, p. 142)

Foucault's theory of resistance (Pickett, 1996) negates the concept of revolution as he claims that "there is no single locus of great Refusal, no soul of revolt, source of all rebellions, or pure law of the revolutionary" (Focault, 1990, pp. 95–96). Only if strategic manipulations of resistance are directed toward a unified attack on a dominant order, not the dispersed local acts of resistance, a revolution can occur.

Then again, Foucault (1977, pp. 86) totally ignores the objectives of resistance as he further claims that resistance with the hope of introducing "another system is to extend our participation in the present system." As Foucault's idea on resistance is significantly influenced by the failed revolutions of 1848 and the events in 1968 in France, it fails to conceive the existential crises felt by the victims of imperialism who view resistance not only to improve their material condition but also as how they are able to regain their lost humanity. Resistance for the oppressed is transformative. Foucault is certainly right in his opinion that "there is no guarantee that the state of affairs brought about by resistance will be better than the present, as any social arrangement or definition of community may become oppressive even if it is instituted by acts of resistance against a previous regime" (Simon, 1995, p. 87).

But Foucault is wrong in his presentation of change and revolution as isolated historical events: Change is a process that requires constant modifications of plans and strategies. Foucault's idea of resistance makes the concept of freedom utopian. It took 20 years for Said to understand

the inadequacy of Foucault's theory of resistance, and Said himself makes
it clear in *Power, Politics, and Culture,*

> one of the things that I think Foucault is wrong about is that he always
> writes from the point of view of power. It's strange, most people think of
> him as a rebel, but he had this side to him which James Miller writes about
> in his book on Foucault, suggesting that all of Foucault's work is really an
> exemplification of his peculiar form of homosexuality and his interest in
> sado-masochism. So you could say that Foucault is always talking about
> power from the point of view, on the one hand, of the way power always
> wins; and then, succumbing to that power, he talks about the victims of
> power with a certain amount of pleasure. And I think that that always
> struck me as wrong, and my attitude to power, in *Orientalism* and else-
> where, has always been deeply suspicious and hostile. It took me another
> ten years to make that more explicit in *Culture and Imperialism,* where I
> was very interested not only talking about the formation of imperialism,
> but also of resistances to it, and the fact that imperialism could be over-
> thrown and was—as a result of resistance and decolonization and
> nationalism. (Viswanathan, 2002, p. 193

It is ironic that Said, borrowing Foucault's (2001, p. 7) concept of the
"Other" within European society constructed and represented linguistically through first "the leper" and then "the mad," developed his
methodology in investigating orientalism as a European discourse of
silencing the orient. Extending Europe's "othering" strategy explained by
Foucault, Said in *Orientalism* demonstrates that the medieval other in
the figure of the leper and the mad has been replaced by the 19th century
figure of the "oriental subject."

Moreover, Said's concepts of knowledge and power, and the way
Europeans constructed knowledge that enabled them to have power over
the Orient, and his subsequent objective of de-orientalizing the Orient
echo Foucault's idea of "... re-do[ing], in opposite direction, the work of
expression: to go back from statements preserved through time and dispersed in space, towards that interior secret that preceded them, left its
mark in them, and (in every sense of the term) is betrayed by them"
(Foucault, 1972 , p. 121). The issue here is not to represent Foucault as

unworthy of borrowing nor to question the originality of Said's discourse on orientalism, but to clarify that, despite his effort in correcting the misrepresentations of the Orient, Said ends up in reproducing the same patterns of misrepresentation. Like Foucault, Said ignores the fact that resistance is an immediate and inseparable reaction to power and that sooner or later all power succumbs to resistance by the oppressed.

In contrast to Foucault and Said, resistance for Asante is the primary objective of an activist scholar who shoulders the solemn responsibility of speaking for and about the marginalized. As an African American, Asante views resistance as a logical response to repression. A clear historical understanding of one's reality is the fundamental requirement for one to resist against the forces that changed the trajectory of his reality in the past and continue to do so in the present. Asante is aware of the discursive forces of white supremacy manifested in the postmodern branding of resistance that blurs the line between the oppressed and the oppressor, and this is why he boldly claims:

> There are no post-modern gray lines here; you either stand with the oppressed and against the oppressor or you stand with the oppressor against liberation. ... If the resistance has been intricately connected to African Americans, it is only that we have suffered the most from the promulgation of the doctrines of white supremacy. It is reasonable to assume that a major part for the human liberation would be waged on the line of black people. (Asante, 2007, p. 164)

Asante's perspective on resistance differs from that of Foucault's because it is relevant to any marginalized groups. The very idea of "blackness" conjures up the notion of resistance as white Europeans have historically associated all the negative connotations with this signifier. Asante questions the very process of this signification and rejects the meanings of "black" deployed as a sign from European perspective. For Asante, black is the new face of resistance and blackness is new value that

> ...possesses a political and social sensitivity directed against all forms of oppression. Therefore, a new people is created and by maintaining the critical themes of blackness they become the new blacks, new Africans, marked or typed by an identity rooted in their fierce opposition to all

forms of domination: racism, sexism, classism, pedophilia, national terror, and white national supremacy. These new blacks are discovered in every nation and among all ethnic groups. (Asante, 2007, p. 165)

For Asante, the oppressed and misrepresented is not necessarily the spurious oriental subject that Said traces in European texts, rather the oriental subject is a subject-as-agent with a history of resistance against imperialism. Asante is interested in retrieving the past of this human subject and using his critical framework through which he wants this subject to speak. While Said has "no patience with the position that 'we' should only or mainly be concerned with what is "ours," any more than I can condone reactions to such a view that require Arabs to read Arab books, use Arab methods, and the like" (Said, 1993, p. xxv).

Asante devotes his scholarship to particularly understand how Africans look at themselves and the world around them. Said's so-called liberal humanism disguised in anti-humanist tropes totally negates the long history of epistemic violence perpetuated by European discourses, which are challenged by groups like feminists and Marxists formed by marginalized Europeans. Asante is not against reading books by people of other cultures so long as those books maintain historical truths, advocate racial equality, and recognize all people's contributions to mankind. Said in *Orientalism* criticizes canonical European books for failing the basic qualities that make a text universally acceptable, but ironically in *Culture and Imperialism* he changes his tone and finds great aesthetic qualities in books which he would readily label as racist. The oppositional stance that Said takes in *Orientalism,* even though that opposition does little service in voicing the oriental self, silenced by European discourses, is neutralized by the contradictory statements he makes in *Culture and Imperialism,* which is considered as corrective to *Orientalism.*

The corrections are evident in Said's decision to include what he "left out of Orientalism": Said decides to provide textual space to Ngugi wa Thiong'o and Tayeb Salih, two African writers who, in Said's word, "redo *Heart of Darkness* by inducing life into Conrad's river" (Said, 1993, p. 211). Said's contrapuntal reading of European and African writers places the former as the predecessors to the latter and provides serious critical analysis and spatial allocation to the canonical European texts in *Culture and Imperialism,* whereas texts by African writers are attributed just perfunctory discussions. For instance, Ngugi wa Thiong'o and Tayeb Salih are contained in one paragraph, and Chinua Achebe is made happy with just one sentence (Said, 2012, p. 211). Moreover, Said accuses Achebe for not discussing Conrad's limitations in using the novel as form in dealing with the evils of colonization: "when in a celebrated essay Chinua Achebe criticizes Conrad's racism, he either says nothing about or overrides the limitations placed on Conrad by the novel as an aesthetic form" (Said, 2012, p. 76).

The critical analysis that Said (2012, p. 96) puts Jane Austen's *Mansfield Park* through is missing from his perfunctory readings of postcolonial writers and surprisingly defends Austen's racist and/or pro-slavery views as shaped by her time. Said (p. 76) states "Austen belonged to a slave-owning society," and asks whether for this we should "jettison her novels as so many trivial exercises in aesthetic frumpery?" Through the characters of the novel, Said (p. 96) is interested in understanding the "connections, to deal with as much of the evidence as possible, fully and actually, to read what is there or not there." Contrary to providing similar critical importance to the postcolonial writers, Said (p. 212) reads them with "Conrad's majestic prose" in the background and claims:

> The post-imperial writers of the Third World therefore bear their past within them—as scars of humiliating wounds, as instigation for different practices, as potentially revised visions of the past tending toward a post-colonial future, as urgently reinterpretable and redeployable experiences, in which the formerly silent native speaks and acts on territory reclaimed as pan of a general movement of resistance, from the colonist.

Asante, unlike Said, does not view the past consisting only of "scars of humiliating wounds," because for him the past did not start with European colonization. Asante locates the origin of humanity in Africa and disregards the artificial concept of shame colonization inculcated in the psyche of the colonized. While Said's thesis begins with the acceptance of the imposed inferiority of the oriental, Asante's Afrocentricity discards all the myths of inferiority and reinstates the historical truths discovered by Cheikh Anta Diop. As Asante states:

> It was on the African continent that humans originated and on the same continent that the most majestic civilizations of antiquity arose in the Nile Valley (Diop, 1991). It was also in Africa that the first flourishing of religion occurred and even the naming of the Gods was said to be an African event (Herodotus, Book II). The mighty kingdoms of the West and South developed and maintained themselves for centuries without the presence of either Arabs or Europeans. (Asante, 1998)

While Said sees scars of humiliation in the past, Asante finds strengths for transformation; while Said informs his readers about the sheer strengths of imperial discourses, Asante fosters the certainty of victory; while Said uses the European methodologies, he himself criticizes, Asante develops his own methodology grounded on the experiences of Africans as agents and subjects in their own history.

This methodology culminates in the Africological model Asante finally develops in *African Pyramids of Knowledge: Kemet, Afrocentricity and Africology* published in 2015 (Asante, 2015). An integral part of this methodology is the "Location Theory" that can precisely locate a text in terms of the author's ideological affiliations, political associations and aesthetic expressions manifested in the very words in the text itself. In his words, Location Theory is:

> a branch of centric theory and reflects the same interest as centric theory on the question of place. It is essentially a process of explaining how human beings come to make decisions about the external world which takes into consideration all of the attitudes and behaviors which constitute psychological and cultural place. (Asante, 1993, p. 57)

Using "Location Theory," an Afrocentrist can locate any text by investigating the "cultural and intellectual address of [its] author" (Asante, 2003, pp. 236–244). Although Said's *Orientalism* might not be strictly categorized as a "decapitated" or "lynched" text defined by Asante, it demonstrates some features of both categories. Said, to use Asante's words, "remained fundamentally committed to a style of writing which placed him [partially] outside of his own historical experiences." Asante defines a decapitated text as one that fails to represent the author's cultural self as well as the collective cultural self of the people it is about.

On the other hand, a lynched text is one that reproduces ideologies of the oppressor it sets out to criticize. *Orientalism* is a partially decapitated text because it uses the framework of the oppressor and, despite honest intentions, fails to rescue the oppressed from objects to the position of subjects in their own history. Said attacked Eurocentrism with a mistaken objective, and hence, his text is "lynched" one. From Edward Said's discursive analysis of the orient, it is difficult to determine whether imperialism invented orientalism or it is orientalism that led to imperialism. Said's position here is postmodernist as he defines the orient neither as an idea nor as a reality.

However, Said is of the opinion that the academic study of the orient is directly related with imperialism. He claims that academic orientalists over two centuries developed a way of thinking about the orient, which is widely embraced by those outside of the academy. This way of thinking always focuses on the ontological and epistemological differences between East and West (Said, 1977, pp. 1–2).

Said's attack on Eurocentrism might sound radical, but it fails to go beyond challenging the attacker and fails to provide any strategies of resistance and reconstruction to those being attacked. Said understood these limitations of his orientalism project, and hence, he envisioned "a post-colonial intellectual project" aimed at "formulat[ing] an alternative to a politics of blame" so that it can "expand the area of overlapping community between metropolitan and formerly colonized societies" (Said, 2023, p. 46). Postcolonialism is significantly indebted to Said's *Orientalism* as it opened the different terrains like literary, political, and historical discourses from which the early theorists-initiated counterattacks to demythologize the "white men's burden," that is, to expose the hegemonic agendas veiled under European humanism.

Those who theorize on postcolonialism soon found Said guilty of the same crime he accuses the Europeans of: The Other has no place in the Sidian discourse other than as disempowered objects. Postcolonial thinkers like Homi Bhabha (2012) and Gayatri Spivak (1999) have capitalized Said's limitations in rebranding their versions of postcolonialism. The absent and mute Other in Said's *Orientalism* emerges and threatens to reclaim his lost place in the discourses. This "Other" becomes the "hybrid mimic man" in Bhabha and the voiceless "subaltern" in Spivak, both theorists are inspired by Said.

Like Said, both Bhabha and Spivak are based in the United States, and like Said, they heavily rely on French poststructural theorists in understanding the formation of subjectivity during and after colonization. And, like Said, they gained wide recognition and still now qualify as major postcolonial thinkers. Said soon grew bitter with the trajectory postcolonialism took in the hands of theorists for whom colonization, in his words, "delivered the benefits of a national self-consciousness, liberal ideas, and technological goods ... that have turned colonialism into a much less unpleasant thing" (Said, 1986, p. 45). Said stands guilty of the same offenses, and he too made imperialism sound like a two-way traffic, a process by which the colonized nations got the gifts of invaluable European knowledge and rich cultural heritage conveyed through the works of his ideological gurus.

It is no surprise that Said's first book *Joseph Conrad and the Fiction of Autobiography* (Said, 2008) traces this indebtedness right in his Joseph Conrad who is, as he remarks, "like a *cantus firmus*, a steady ground bass to much that I have experienced ... No one could represent the fate of lostness, and disorientation better than Conrad did, and no one was more ironic about the effort of trying to replace that condition with arrangements and accommodations" (Said, 1998, p. 3). Said shares Conrad's life as an exile doomed to write in a language other than his mother tongue and the predicament of belonging to two worlds simultaneously. Postcolonial theorists are guilty as charged by Said, so is Said as charged by San Juan (2002), Aijaz Ahmad (1995), Arif Dirlik (1999), among others. The Said who rejected the Western canon is now ambivalent about his radical past: Said now provides nuanced reappraisals of controversial authors like Conrad and Kipling because he redefines his ideological position, which is evident in the following statement:

> One of the legacies of Orientalism, and indeed one of its epistemological foundations, is historicism, that is, the view propounded by Vico, Hegel, Marx, Ranke, Dilthey, and others, that if humankind has a history it is produced by men and women, and can be understood historically as, at each given period, epoch, or moment, possessing a complex, but coherent unity. So far as Orientalism in particular and the European knowledge of

other societies in general have been concerned, historicism meant that the one human history uniting humanity either culminated in or was observed from the vantage point of Europe, or the West. What was neither observed by Europe nor documented by it was therefore "lost" until, at some later date, it too could be incorporated by the new sciences of anthropology, political economics, and linguistics. (Said, 1985, p. 101)

Said is now hopeful that the gaps in Eurocentric history will be filled up by the same disciplines he was suspicious of then, but he is lenient about the false versions of history these disciplines constructed. Said's radicalism is now transformed into humanism (Copson, 2015), a humanism that is fundamentally Eurocentric. Said's solution to the very problems of "orientalism" as a discourse, as the above statement indicates, is not possible to come outside of it.

This solution, or rather a suggestion, is unconditionally accepted by Homi Bhabha (Greedharry, 2008) who, like Said, uses poststructuralist Lacanian psychoanalysis (Parker, 2010), through which he takes the "oriental subject" and his struggle to a whole new dimension that disregards the brutalities of imperialism and reduces the anti-colonial struggle to a mere psycho-linguistic process devoid of any historical specificities. Bhabhaesque approach to the long and rich history of resistance to imperialism in its diverse forms makes the postcolonial pedagogy highly controversial as it aspires to promote the idea that cultural purity does not exist. The issue at hand is postcolonialism and its lack of location in terms of time and space, and the applicability of Asante's Afrocentricity in solving it. Because of the uneven development of colonization globally and the impacts of decolonization across the colonies, it would be historically inaccurate to proclaim that all ex-colonies share a common past.

Hence, it is impossible to locate a unified colonial subject: Universal colonial experience is thus a myth. This view is flawed because, despite diversities, there is at least one aspect of colonization shared by all irrespective of time and space. That shared element is violence. What unifies the inherent diversity in postcolonial experiences is the common past of colonial oppression. It is because of this shared traumatic past that postcolonial critics often tend to apply the term "postcolonialism" uncritically to refer to a unified colonial experience.

Hence, the location of the colonial experience as well as the location of the theorist who theorizes on it is of crucial importance to give authenticity to that theorization. With a firm historical and cultural location in time and space, one can unveil the masks behind the rhetoric of power, privilege, and position. However, there is something more than knowing and showing from one's "—centric" perspective; there is also *doing*, and one of the chief action-based arenas for *doing* is the educational system.

According to Asante, establishing a new intellectual *djed* or stasis is an act of revolution, because it fundamentally exists as a critique of 500 years of Eurocentric mental enslavement prosecuted through language. With our realization that all phenomena are expressed in space and time, we can redefine our "centricity" as "a consciousness, quality of thought, mode of analysis, and an actionable perspective where [we] seek, from agency, to assert subject place within the context of [our] history" (Asante, 2007, p. 16). As an Afrocentrist, Asante is not obsessed with rescuing the past alone: His views on the problems in the present are also of serious critical insight.

Living in a racially polarized American society, he is aware of the roots of problems in the Black community. He thus says, "The little African American child who sits in a classroom and is made to accept as heroes and heroines who defamed her people during their lifetime is being decentered, marginalized, and made a non-person, one whose aim in life might be some day to 'shed her blackness' as a badge of inferiority" (Asante, 2007a, p. 80). He further states, "Few contemporary schools teach history the way it should be taught to transform students who enter schools and colleges" (Asante, 2007a, p. 86). According to him, what is needed is a pedagogy of veracity built upon the facts of history as far as we know them. To operationalize his ideas, Asante created the first PhD program in African American Studies at Temple University in 1988 (Reid-Merritt, 2018) and, in 2003, proposed a curriculum for the Philadelphia School District. Unfortunately, but not surprisingly, his proposals on teaching African American History, African History, and African Diaspora have agitated Schools District's administrators and boards of education. Asante (2007a, p. 140) explains, "They are those people who seem to insist that the only legitimate history is European history and that nothing written by Africans, Asians, Latinos, or First Nations people really matters". In another article, Asante (1996, p. 22) asserts that:

Whiteness in the university is not found merely in the lack of matriculating African, Latino, or Asian students, but in the whiteness of the curriculum, the very heart of what we as professors teach, research, and otherwise transmit to our students. The fundamental dogma of the American academy seems to rest upon the belief that the European culture is the world's only source of rational thought. Every sequence of courses in the disciplines seems to assume that whites created the foundations of all knowledge on the basis of European values. And there is rarely anything in the structure of the curriculum to challenge that assumption.

In his criticism of the universities as the agents of Eurocentrism, Asante's position is like that of Ngugi wa Thiong'o's critical stance against the English department: In *Decolonizing the Mind*, Ngugi demands the abolition of the English department because of its prioritizing "one single culture." Joseph McLaren elaborately discusses the similarities between these two famous Africans in their courageous fight against the White supremacy in the academy and outside in the greater world. As he states:

Ngugi's ideas in *Moving the Centre* have relevance to the debate over Eurocentrism, Afrocentrism, and multiculturalism. His critique of Eurocentrism can be examined in relation to Afrocentric critical theory and the writings of its foremost exponent, Molefi Kete Asante. Asante's *Afrocentricity: The theory of Social Change* (1988), *The Afrocentric Idea* (1987), and *Kemet, Afrocentricity and Knowledge* (1990) can be paralleled to Ngugi's *Moving the Centre* in that both writers engage the center as a locus of cultural and political transformation. Of particular interest is the way Ngugi views language and the role of the African writer in the face of neocolonialism. Ngugi's support of indigenous African languages has parallels to Asante's exploration of Ebonics, or Black English, as a mode of discourse and expression. An additional relationship between both writers is the inherent political nature of their works.

"Afrocentricity" is now widely accepted as a critical theory with a firm philosophical basis in addressing fundamental issues related to identity, agency, and history. The transformative power of Afrocentricity has already surpassed the four walls of the academy and gained much traction in wider cultural, social, and ideological dialogues and debates. Asante's steadfast stance as a scholar-activist propelled the repositioning of the African people and their culture from the margin to the center of analysis.

Implications of Afrocentricity are not limited to Africa or the African diaspora: In response to imperialism and Eurocentrism, diverse scholars from around the globe now apply Afrocentric ideas in historical reclamation and cultural transformation. Despite its ethnocentric declaration of rescuing the past of the ex-colonized people from the debris of Eurocentric misrepresentations, postcolonialism is dwarfed when faced with authorized European history. Afrocentricity, as it is developed by Molefi Kete Asante in his numerous books, prioritizes the importance of identity, agency, and location of the writer/narrator/theorist while saying anything about Africa and the non-western world in general. Without the proper sense of agency and location, according to Asante, "we permit a dysfunction between who we are and who we are told we ought to be" (Asante, 2007, p. 158). This dysfunction is what characterizes present postcolonial studies as most theorists of the discourse are more inclined to look at the ex-colonized world primarily from outside. This is the result of the education they receive in the Euro-American system. Afrocentric methodologies and scholarship advanced by Molefi Kete Asante and others is designed to expose the factual inaccuracies and cultural contradictions of a system that deliberately excludes the true history of disempowered people.

## REFERENCES

Ahmad, A. (1995). The politics of literary postcoloniality. *Race & Class*, *36*(3), 1–20.

Alexiadou, N. (2005). Europeanization and education policy. In *World Yearbook of Education 2005* (pp. 106–121). Routledge.

Archie, M. M. (2009). An Afrocentric critique or the locating of dislocation: an example from contemporary practice. *Journal of Black Studies*, *39*(3), 356–370.

Asante, M. K. (1993). Location theory and African aesthetics. In K. Welsh-Asante (Ed.), *The African aesthetic* (pp. 53–62). Greenwood Press.

Asante, M. K. (1990). *Kemet, Afrocentricity and knowledge*. Africa World Press.

Asante, M. (1998) *The ideology of racial hierarchy and the construction of the European slave trade*. An International Conference Sponsored by UNESCO. https://unesdoc.unesco.org/ark:/48223/pf0000156750

Asante, M. K. (2003). The Afrocentric idea. In A. Mazama (Ed.), *The Afrocentric paradigm*. Africa World Press.

Asante, M. K. (2007). *An Afrocentric manifesto*. Polity Press.

Asante, M. K. (2013) Academic affairs distinguished lecture series. The full audio tape of the lecture is available on YouTube at https://youtu.be/bdCuVr4TEvw

Asante, M. K. (2015). *African pyramids of knowledge: Kemet, Afrocentricity, and Africology.* Universal Write Publications LLC.

Asante, M. K. (2013). *Academic affairs distinguished lecture series.* YouTube https://youtu.be/bdCuVr4TEvw

Asante, M. K. (2003). Locating a text: Implications of Afrocentric theory. In A. Mazama (Ed.), *The Afrocentric paradigm* (pp. 236–244). Africa World Press.

Asante, M. K. (1996). Multiculturalism and the academy. *Academe, 82*(3), 20–23.

Asante, M. K. (2003). *Afrocentricity: The theory of social change.* African American Images. Chicago.

Ashcroft, B., Griffiths, G., & Tiffin, H. (Eds.). (2024). *The postcolonial studies reader* (3rd ed.). Routledge. https://doi.org/10.4324/9780429469039

Auerbach, E., & Porter, J. I. (2021). *Time, history, and literature: Selected essays of Erich Auerbach.*

Ben-Jochannan, Y. (1991). *African origins of the major "Western Religions"* (Vol. 1). Black Classic Press.

Bhabha, H. K. (2012). *The location of culture.* Routledge.

Césaire, A. (2023). Discourse on colonialism. In *Postcolonialism* (pp. 310–339). Routledge.

Chinua, A. (1958). *Things fall apart.* Heinemann.

Conrad, J. (1901). *Heart of darkness.* Рипол Классик.

Copson, A. (2015). What is humanism? In *The Wiley Blackwell handbook of humanism* (pp. 1–33). John Wiley & Sons, Ltd.

Dilthey, W., Rodi, F., & Makkreel, R. A. (2018). *Wilhelm Dilthey: Selected works: Hermeneutics and the study of history.* Princeton University Press.

Diop, C. A. (1991). *Civilization or barbarism.* Chicago Review Press.

Dirlik, A. (1999). Is there history after Eurocentrism?: Globalism, postcolonialism, and the disavowal of history. *Cultural Critique* (42), 1–34.

Donnel, A., & Welsh, S. L. (Eds). (1996). *The Routledge reader in Caribbean literature* (p. 131). Routledge.

Egerton, H. E. (2018). *A short history of British colonial policy.* Routledge.

Fanon, F., Sartre, J. P., & Farrington, C. (1963). *The wretched of the earth* (Vol. 36, pp. 3–317). Grove Press.

Foucault, M. (1977). *Language, counter-memory, practice, ed. Donald F. Bouchard* (Trans. Donald F. Bouchard and Sherry Simon). Cornell UP.

Foucault, M. (1980). *Power and strategies. Power/knowledge: Selected interviews and other writings, 1972–1977* (ed. Colin Gordon). Harvester, 142.

Foucault, M. (1972). *Archaeology of knowledge and the discourse on language* (p. 121). Pantheon Books. p. 121.

Foucault, M. (1990). *The history of sexuality—Volume I: An introduction* (Trans. R. Hurley) (pp. 1–160.). Vintage.

Foucault, M. (2001). *A history of insanity in the age of reason*. Routledge.

Gadamer, H. G. (1977). *Philosophical hermeneutics*. University of California Press.

Garvey, M., & Garvey, A. J. (2022). *Africa for Africans: Or, the philosophy and opinions of Marcus Garvey*. Graphic Arts Books.

Goethe, J. W. (2014). *Johann Wolfgang Goethe*. Kriterion-Verlag.

Golding, W. (2012). *The inheritors: Introduced by Ben Okri*. Faber & Faber.

Goldberg, T. D. (2006). Racial Europeanization. *Ethnic and Racial Studies*, 29(2), 331–364.

Gottlieb, D. (1976). Ontological reduction. *The Journal of Philosophy*, 73(3), 57–76.

Greedharry, M. (2008). Homi Bhabha and the psychoanalytic truth. In *Postcolonial theory and psychoanalysis: From uneasy engagements to effective critique* (pp. 73–104). Palgrave Macmillan.

Harrison, G. B. (2013). *Shakespeare's tragedies*. Routledge.

Hindle, J. (Ed.). (1996). *London review of books: An anthology*. Verso.

Juan Jr, E. S. (2002). The poverty of postcolonialism. *Pretexts: literary and cultural studies*, 11(1), 57–74.

Juan, S. (1998). The limits of postcolonial criticism: The discourse of Edward Said. *Solidarity*. https://www.solidarity-us.org/node/1781

Kipling, R., & Wise, T. J. (1899). *The white man's burden*.

Lee, K.-W. (1997). Is the glass half-empty or half-full? Rethinking the problems of postcolonial revisionism. *Cultural Critique*, 36, 89–117.

Loomba, A. (2002). *Colonialism/postcolonialism*. Routledge.

Macaulay, T. (1835). Minute on Indian Education. Retrieved January 17, 2013, from http://www.columbia.edu/itc/mealac/pritchett/00generallinks/macaulay/txt_minute_education_1835.html

Nayar, P. K. (2008). *Postcolonial literature: An introduction*. Pearson Education India.

Nietzsche, F. (2000). *Basic writings of Nietzsche*. Modern Library.

Nobles, W. (1978). *African consciousness and liberation struggles: Implications for the development and construction of scientific paradigms* [Conference session]. Fanon Research and Development Conference, Port of Spain, Trinidad.

Obenga, T. (2004). Egypt: Ancient history of African philosophy. *A companion to African philosophy*, 28, 31–49.

Paranjape, M. R., & Paranjape, M. R. (2012). Michael Madhusudan Dutt: The prodigal's progress. In *Making India: Colonialism, national culture, and the afterlife of Indian English authority* (pp. 65–83).

Parker, I. (2010). *Lacanian psychoanalysis: Revolutions in subjectivity*. Routledge.

Parry, B. (2023). Problems in current theories of colonial discourse. In *Postcolonlsm* (pp. 714–747). Routledge.

Patterson, L. (1991). *Chaucer and the subject of history*. University of Wisconsin Press.

Petras, J. (2010). *Zionism, militarism and the decline of US power*. SCB Distributors.

Pickett, B. L. (1996). Foucault and the politics of resistance. *Polity, 28*(4), 445–466.

Prasad, M. (1997). On the question of a theory of (third) world literature. *Cultural Politics, 11*, 141–162.

Prasad, S. (2005). Colonialism as civilizing mission: Cultural ideology in British India. *Journal of Colonialism and Colonial History, 6*(1).

Reid-Merritt, P. (2018). Temple University's African American Studies PhD Program@ 30: Assessing the Asante affect. *Journal of Black Studies, 49*(6), 559–575.

Rushdie, S. (1983). The Indian writer in England. In M. Butcher (Ed.), *The eye of the beholder: Indian writing in English*. Commonwealth Institute.

Rushdie, S. (1991). *Imaginary homelands: Essays and criticism, 1981–1991* (pp. 9–21). Viking, 1991.

Said, E. W. (1985, May 7). Orientalism reconsidered. *Cultural Critique*, 1: 101.

Said, E. W. (1986). Intellectuals in the post-colonial world. *Salmagundi, 70–71*, 44–64.

Said, E. W. (1977). Orientalism. *The Georgia Review, 31*(1), 162–206.

Said, E. W. (1985). Orientalism reconsidered. *Cultural Critique*, 1, 101.

Said, E. (1986). *Intellectuals in the post-colonial world* (p. 45).

Said, E. W. (1993). *Culture and Imperialism*. Chatto and Windus.

Said, E. W. (1998). Between worlds. *London Review of Books, 20*(9), 3.

Said, E. W. (2003). *Orientalism*. Penguin Books.

Said, E. W. (2008). *Joseph Conrad and the fiction of autobiography*. Columbia University Press.

Said, E. W. (2012). *Culture and imperialism*. Vintage.

San Juan, E. (1998). The limits of postcolonial criticism: The discourse of Edward Said. *Against the Current, 13*(5), 28.

Schiele, J. H. (1994). Afrocentricity: Implications for higher education. *Journal of Black Studies, 25*(2), 150–169.

Sheorey, R. (2006). *Learning and teaching English in India* (Vol. 7). Sage.

Simon, J. (1995). *Foucault and the political* (1995). Routledge.

Smith, A., & Asante, M. (2025). *Reading Du Bois: An Afrocentric critique of the color line*. SUNY Press.

Spivak, G. C. (1998). Race before racism: The disappearance of the American. *boundary 2, 25*(2), 35–53.

Spivak, G. C. (1999). *A critique of postcolonial reason: Toward a history of the vanishing present*. Harvard University Press.

Tiffin, H. (1983). *Commonwealth literature: comparison and judgement* (pp. 19–35).

Vico, G. (1916). *La scienza nuova* (Vol. 14). G. Laterza & Figli.

Viswanathan, G. (1989). *Masks of conquest: Literary study and British rule in India*. Columbia UP.

Viswanathan, G. (Ed). (2002). P*ower, politics, and culture: Interviews with Edward W. Said*. Vintage Books, Random House.

Von Humboldt, W. (1999). *Humboldt: 'On language': On the diversity of human language construction and its influence on the mental development of the human species*. Cambridge University Press.

Walcott, D. (1974). The Caribbean: Culture or mimicry? *Journal of Interamerican Studies and World Affairs, 16*(1), 3–14.

Wa Thiong'o, N. (1986). *Decolonizing the mind: The politics of language in African literature*. Portsmouth: Heinemann.

Wa Thiong'o, N. (1993). Moving the centre: The struggle for cultural freedoms. Heinemann.

Wa Thiong'o, N. (1998). Decolonising the mind. *Diogenes, 46*(184), 101–104.

Wa Thiong'o, N. (2005). *Petals of blood* (Vol. 1). Penguin.

Wa Thiong'o, N. (2018). On the abolition of the English department. *Présence Africaine, 197*(1), 103–109.

# CHAPTER 9

## *Aiming at the Cannon: Afrocentricity as a Disruptive Technology*

### Aaron X. Smith (bka) Jabali Adé, PhD

ABSTRACT

Within this increasingly polarized and intentionally distorted technological matrix, the value of Afrocentric historical accuracy and contextual interpretation becomes increasingly vital. Understanding and implementing Afrocentricity as a disruptive technology posits it perfectly within the contemporary context as a viable tool for liberating transformative change. This chapter interrogate the continued quest to utilize Afrocentric methodologies as a corrective for the consequences of inaccuracies and omissions from the popular chronology of traditional education. Focusing on academic institutional development in the founding of prominent academic institutions such as Harvard and Georgetown and their connections with race and equality and exploitation will further punctuate the primary arguments in this chapter. This following chapter highlights the importance of self-determined Afrocentric paradigms, curriculums, and historical understandings. There are several obstacles to Afrocentric evolution explored here, which include fears of change, misunderstanding the value of African resistance in the protracted quest for liberation, and misinformation that prevents clear understandings capable of promoting sound theoretical options moving forward. Lastly, possibilities for a brighter, freer, and Afrocentrically located future are interrogated.

**Keywords:** Afrocentric, Technology, College, Chronology, Context

"Afrocentricity refers to the intellectual work of a group of African philosophers, historians, and sociologists during the late 20th century with varying degrees of attachment to the central idea that the key crisis in the

African world is the profoundly disturbing decentering of African people from a subject position within their own narrative. In Afrocentricity the opening consciousness is assumed to be an awareness of the off centeredness of Africans as a result of Arab and European and military, cultural, and social intrusions that have dislocated African people" (Asante, 2017b, p. 231). The apex of Afrocentric engagement is approaching. We are about to witness, shape, and experience the Afrocentric future. In preparation for this transformative renaissance, this chapter articulates three critical facets of preparatory Afrocentric engagement:

1    the need and benefits of increased Afrocentric context within education;
2    the chronological corrective components of Afrocentric historical analysis; and
3    potential opportunities to implement Afrocentric methodologies to improve our collective future.

When Molefi Kete Asante is discussed because, most often, in context concerning deficiency and effectiveness in the production of scholarship and his groundbreaking academic contribution of creating the first doctoral program in African American studies, less attention is given to the bravery and boundless boldness necessary to step into the four advocacies for African people understanding what such positioning has cost many freedom fighters who struggled before us. "Intellectuals have been summarily put in prison for voicing their concerns or thrown into jails for suggesting the possibility of an African orientation in government, in architecture, in economics, in education, and in culture. Our economic, political, and cultural motifs must remain African; otherwise, we are moved off of our strengths. In this century we must refute the critics of our ancestors and say that, while we do not want to follow everything done in the past we do want to build upon the foundation of the past (…) Despite the bitter antagonisms against the culture of our ancestors, we must seek to interpret contemporary developments in every sector and every field in the light of our own terms" (Asante, 2020, pp. 3–4).

Asante established a model of courage and diligence through remaining focused and productive under fire from critics and others who were fearful of change. It does require the expertise of veteran historians or deep political and scientific thinkers to recognize that these are transformative times.

The winds of transition are raging swiftly throughout academia and the larger society. Today, one of the most popular critical catchphrases in conservative spaces is semantic alteration of *diversity, equity, and inclusion* (Barnett, 2020; Beavers, 2018). With increasing attention being paid to issues of academic inclusion in modern times, the viewpoints, experiences, and identities of marginalized or completely excluded take on more significant degrees of importance. Few methodologies can manifest the accomplishments of sincere and effective engagement in all three areas of DEI as Afrocentricity can boast. An important distinction that must be made concerning Afrocentric scholars involves their willingness to go outside of and against the tenets of traditional education concerning the subject matter and traditionally acceptable points of view.

This unique level of criticism begins from an Afrocentric location with a more candid critique of educational systems and their history. Asante daringly demonstrates the deficiencies of modern traditional educational institutions with critical assessments and suggestions for reform in his work *Revolutionary Pedagogy: Primer for Teachers of Black Children.* Asante explains, "There is a general opinion among educators, politicians, and the public that in the United States urban education is a failure period using various indices of the new educational regime researchers have found that schools in larger urban communities demonstrate lower scores on standardized tests, lower levels of discipline, more school absences, and often less motivation to learn period in an executive summary of school conditions, the National Center for education statistics state quote many Americans believe that urban schools are failing to educate students they serve" (Asante, 2017c, p. 1). The original concept of universities as elite houses of upper-class future leaders and forward thinkers of the world emanating from a particular class alone is certainly a vision of the past within most collegiate spaces in the United States.

Long gone are the days of Harvard and William and Mary's monopoly and later disproportionate combined influence on the definition of institutional governance related to students, teachers, and administrators within the university system. Whether for more excellent pursuits of profits or genuine evidence of a more progressive and inclusive society, a multiplicity of manifestations of greater diversity continues to permeate the space. Shared governance speaks to how agency is institutionalized structurally.

Increased equity through mutually beneficial partnerships and tempering responsibilities and hierarchies with agency allocations and diversified authority all represent shared governance organizational structures (Riggs, 1975). To achieve increases in institutional equity and honestly share power, it is essential to seriously consider the larger cultural contexts that inform and influence institutions, and it is beneficial to implement an Afrocentric victorious consciousness to have the courage to enact positive change and to ask relevant and potentially transformative questions.

## THE PRICE OF EDUCATION AND THE COST OF IGNORANCE: AFROCENTRICITY, CONTEXT, AND CORRECTING CHRONOLOGY

When contextualizing the importance and power of Afrocentric context within the education paradigm, it becomes abundantly clear why this work is less of a victory lap in honor of Molefi Kete Asante and more of a call to action based on his work. This clarion call of Afrocentric theoretical application is designed for those willing to implement his teachings in the present day for a more inclusive and edifying tomorrow. As a professor and protégé of Molefi Kete Asante, my primary battlefield of struggle is academia, and my weapon of choice is Afrocentric stratagem (Long, 1992).

Worlds of historical distortion, class disparities, and racial justice continue to collide on college campuses throughout the nation. When engaging significant yet subtle differences, we must effectively define terms to achieve clarity and mutual understanding.

In his work, *Points of View: Writing on Race from Diverse Perspectives*, Asante brought together a collection of authors willing to share ideas and perspectives that could enhance racial discourse. In a section titled "Definitions of critical terms in the discourse on racism," the contributions of Carlos Hoyt Junior are highlighted.

**Prejudice:** Preconceived opinion not based on reason or actual experience, bias, partiality.

**Racism:** The belief that all members of a purported race possess characteristics, abilities, or qualities specific to that race, especially so as to distinguish it as inferior or superior to another race or other races. Racism is a particular form of prejudice defined by preconceived erroneous beliefs about race and members of racial groups.

**Power:** The capacity to exert force on or over something or someone.

**Oppression:** The exercise of authority or power in a burdensome, cruel, or unjust manner (Asante, 2012, p. 22).

Afrocentricity focuses more on critiques of racial hierarchy while acknowledging the universality of various forms of oppression. Intersections of inequality have brought me to my current emphasis on the importance of understanding the depth and nuance of historical context when analyzing disparate outcomes in society. We suffer from a collective truth deficiency within educational spaces and beyond, which further divides us while denying us the opportunity to engage the full humanity of others. Eurocentric distortion plays a crucial role in our collective deception. Afrocentricity provides a corrected chronology that connects our cultural, genetic memory with the most significant possibilities for envisioning a more robust future by accessing information and wisdom from the past.

It seems counterintuitive to assume that we could rightfully be made whole through history without being provided with the full story of our origins and evolution. Two-thirds of human history occurred in Africa before the inhabitants migrated throughout the world. "Africa stands at the very beginning of the origin of humanity. In no other continent have scientists found such extensive evidence of our origins as in Africa (…). Since the 1920s, scholars and scientists have been investigating the various links in the chain of human evolution, looking at the archaeological record as well as the biological record" (Asante, 2024, pp. 6–7). When Afrocentric scholars discuss the returning and gathering of the Sankofa principle, we refer not only to that which is suppressed or denied but also to the abundance of historical information yet to be uncovered, which we endeavor to unearth in efforts to resurrect the full African connection and potential of our people. Historical context plays a significant role in accessibility, affordability, positive student outcomes, comfortability, and safety. The absence of such context raises additional questions.

What are the effects of Eurocentric worldviews and Whitewashed historical contextualization within the educational gaps of equity, access, and quality of experience? Whether we look at financial aid, demographic inclusion along racial lines, academic performance, student retention, and graduation rates, a racial subtext exists. Contextually framing an issue, institution, subject, or people is critical to better understand observed phenomenon. We need to look no further than the ivory towers and hallowed halls of academia for institutional evidence of racial divides. *Ebony and Ivy: Race, Slavery, and the Troubled History of America's Universities* (Wilder, 2013) helps to provide the necessary fundamental framing for an analysis of racial disparities in higher education. The international connections between higher learning institutions and geopolitical engagement throughout the years have been significant.

This work details the relationship between the hierarchical racial ladder, limited educational opportunities, and the emerging collegiate class beginning in the 17th century with the founding of Harvard in 1636. "The founding, financing, and development of higher education in the colonies were thoroughly intertwined with the economic and social forces that transformed West and Central Africa through the slave trade and devastated indigenous nations in the Americas. The academy was a beneficiary and defender of these processes" (Wilder, 2013, p. 2). Wilder skillfully details the exploitative human trafficking of Africans. In the foundational aspects of higher education in America. While there's an in-depth chronology of the development of educational institutions, I recognize the Afrocentric seeds of educational disruption, which continue to benefit authors, scholars, and students from all fields and disciplines within the academy.

Through several Afrocentric sacrifices, which in some instances cost scholars their careers greater space for Black truth telling, African-focused accounts of history have been created. While he graciously accepts this mantle of boldness, he refuses to unchain early colleges from their connections with colonial conquest. The chapter titled "Race and the rise of the American college" examines the influence of slavery on the production of knowledge and the intellectual cultures of the United States. College founders and officers used enslaved people to raise buildings, maintain campuses, and enhance their institutional wealth. However, the relationship between colleges and slavery was not limited to the presence of slaves on campus. The American college trained the personnel and cultivated the ideas that accelerated and legitimated the dispossession of

Native Americans and the enslavement of Africans. Modern slavery required the acquiescence of scholars and the cooperation of academic institutions (Wilder, 2013, p. 10).

When institutions of higher learning are recognized as tangible extensions of a destructive yet funk institution that was racially codified to exploit human capital, how engaging with Education often changes. The work of Asante and other Afrocentric scholars has created a broader vision of topics worthy and fit to publish due to our persistent production of widespread scholarship. Publishing houses such as Third World Press and newer companies such as Universal Wright continue to provide outlets and balance to a widely Eurocentric industry (Pelizzon & Somel, 2021). Writers from other disciplines have directly and indirectly benefited from these collaborations and scholarly steadfastness, knowingly or unknowingly. Afrocentricity has helped to set ideas free from every discipline. The links between learning and liberation become more apparent in the minds and spirit of Afrocentric thinkers who cherish a sense of obligation to their ancestors to march on with a victorious consciousness. We, the intellectual children from Asante to Yaa Asantewa (Aikins, 2009), consider ourselves blessed to carry such a courageous and consequential tradition as scholar-activists, soldier scribes, and spiritual educators. We focus more on who we can heal rather than what we can have and hold for ourselves based on our gifts of knowledge. We recognize our position in a never-ending cycle of chronicling history, analyzing past, present, and potential while diligently endeavoring to create our legacy. We labor to have my contributions fit into the lineage of unwavering determination and dedication to our people and elevating the human family, which Afrocentric engagement personifies. "What we are witnessing in the development of an intellectual communication as a field of inquiry is the creation of theoretical postures from which to survey the whole of human interaction between cultures" (Asante, 1983, p. 4).

## BLACK HISTORY AND THE AFROCENTRIC PRESENT

As a microcosmic example of the relevance of Black history, a candid Afrocentric analysis of the roots of the university reveals how racist worldviews permeated the construction, culture, and accessibility of the ivory tower. Several scholars have effectively displayed how universities leveraged the cruel institution of enslavement to fund, find, and expand many aspects of the university system. From exclusion and exploitative service roles to being sold to remedy outstanding university debts, there exists a long, sordid history between racialized cultural ignorance and the pursuit of higher intelligence in America. An Afrocentric understanding of the historical evolution of institutions of learning creates opportunities for insights concerning disparities within the racial and economic wealth gaps, which were not significantly altered by integrating schools or other displays of increased cross-racial tolerance. "Afrocentricity seeks the agency of Africans in economics religion, institutions, history, culture, and communication. (…) Black people know what the problems are, and they know how the solutions must come. Thus, the Afrocentrists stand with the people for the rhetoric of African agency, the establishment of African institutions, critical attacks on all forms of oppression, pan Africanism, and the bringing into existence of an African diasporic vision that includes south America and the Caribbean there is a true choice for the African community in the United States, as there is for Africans on the continent and throughout the diaspora dash either we become people who seek self-determination, or we become brown and Black imitators of Europeans" (Asante, 2020, pp. 22, 23).

Revisionist history and denial of access and opportunity contribute to situations when certain people are treated less than others. For generations, her fundamental disregard for the humanity of African people has been a hallmark of a conflicted Republic (Slavery: Weld, 1839; Convict Leasing: Blackmon, 2009; *Human Zoo's*: Blanchard, 2008; Three-Fifths Compromise: Flynn & Jackson, 2020).

Afrocentricity has continuously challenged the inhumanity of racism, often emphasizing the profound contradiction of rejecting our collective African origins. The primary function of recognizing members of your species (e.g., dogs recognize other dogs, cats recognize other cats) appears intrinsic to most mammals. However, there has been great confusion for humans afflicted by the perceptual distortions of the problematic paradigm of racial hierarchy. Unfortunately for millions of Black people, being academically inclined has not caused them to become less racially

depraved in their thinking. In a twist of tragic irony, degrees have no relationship to the national temperature concerning diversity, equity, and
inclusion at college. In closing, I suggest the remedy to this layered issue of
racial and collegiate problematics involves an Afrocentric-nuanced
approach that centers on effectively contextualized, solution-based action.
Eurocentric educational systems have struggled to provide the levels of
honesty and context surrounding racism, which could properly prepare
students to positively engage the existence of such problems and respond
effectively according to their awareness. We must understand how we
have reached this point in our academic history to view the related challenges in a manner that could inspire transformative change concerning
racial disparities in colleges and universities. Afrocentric thought and
analysis provide the clarity necessary. "Afrocentric education is not against
history: it is for history-correct accurate history. If it is against anything, it
is against marginalizing African American children, Latino children, Asian
American, Native American children—a true centric education is different
from a racist education, that is, a white supremacist education. (...)
African American scholars trained in the best universities and with some
of the most impressive credentials have now emerged with ideas about
how to change the curriculum Afrocentricity" (Asante, 2007, p. 82).

Three of the specific issues in education where clarity could be particularly beneficial include the legacy system, histories of university
endowments, and the more significant legacy of inequality that informs
these contemporary realities. There are numerous questions of how more
accurate context can assist in providing more significant degrees of equity
in education among racial groups are numerous. How would institutions
positively respond (possibly engaging the Kemetic principle of Ma'at,
Karenga, 2003) to increase awareness concerning the origins and ongoing
perpetuation of various inequalities surrounding colleges and universities? How can Afrocentric analysis show whether racism within academic
institutions in the form of exclusionary and exploitative practices and
policies concerning access and quality of education contributed to the
racial gaps? "Many of the principles that govern the development of the
Afrocentric idea in education were first established by Carter G Woodson
in the miseducation of the Negro (1933). Indeed, Woodson's classic
reveals the fundamental problems pertaining to the education of the

African person in America" (Asante, 1991, p. 170). In many instances, these challenges are presented in complex numbers without influencing historical realities and contemporary inequalities, which could more powerfully inform the causes for the existence and perpetuation of the differences in higher education (Kezar & Eckel 2002).

The history of such an impersonal reductionist evaluation has its roots in preconceived negative notions related to racial difference and the consistent denial of the full humanity of African Americans and throughout the diaspora, which Afrocentric scholars such as Asante and Dove seek to reveal and remedy. Many of these organizational challenges have long-standing, deep-seated historical implications. "That is why he [Woodson] places on education, and particularly on the traditionally African American colleges, the burden of teaching the African American to be responsive to the long traditions and history of Africa as well as America" (Asante, 1991, p. 170). Several authors outside of Afrocentric spaces have understood and expressed the value of context and nuance in creating more relevant strategies for problem solving and understanding.

## DISTRUST OF THE OFFICIAL STORY

As an African American studies professor, I gravitated toward the general air of distrust concerning several aspects of traditional education. I have often said that the original official story is seldom believed to be correct over time. Just as there is political spin and the manipulation of people through propagandizing phenomena and perspectives, academic, intellectual, and analytical spin. This whirling and disorientating design can be viewed as a tightly coiled conceptual centrifuge when interrogating the circular paradigm of Eurocentric thought, which Afrocentric thinkers consistently seek to break free from, expand beyond, and ultimately revolutionize. My distrust for official stories has increased exponentially throughout my history studies from an Afrocentric perspective. From Phrenology (Greenblatt, 1995) to Eugenics (Kevles, 1999) Drapetomania to dreams of Democracy denied, an unfortunate pattern persists. Racialized pseudo-sciences and other expressions of scientific racism serve as institutional examples of preconceived racist notions run amuck and the institutionalization of ignorance.

The types of universities that tend to embody these problems may be less progressive and diverse, and those that have more intimate connections to an exclusionary history that informs their historical mission and modern vision. For example, the history of an institution founded by enslavers may contextualize educational disparities in education and their causes far differently than an institution established by abolitionist religious leaders. In addition to the significance of the mission and history of institutions of higher learning, there are other factors that Afrocentric analysis and engagement can help to rectify. This approach is when Eurocentric academic sources are subjected to Afrocentric scrutiny, revealing more manufacturing than meaning, more filibustering than fact, and more artificial than intelligence when most. Afrocentricity is designed to produce thinkers who, by virtue of their centeredness, are committed to sanity. "The idea of conscientization is at the center of Afrocentricity because this is what makes it different from Africanity. One can practice African customs and mores and not be Afrocentric. Afrocentricity is conscientization related to the agency of African people. One cannot be Afrocentric without being a conscious human being. This is the key to re-orientation and re-centering. Africans have been negated in the system of white racial domination. This is not mere marginalization, but the obliteration of the presence, meaning, activities, or images of the African. This is negated reality, a destruction of the spiritual and material personality of the African person" (Asante, 2017a, p. 2). I've long believed, as an Afrocentric scholar, that one of the primary problems we face in academia is the lack of diversity in subject matter and discourse direction, an unfortunate phenomenon that I label as the monopolization of the mind. This often occurs concerning the disproportionate attention paid by educators to European thinkers from Greece.

As a result, I welcome current ideological shifts prioritizing the thoughts of indigenous shamans or female pharaohs of ancient Africa, Chinese emperors and military strategists, or Inuit fishers who have expressed ideals and concepts that can inform and advance human philosophy. Afrocentricity is not designed to displace or devalue the perspective of others but rather to manifest the importance of various identities speaking from within their own historical and cultural context and from their center. In my work, I begin considering a young African American population, which arguably suffers significant underrepresentation in the

American academy; I seek to use Afrocentric educational tools to expand the notion of belonging while reaffirming diverse conceptualizations of being human beings. There remain persistent concerns about Eurocentric scholars who rely on the convenience of compartmentalization and bear the potential threats of such philosophical organizational distancing.

When recognizing the holistic, communal, and cyclical nature of Afrocentric thought and culture, it becomes evident how viewing Eurocentric standards as universal could be profoundly problematic. "Afrocentricity enters the critique of European hegemony after a series of attempts by European writers to advance critical methods of the construction of reality in the context of Europe itself. But Europe has been unable to satisfactorily critique itself from outside the racist, hegemonic paradigm established as the grand narrative of the European people. It is here that Afrocentricity provides the first deep analysis of the social and political situation inherent in hegemonic societies" (Asante, 2000). For many young African American children and those who identify as children of the African diaspora, the last thing they need concerning their educators and subjects of education is increased distance. In my work with young people throughout Philadelphia, this notion of existing as a nondescript generality despite the uniqueness of their fearful and wonderful makeup creates schisms and other troubling tensions.

My concern for their future and the dissemination of truthful and empowering information is why I am so invested in the transformative power of Afrocentric education. Language is another concern, and Afrocentric analysis helps us better understand and manipulate language. Terms such as People of Color and even minorities are often used in situations that apply directly to anti-Black histories, policies, and behaviors. Despite this reality, an analytical whitewashing that prioritizes European convenience over African pain (and even death) often persists. Afrocentric scholars must continue to address the root causes of the pain, generational curses, and trauma that usually inhibit intellectual growth and make way for the freedom, peace, and preparedness that will carry them through life's journey. Afrocentric methodologies illustrate connections between feelings of ostracization while resisting oppression and invisible barriers to academic ascension.

We also compare, contrast, and synthesize existing methodologies of Afrocentricity with emerging theories and movements, such as Afrofuturism, which consistently update and engage Afrocentric approaches. While compiling information for this text, I was consistently plagued with questions such as how can we most effectively navigate away from the dead ends of academic disparities without a realistic, in-depth roadmap of how we arrived here in the first place? How can you effectively and beneficially serve a person you only understand partially? Despite these questions, I recognize that an essential part of the answers I seek can be found in the practical application of Afrocentric theory. Transforming our understanding of the history of education and current curriculum-related conditions are two approaches that will prove transformative in the future. "Afrocentric Theory allows a writer to structure both the internal and the external world; they are essentially the same worlds. The difference lies mainly in the way both worlds relate to the investiture of cultural vision, that is, whether there is actual difference in vision. Perhaps the only way that the writer can structure both is to see them as one" (Asante, 1990).

# REFERENCES

Aikins, J. K. (2009). Yaa Asantewaa (ca. 1840–1921). In *The international encyclopedia of revolution and protest* (pp. 1–2). Wiley-Blackwell.

Asante, M. K. (1983). The ideological significance of Afrocentricity in intercultural communication. *Journal of Black Studies, 14*(1), 3–19.

Asante, M. K. (1991). The Afrocentric idea in education. *The Journal of Negro Education, 60*(2), 170–180.

Asante, M. K. (2000). Afrocentricity and history: Mediating the meaning of culture in western society. *Souls: Critical Journal of Black Politics & Culture, 2*(3), 50–62.

Asante, M. K. (2007). *An Afrocentric manifesto*. Polity Press.

Asante, M. K. (2012). *Points of view, writings on race from diverse perspectives.* Cognella.

Asante, M. K. (2017a). *Afrocentricity: Notes on a disciplinary position. In Afrocentric traditions* (pp. 1–14). Routledge.

Asante, M. K. (2017b). The philosophy of Afrocentricity. In A. Afolayan & T. Falola. (Eds.), *The Palgrave handbook of African philosophy* (pp. 231–244). Palgrave Macmillan.

Asante, M. K. (2017c). *Revolutionary pedagogy: Primer for teachers of black children.* Universal Write Publications LLC, 2017.

Asante, M. K. (2020). Afrocentricity. In R. Rabaka (Ed.), *Routledge handbook of pan-Africanism* (pp. 147–158). Routledge.

Asante, M. K. (2024). *The history of Africa: The quest for eternal harmony.* Routledge.

Barnett, R. (2020). Leading with meaning: Why diversity, equity, and inclusion matters in US higher education. *Perspectives in Education, 38*(2), 20–35.

Beavers, D. (2018). *Diversity, equity and inclusion Framework.* The Greenlining Institute.

Blackmon, D. A. (2009). *Slavery by another name: The re-enslavement of Black Americans from the Civil War to World War II.* Anchor.

Blanchard, P., Bancel, N., Boëtsch, G., Deroo, E., Lemaire, S., & Forsdick, C. (2008). *Human zoos: Science and spectacle in the age of empire.* Liverpool University Press.

Flynn, J., & Jackson, D. (2020). Extraordinary rule (three-fifths compromise). *Encyclopedia of critical Whiteness studies in education, 2,* 198.

Greenblatt, S. H. (1995). Phrenology in the science and culture of the 19th century. *Neurosurgery, 37*(4), 790–805.

Karenga, M. (2003). *Maat, the moral ideal in ancient Egypt: A study in classical African ethics.* Routledge.

Kevles, D. J. (1999). Eugenics and human rights. *BMJ, 319*(7207), 435–438.

Kezar, A., & Eckel, P. D. (2002). The effect of institutional culture on change strategies in higher education: Universal principles or culturally responsive concepts? *The Journal of Higher Education, 73*(4), 435–460.

Long, L. C. (1992). *An Afrocentric intervention strategy* (pp. 87–92). U.S. Department of Health and Human Services: Center for Substance Abuse Prevention.

Pelizzon, S., & Somel, C. (2021). Eurocentricity. In I. Ness & Z. Cope (Eds.), *The Palgrave encyclopedia of imperialism and anti-imperialism* (pp. 770–776). Springer International Publishing.

Riggs, F. W. (1975). Organizational structures and contexts. *Administration & Society, 7*(2), 150–190.

Weld, T. D. (Ed.). (1839). *American slavery as it is: Testimony of a thousand witnesses* (No. 10). American Anti-Slavery Society.

Wilder, C. S. (2013). *Ebony and ivy: Race, slavery, and the troubled history of America's universities.* Bloomsbury Publishing.

# CHAPTER 10

## *The Diverse Keys to the Creation of PhD in Black Studies: An Interview With Molefi Kete Asante*

### ABSTRACT

This interview conducted between Aaron X. Smith/Jabali Adé, Dr. Molefi Kete Asante, and me in May 2023 offers a unique first-person insight into the motivations, challenges, and triumphs related to the founding of the first PhD program in African American Studies at Temple University in Philadelphia. From creative strategies to unlikely allyship, the nuance of struggle and an Afrocentric victorious consciousness are on full display through the excerpt of an interview transcript, which allows the reader to hear directly from the source of the Enlightenment and inspiration this text is dedicated to. This chapter investigates the evolution of a field of study known by many names, including Black Studies, Africana Studies, African American Studies, and Africology. Utilizing an Afrocentric ethnographic methodological approach, I endeavor to present personalized academic perspectives and experiences through the microcosmic analytical lens of Afrocentricity's founding figure. One aspect of curiosity I sought to elucidate involved lesser known facts concerning opposition to the creation of the doctoral program and unlikely sources of support.

**Keywords:** Ethnographic, African American Studies, Asante, Temple University, Black, Africana, Africology, Allyship, Resilience, Persistence, Education, Ethnic Studies, 1960s

### INTRODUCTION

The triumphs and obstacles overcome within the evolution of Black Studies eerily mirror the tumult and triumphs experienced by Black

America over generations. Scholars from various disciplines, identities, and parts of the world formed a most unlikely and loosely affiliated alliance, making this landmark department possible.

Thoughts of Black Studies often conjure visions of larger progressive protest movements of the 1960s, which created the climate that made its inception a virtual inevitability. Many of the contemporary, national conversations around race, racism, and educations are heavily influenced from scholars affiliated with academic circles connected to Black Studies.

These links are observable through the groundbreaking documentary work of Henry Louis (Skip) Gates from Harvard or the theoretical approaches of Black legal scholars, including Derrick Bell, Alan Freeman, Kimberlé Crenshaw, Richard Delgado, Cheryl Harris, Charles R. Lawrence III, Mari Matsuda, and Patricia J. Williams whose work evolved into Critical Race Theory. Black Studies and the children (and affiliated scholars) of this powerful, paradigm-shifting legacy were empowered significantly through the expansion of the formal structure of their discipline with the development of the first PhD program in African American Studies at Temple University in Philadelphia, PA. The seeds of the university program were established in 1971 through an act of protest where large groups of students would put their bodies on the line to provide educational opportunities from a Black perspective. As the young people entered a busy thoroughfare that served as a primary artery of transport in Philly, the heartbeat of Black self-determination, which plateaued in the 1960s, experienced a cultural defibrillation, jump-starting the next chapter of African American institutional struggle.

## A PARAGON OF ACADEMIC PRODUCTIVITY AND RESILIENCE

Dr. Molefi Kete Asante is the founder of the first doctoral program in African American Studies and author of over 100 books. Born Arthur Smith in Valdosta, Georgia (August 14, 1942), his parents, Arthur Lee Smith and Lillie B. Wilkson-Smith, showered Arthur and his 15 siblings with love and guidance at the center of this ethnographic study. Arthur was identified as a diligent student and capable public speaker at an early age. He was active in the local church the family attended and, for a brief time, aspired to become a preacher. At 18, Arthur received a different calling from his ancestors. He began to embark upon a quest to better understand himself and the history of Black people worldwide. He would be accepted to and enrolled in Southwestern Christian College, where he graduated 2 years later (1962) with an AA degree. Shortly after this achievement, he graduated from Oklahoma Christian University in Oklahoma City, OK. This achievement marked the first time anyone in his family graduated from college. As a student here, he would begin publicizing his life-long passion for writing. His first work to be published was a collection of poems he composed.

The collection was titled *Break of Dawn* and was released during his senior year as an undergraduate student. Upon receiving his BA, Smith left Oklahoma and traveled to Los Angeles, where he enrolled in an MA program at Pepperdine University. He graduated in 3 years with a PhD in communications from the esteemed University of California, LA. After graduating, Smith returned to Purdue where he was employed through the communications department and enjoyed a stint as an assistant professor. It was during this phase of his professional journey Smith became the founding editor of *Journal of Black Studies*. This display of innovative, academic ingenuity foreshadowed the creation of intellectual space creation, which served as the motivation for this person-centered ethnographic study. While back at Purdue, Smith (1970) was able to have a second book published, *The Rhetoric of Black Revolution*. Smith/Asante returned to UCLA shortly after that to work as an assistant professor. His resilient, innovative spirit resurfaced when he became the first editor to be a permanent fixture for the Center for Afro-American Studies.

During this time, Asante designed a master's program run through the center. These achievements undoubtedly increased Asante's faith in his ability to expand the potential of institutions to educate and empower according to the needs of African American students and those interested in their history and contributions. After several additional publications, he relocated to Philadelphia to work as a professor and department chair at Temple University in 1984. Two years after this appointment, Asante successfully established the first PhD program in African American Studies.

# FIELDWORK

To gain a better understanding of Dr. Asante's tastes concerning programming, aesthetics, and scholarship, I traveled to the institute he founded to conduct field research and an interview with the namesake of the Molefi Kete Asante Institute (5535 Germantown Avenue in Philadelphia). Parked just outside of the center, I observed several people walking by. Almost all of them were of African descent or would be classified as Black without additional interrogation concerning their identifications. Most people who passed by were in conversation with other people (directly or through a device). The outside of the building is adorned with thick glass panels allowing passersby to see directly into the center. A sign above the entranceway displays the name of the center/institute, including the name of the center's founder. The sign's colors are those popularized by Pan-Africanists and freedom fighters for liberation: red, black, and green. Upon entering, I was immediately greeted by a Black woman with an African accent adorned in traditional African clothing with intricately sewn patterns in green, yellow, red, and brown colors. The title of today's event was "Defending and protecting all African People from Abuse."

The structure of the building was narrow and aesthetically pleasing. There were African/African-inspired art and wooden bookcases lining the walls. Most book titles focused on Black history and culture, including words such as Afrocentric, Black, African, Freedom, Africa, Consciousness, and Liberation. The back of the center is filled with rows of burgundy cushioned chairs with metal/metallic legs. There were about three rows filled with people who mostly seemed previously familiar with each other. Most of the people present had gray or partially gray heads of hair. They seemingly enjoyed the space in preparation for the lecture, discussing phrases such as, "Hotep, good to see you, sister," as they embraced. Many of the audience members were in African cultural garb with various patterns: two wore Kente clothe accents, others were adorned with African mud cloth, some bearing adinkra symbols.

# INTERVIEW TRANSCRIPT

In the interview transcript, Dr. Asante discussed the diversity and climate of protest and self-determination that defined an era and gave birth to Black Studies. The interview lasted roughly 40 min. The focus of the interview was the story/stories related to the founding of the first PhD program in African American Studies in the world. Names of supporter's information about detractors and other challenges were discussed. Questions about basic information, resilience, and advice for the future are all included in the larger discussion from which a portion was extracted from the reading below. I pray that you find beneficial connections and understanding regarding Africology as you find inspiration from the determination of will and connections to ancestral spirits displayed throughout the following transcribed conversation.

**Interviewer: Aaron X. Smith; Interviewee: Molefi Kete Asante**

Interviewer:   Can you tell me what impact if any, the location of the department's PhD founding had on your journey and innovative contribution to the Academy?

Interviewee:   Temple University is in the beating heart of Philadelphia, one of the great black communities in this country. When I arrived from Buffalo, New York, in 1984, Philadelphia had elected its first African mayor, Wilson Goode. The city was increasingly populated by African people from all over the nation and the world. Temple University was led by a second generation Greek-American named Peter Liacouras, one of the iconic university presidents of the era. He was liberal, progressive, and courageous. When he interviewed me for the job as chair of African American Studies, he said, "Temple should have the best African American Studies program in the nation. We are in one of the most dynamic centers of African American culture."

Quite honestly, I was shocked at his directness and earnestness. I told him that if I came to Temple University, we would build the best department in the country. I said, "Mr. President, I'm going to come and help you create a formidable department right here in North Philly." I did not think that Boston or Berkeley should or could beat Philadelphia in supporting such a program. I had been chair of the Department of Communication at SUNY Buffalo for almost ten years. For a couple of those years I had simultaneously chaired the Department of African American Studies. I went to Buffalo from the University of

California, Los Angeles where I was the first director of the Center for African American Studies from 1969–1973.

When I came to Temple to take the reins of the department of African American Studies, I had only three other faculty members in the program. Dr. Odeyo Ayaga who lived in Willingboro, New Jersey, Dr. Alfred Moleah who lived in Wilmington, Delaware, and Dr. Tran Van Dinh who lived in Washington, DC. Tran Van Dinh who lived in Washington DC and me.

The head of our PASCEP (Pan-African Studies Community Education Program) was Maisha Sullivan Onganza. She lived in Philadelphia and was responsible for holding the entire program together until I was hired. The PASCEP was an academic as well as an activist platform for the local community. Faculty members would teach without pay courses on basic subjects to community people who gave the program a nominal fee for transportation for the teachers. Founded by Annie Hyman, the PASCEP program had become one of the centers for community education, activism and discourse.

Accessing the situation at Temple, the first thing I needed to do was to augment the faculty. The person who had led the search committee for the chair position was a historian named C. Tsehloane Keto. He was a South African intellectual who was deeply entrenched in the African American community.

I had learned early from my father that if you wanted something you had to ask. You would only hear "Yes" or "No". So, I went to Keto's office and asked him to join our faculty. He said, "Yes, I would be happy to move my position to the Department of African American Studies." I was pleased. After working it out with the Dean of the College and the history department, Professor Keto joined our faculty. He was elevated to the position of full professor and made a massive contribution to the department. I also asked the famous poet, Sonia Sanchez to rejoin the department after hearing that she had once been on the department's faculty. I sincerely believe that she would have joined us if she had not been fearful that some future dean would try to destroy the program as the former dean had done. She remained our supporter but kept her position in the Department of English. Her eminence continued to grow at Temple and she was awarded the highest distinction at the university. On several occasions she sat on our dissertations and spoke highly of our work.

Interviewer: Were there other professors you recruited or who filled the void left by Sanchez's declined offer?

Interviewee: The department had seen the likes of Molara Ogundipe-Leslie, Yosef ben Jochannon, Wilbert Roget, Rita Smith, Barbara Hampton, and others who had emerged after the students demanded a Black Studies program. A previous dean had tried to disband the department by pushing people to other departments. Roget, for example, went to French; Sanchez to English. That is why the program had only three faculty members when I arrived. Maisha Ongonza was not on the faculty, she was an administrator. Eventually, I was able to hire Muriel Feeling to direct PASCEP and teach an occasional class.

I was able to recruit Kariamu Welsh, the founder of the Zimbabwe National Dance Company, Sonja Peterson-Lewis, Nah Dove, and others in the 1990s.

When I came to Temple, only Tran Van Din was a full professor. The chair before me, Odeyo Ayaga from Kenya, was an assistant professor, and Alfred Moleah was an associate professor. I tried to convince Moleah to play a stronger role in our program, but he was concerned only with positioning himself to return to South Africa. I told him and Tran that I was going to propose a doctoral program. They did not much believe the university would support it. Well, they were wrong because the university administration was supportive although we did have difficulty with some faculty members in other departments.

Interviewer: What was the process of that decision? Was it more collective or an individual vision?

Interviewee: I made the decision that I wanted to have a graduate program. I wanted to have a master's degree program first, to be honest with you. I proposed it to the president and to the board of trustees. This was the pattern at most universities. But as I looked around there were seven other MA programs in African American Studies, nationally.

I decided, to make Temple's department distinctive. Our objective was to be rigorous enough to qualify our own scholars. I then wrote the proposal for the PhD program. We had a small faculty member to be proposing a doctoral program. Two of the faculty members retired almost immediately, Tran Van Dinh and Odeyo Ayaga. Although I was embolden to go for the PhD, I also knew that some people would question our ability to deliver the program with only three faculty members.

There was a delegation from the college, led by history and sociology, who came to see me in my office, and they said we just don't think you have enough people here to contemplate a PhD. Back in those days you could look up the catalogs of most universities and find what majors and degrees they offered and who they had on faculty. I found two or three universities that gave PhD's in classics with only two faculty members. Why couldn't we do it with three or four faculty? I answered the committee that had come to me with data collected from those catalogs. Then, the proposal had to be submitted to the college graduate committee comprised of 12 faculty members, none of them African Americans.

All the people on the Graduate Committee representing various departments were white except one person. Professor Jitendra Nath Mohanty. That one person was an Indian and he was a fine scholar of intuition and aesthetics from the philosophy department. I never forgot him and always respected his courage and insight. When I appeared before the Graduate Committee of the College with my proposal, it was Professor Mohanty who understood it immediately and went to battle for our doctoral program. Mohanty said, "Dr. Asante, I understand precisely what you're asking for, and I believe it's necessary in this university, and I would be willing to support you." That took the tension down in the room because Mohanty, an Indian scholar of world renown, was speaking up. Although I had been questioned by several white scholars prior to Dr. Mohanty's approving statement, after he spoke, no one else had any questions. J. N. Mohanty continued, "You're trying to look at things from inside out; they don't understand when you talk about Afrocentricity," The committee accepted the proposal and passed it on to Dean Lois Cronholm, Provost Barbara Brownstein, and the board of trustees. However, the head of the Sociology department, Magali Sarfatti-Larson met me at the entry to Gladfelter Hall, where both of us had offices, and said "Molefi, it would be over my dead body that you get a PhD in African American Studies."

I vowed to myself; this will be done. All the administrative above the college level supported the idea, including Vice President Patrick Swygert, the lone black administrator. The College of Liberal Arts (at one time the College of Arts and Sciences) could hardly find the strength and will to fully fund the program. We fought annually and were able to eventually get ten teaching assistantships.

Interviewer:     What was it like working with Bill Cosby, did you interact with him often?

Interviewee:     I didn't know him well and I don't think he knew me well, but he knew the experience that we had at Temple and as a board member he respected what I was trying to do. In the 1970s I was a professor at UCLA when I met Bill Cosby. He was working with "Fat Albert and the Cosby Kids" and a colleague, Gordon Berry, and I, were consultants to the CBS program. I was very young, this was maybe 1971 or 1972 and I was director of the UCLA Center for African American Studies, and in the Department of Communications, and Dr. Gordon Berry was in the school of education. I studied the script's language, and Berry its educational objective. We sat with Cosby and his writers to make sure that the language was right and message was clear.

Cosby would tell stories, and we would have to put meat on the story.

The fact is that he knew me, and I knew him from these few interactions around his television series, but we were never social acquaintances. However, he was a great supporter of the doctoral program in African American Studies at Temple during the time of our struggle.

On Temple's Board of Trustees, Cosby worked with Bishop Nicholas, a leading African American preacher on the board, to argue for our doctoral program. Reverend Nicholas was head of the education committee for Temple's board of trustees, so I had Cosby and Nicholas as strong soldiers on the board. The PhD program was approved in 1987 and the next year we opened up to accept students.

Provost Barbara Brooke Brownstein asked me how many people you need, and I said, give us three faculty members. I should have said ten people, but I was euphoric about the approval and the fact that they wanted to know how many faculty we needed.

I hired Sonja Peterson Lewis because the students were saying we need a woman. I had spoken at the University of Utah for black history month, and the Dean at Utah recommended a young black woman who had a Rockefeller grant. I talked to Sonja and we were soon able to invite her to Temple. We hired her and she was the first person hired from outside Temple. She would be followed by C. T. Keto, Kariamu Welsh, Nah Dove, and nearly ten other scholars.

Ave rarely had strong knowledgeable and supportive deans. Only one stands out and she was Lois Cronholm. She was the most sympathetic Dean we've ever had toward this department. I got a note from her maybe three or four years ago when she wrote me and said the greatest achievement of my academic career, after she became President of Baruch College, she said this) the greatest achievement of my academic career was to work with you in getting the PhD program in African American Studies. Lois Cronholm was coming from the Kentucky, and she was a liberal from the South and she had a cross burned on her yard by the Ku Klux Klan. Dean. Cronholm was an emotional and sincere person. She recognized the struggle for justice and equality and worked to support the program. We eventually reached 14 faculty members, hired the eminent scholar Theophile Obenga, and brought on Bobby Seale as a liaison between the department and community.

I also asked her Dean Cronholm to let me go out and hire Charles Fuller. He was a Pulitzer Prize winner. He lived in Philadelphia and ironically, our theater department had never asked him to come and work with them although he had written several plays, including "A Soldier's Story," and other important works. He agreed to take a professorship with us at Temple and was a major attraction for students.

In 1990 we graduated our first doctoral student, Adeniyi Coker. He was the first person to get a PhD in African American Studies in the world.

Interviewer: Can you tell me a little bit about those moments where maybe you expected to get some support or it's coming from different places than what you expected? What pushes you forward because you know this to most people would seem like a long time to be persistent towards these efforts.

Interviewee: I think you must believe in your project and if you believe in the project strongly enough then you must be relentless. I believe that there is nothing greater for a university than to express somewhere in its curriculum this unique struggle and constant agitation for democracy, for justice and for humanity that our people have always shown. I mean, there is no force that I saw in moving in this direction that was equal to our force. In other words, I didn't think that they had a good footing, and I still believe that way. I still believe that ultimately there must be somewhere in the university where African American Studies is a whole college. There are possibilities in music, art, theater, dance, scientific discovery and other fields. The extent of our interests, contributions, and achievements is equal to any other group in the world. African Studies or African American Studies as a subset of that grand title must be seen as stretching across all disciplines.

Interviewer: Can you speak to the diverse academic appetites of the students who take courses in the Department?

Interviewee: Our students are interested in the world, they are curious, questing individuals, and they come from all communities, genders, and cultures. Their appetite is for truth, facts, dignity, and respect for humanity.

Interviewer: You talk about a theory of victorious consciousness. Can you talk a bit about how that theory and some of the comments you made about staying persistent all play a part in believing in your program?

Interviewee: I think because you must model the behavior you believe, and for me what I saw and what I can still see, is a lot of people who are cautious. I will just tell you that I will defeat it, I will tell you not only am I conscious of my oppression, but I am also conscious of my victory.

## REFLECTIVE THOUGHTS

This interview and the related field notes represent a revealing journey, through the history of the first PhD in African American Studies offered in the world at Temple University. The diverse nature of the contributors and their contributions involved in the formation and maintenance of the Africology and African American Studies department were. It was inspiring to see that through diligence and teamwork, so many lives could be transformed in a positive way. There were revelatory aspects of the transcript dealing with the need for consistent vigilance in preparation for what seems like inevitable attacks. The value of international perspectives from those who have lived outside of the United States appears to be a critical part to the ability to see beyond themselves and appreciate the perspectives and academic self-determination of others. My firm belief is that the standard traditional approaches to research and higher education have not been working significantly to resolve modern issues in higher education. I prefer to implement alternative methodologies and innovative analytical approaches as my academic investigation and interrogation tools.

## REFERENCES

Smith, A. L. (1970). *Rhetoric of black revolution*. Allyn and Bacon.

Molefi Kete Asante. https://www.thehistorymakers.org/biography/molefi-kete-asante

Yosef Ben Jochannan. https://www.nytimes.com/2015/03/29/nyregion/contested-legacy-of-dr-ben-a-father-of-african-studies.html

Tran Van Dinh. https://en.wikipedia.org/wiki/Tr%E1%BA%A7n_V%C4%83n_D%C4%A9nh

Sonia Sanchez. https://poets.org/poet/sonia-sanchez

# *Afterword*

This text emerges on the occasion of the First International Congress of Afrocentric Education held at UNEB (Universidade do Estado da Bahia)—from May 5 to 9, 2025—and at UNILAB (Universidade da Integração Internacional da Lusofonia Afro-Brasileira) located, respectively, in Salvador and São Francisco do Conde in the State of Bahia—Brazil. At this Congress, I had the pleasure of meeting personally Dr. Molefi Kete Asante, the father of Afrocentricity, who has propelled and enhanced the research and studies of Afrocentric students in Brazil, and keynote the opening ceremony, and Dr. Nah Dove, the creator of Womanism, and the author of the Afrocentric School, who spoke passionately about the impact and power of Afrocentricity globally and the power of the woman as the foundation of humanity.

The event was promoted by the Afrocentrada Education Research Group (Grupeafro/Unilab Malês) and by the Afrocentric Health Research Group. Inaugural participants include Ilera Dudu (UNEB),coordinated by Professor Dra. Suiane Costa Ferreira, in partnership with the Education Laboratory for Ethnic Racial Relations of Federal University of Pernambuco (UFPE). Others include Professor Dra. Maria da Conceição dos Reis and the Afro Perspectives Knowledge and Childhood Research Group from the Federal Rural University of Rio de Janeiro (UFRRJ) as well as Professor Dr. Renato Noguera. These groups and Ubuntu Extension Program African-Based Studies coordinated by Professor Dr. Gabriel Swahili have been producing research with an emphasis on discussions about teacher training, pedagogical practices, education for ethnic-racial relations, Afrocentric education, health education, and its articulation with basic education and higher education. These discussions have also been promoted in schools, universities, communities, and other spaces by educators, researchers, and organizations from different places in the country.

To our joy the congress met the expectations of the participants of the event. That the Father Founder of Afrocentricity was at the foreground of this congress, amplified the impact and success. We are proud that Dr. Dove, Dr. Ayo Sekai, and Dr. Asante were very impressed by the knowledge that Unilab students have of their works and by the fact that most of the students are from Angola, Cape Verde, Guinea-Bissau, Mozambique, and São Tomé and Príncipe. In view of this, Dr. Ayo Sekai, who presented as the number one publisher of Afrocentric works and the majority of Dr. Asante's books from any one publisher, spoke about the imperative of publishing and applying research from Black Scholars. Through her vision and powerful lens, she invited me to write the poster of this important work edited by Professor Dr. Aaron X. Smith in order that the Afrocentric educational debate in Brazil be represented in this work of such enormous scale.

In Brazil, the Afrocentric debate begins with Abdias Nascimento and the publication of his classic *The Quilombism*, published originally in 1980. Another important text is the Lélia Gonçalves's *The political cultural category of Amefricanity* by Elisa Nascimento, 1981, with *Pan-Africanism in South America* and the publication of the Sankofa collection in 2009, whose volume four contains a set of articles on Afrocentricity, continuing the work started by Abdias. More recently, Professor Renato Noguera[1] with his articles and books has brought this debate to the academy. Although the discussion is still extremely marginalized in this environment.

In 1899, José Verssimo wrote in the *Journal of Commerce* that due to the mix of races and European immigration the Black races would be extinct from Brazil. A violent statement like this written in an important periodic of the country shows us that the Brazilian Republic was born under the guidance of a policy of extermination of the African Brazilian population.

The only divergence that existed among the advocates of the policy of whitening concerned the time in which the country would become, in fact, white. The most optimistic, such as João Batista de Lacerda estimated the

---

[1]Look at the works, for example. *O Ensino de Filosofia e a Lei 10.639*, Rio de Janeiro: CEAP, 2011, Afrocentricidade e Educação: os princípios gerais para um currículo afrocentrado. *Revista África de Africanidades,* Ano 3, n. 11, novembro, 2010. Available at: http://www. africaeafricanidades. com. br/documentos/01112010_02. pdf.2025/05/16

end of the process in a century. Lacerda was director of the National Museum of Rio de Janeiro and in this condition represented Brazil at the First Universal Races Congress that took place in 1911 in London. At this event he presented the topic *About the mixed-race people in Brazil* and said: "thanks to this ethnic reduction procedure, it is logical to assume that, within the span of a new century, mixed-race people will disappear from Brazil, a fact that will coincide with the parallel *extinction* of the Black race between us."[2] One of the most pessimistic, such as one by Afrnio Peixoto, states that extermination would be complete in three centuries. Let's see your eloquent words: "it may take us three hundred years to change our soul and bleach our skin, and, if not white, at least disguised, we lose our mestizo character. We have already purged so many years."[3]

It is worth noting that throughout the 20th and 21st centuries, the Brazilian state did not apologize and did not repudiate this genocidal policy. In fact, many of its defenders are still revered today as great abolitionists, republicans, and democrats.

We can perceive a similar phenomenon when we analyze the history of the public education system of the country. The structuring of public, universal, and free took place in Brazil from the 1930s of the past century. The pioneers of educao nova were responsible for the foundations of the educational model of the country. Model, this, founded on eugnical bases. Jerry Dvila, who studied the educational policy of Brazil in the period from 1917 to 1945, wrote in the introduction of his work *Diploma of Whiteness*: "the so-called educational pioneers of Brazil transformed the emerging public schools into spaces in which centuries of white-European suprematism were rewritten in the language of merit, science and modernity."[4]

---

[2]See the work Sobre os  mestiços no Brasil. In: *Revista História, Ciências, Saúde-Manguinhos*

[3]See the *Annals of the Chamber of Deputies*, Sesso, December 27, 1923, pp. 383–384.

[4]See the work *Diploma of Whiteness: Race and Social Policy in Brazil, 1917–1945*. São Paulo: UNESP, 2006, p. 24.

Fernando de Azevedo, writer of *The Pioneers of New Education*, one of the main thinkers of Brazilian education was also the first secretariat of the Eugenic Society of São Paulo founded by Renato Kehl. Considered by Monteiro Lobato as the father of eugenics in the country, Renato Kehl was also a defender of Hitler's policies. Fervent eugenist, Azevedo never reconsidered his positions on eugenics even after the advent of Nazism. In his work *From Physical Education: What It Is, What It Has Been, and What It Should Be*, in the third edition, which was published in 1960, he wrote that he wasn't pessimistic about the future of Brazil, noting that his educational eugenics action plan would succeed because it would integrate into the national currents forming the nation. The shaping force of physical education would guarantee this process.

Just as it happened in relation to politics of extermination of the Afro-Brazilian, the Brazilian State at no time repudiated or apologized for imposing on this people an educational system based on eugenics. It is worth highlighting that, according to Davila, the Brazilian educational institutions till today retain their eugenic character: "eugenia lost its scientific legitimacy during World War II, but the institutes, practices and assumptions to which it originated in fact, its spirit survive."

Critics of this educational system, such as Darcy Ribeiro and Paulo Freire, have never evidenced or criticized the eugnic charter of education practiced in the country. In fact, Fernando de Azevedo's educational ideas, in general, are not associated with eugenics by the Brazilian academy and the author is often revered for defending a democratic school model.

In the face of this scenery, I think some quests are inevitable. A racist educational system born in the Vargas era,[5] which maintains this racism in the democratic period from 1945 to 1961, remains racist during the military dictatorship, continues with the same charter in the period of redemocratization and in the last 22 years solemnly ignores a federal legislation[6]—can it be reformed to the point of ceasing to be racist? If the answer is

---

[5]Getúlio Vargas was the President of Brazil from 1930 to 1945.

[6]In 2003, Law 10.639/2003 was published, which amended the Law of Guidelines and Bases of Brazil, obliging public and private establishments in the country to teach African and Afro-Brazilian History and Culture.

affirmative, it is up to us to investigate how this reform would be possible and what time would be reasonable to implement it. We cannot lose sight of the fact that in the next decade the public education system will become a centennial.

If the answer is negative, it means admitting that racism is a permanent reality in Brazilian society. As it is hegemonized by whites, we are naturally led to ask ourselves: what should we do to educate our children and young people satisfactorily?

I think this is a debate that we cannot avoid. This text is also an invitation for us to conduct it in the best style of African traditions. Our position, although minority, can be inferred from the excerpt by Jacob Carruthers:

> In the view of the dismal of Project of Eurocentric or European-centered for our Black youth, we ought as a matter of common sense consider African-centered education. (I will dismiss without comment the absurd notion that a universalistic curriculum is the solution). Let us now make the case a bit clearer.

> The crisis endemic in Black education is the basis of what Bobby Wright calls "Menticide". Menticide is the most sophisticated phase of the white supremacist war strategy against the Black race. If we lose that war, there will be no more problems in Black education, no more Black education, and no more Blacks. [. ] If we want to win the war against white supremacism, if we want to live, then we must take the education away from our enemies. We must build true African education on a life-giving base. Only an African-centered education offers such a base.

Therefore, in 2016 in my doctoral thesis I coined, inspired by the Quilombism of Abdias Nascimento, the concept of Quilombist Education. This can be interpreted as an Afrocentric education applied to the Brazilian reality. It defined as follows:

> [...] a process of transmitting values, beliefs, customs, and knowledge so that Afro-Brazilians can live adequately in this society, thus ensuring the continuity of their people and culture. This education should be inspired by the experience of the quilombos, since these societies allowed Africans to exist on this land without renouncing their Africanity, as well as being open to indigenous and white excluded from the colonial system. Just as quilombos were constituted as spaces for the construction of Afro-Brazilian

identity and resistance to European acculturation quilombist education, today, must be conceived as a process of formation of the Amefrican of Brazil[7] and resistance to the historically constituted eugenic and Eurocentric model of education with a view to the construction of the quilombista intercultural society.

To achieve these goals, we need to develop school institutions, that is, educational and socialization processes inspired by African traditions; take control of these institutions; and draw up a curriculum. Dr. Ayo Sekai with Universal Write Publications is a prime example of an institution focused on African consciousness and research on Afrocentric Scholarship. It is also important to note that, in order to enable these needs and prepare teachers to minister the contents necessary for the formation of the Afro-Brazilian. With regard to the curriculum, the text by philosopher Renato Noguera in *Afrocentricity and Education: The general principles of an Afrocentric curriculum* offers us a good starting point to think of a curriculum inspired by African principles and values. In it we can read:

> What would be the principles or parameters for an Afrocentric curriculum? Asante wrote a brief srie of organizing elements of the curriculum named *Princpios Asante for the Afrocentric curriculum.* The article contains 10 principles: 1) You and your community; 2) Well-being and biology, 3) Tradition and Innovation; 4) Artistic expression and creation; 5) Location in time and space; 6) Production and distribution; 7) Power and Authority; 8) Technology and Science; 9) Choices and Consequences; 10) World and society. Starting from the reading of these constituent elements of each principle and an articulation with Nguzo Saba makes it possible an Afrocentric exploration of the foundations of education, this, we can analyze the philosophical, historical, psychological and sociological elements in an African perspective to compose the multi-faceted field of education. Therefore, a careful reading of Nguzo Saba and *Afrocentric curriculum* principles leaves no doubt, Karenga and Asante agree that knowledge is measured by its potential to serve the community, integrate people and provide a life without opposition to the environment.

---

[7]The Afro-Brazilian intellectual Lélia Gonzalez coined the concept of Africanity to help us understand the reality of Africans in the Americas.

Although Noguera is not thinking of independent schools, his work presents a valuable reflection on how the Brazilian curriculum can be Afrocentric. His analysis recognizes that the "hegemonic educational system permeated by values that locate nature as an object, knowledge as a weapon and property, and, the human being as a being that controls and requires everything to gravitate around it" and thus understands that in an Afrocentric education it is necessary to lighten and articulate the Seven Principles of African tactics throughout the entire curriculum.

To conclude, it is worth highlighting that despite our understanding that Brazilian public and private schools do not meet the needs of Afro-Brazilians, we cannot ignore the fact that most Afro-descendants study in the public system. Moreover, the quilombista model proposed here does not exist. Therefore, I think we have challenges to prepare teachers for quilombista education, to develop theoretically and practically a quilombista pedagogy. Fundamentally we must protect our children and youth in the public eugenic system while working for the development of quilombista education models.

Ricardo Matheus Benedicto, PhD

Professor of the Institute of Humanities and Letters of
Unilab—Campus dos Malês,

Coordinator of the Research Group on Afrocentrada Education

# *Conclusion*

Today's social justice movements have spotlighted on the need for drastic improvements in diversity, equity, inclusion, agency, access, and success concerning students and leadership within society. Changing demographics are a biological, geographical certainty that should be embraced as we remain prepared to maximize these unavoidable conditions rather than be left behind due to obsolete assertions about best serving changing populations. I genuinely believe that a more accurately informed population will create a fairer society for all. If we knew better, we would do better. Lacking knowledge about these lesser known, alternative historiographies could create cultural, economic, and academic blind spots, which could obstruct the maximum effectiveness of even the most well-meaning progressives.

For example, in my field of higher education, administrators and others in positions of leadership can also value greatly from being part of institutional shifts, which could increase the value they bring to their respective professions. The growth added to an administration that improves its ability to support humane, culturally relevant connections with students could be exponential. One of the most advantageous aspects of the college experience involves creating an encouraging, challenging, and growth-oriented network that can potentially be accessed for the life of a graduate. These forms of expanding the culturally sensitive reach of various communities should have powerfully positive impacts upon student populations who previously may have felt less recognized or valued.

Afrocentricity encourages us to move away from the fears of polarization and demonization through a collective commitment to working in tandem as a team dedicated to attacking problems rather than people. We must create policies and legislation that offset the current ones that are contributing to the negative conditions we experience. Honest Afrocentric, layered innovative approaches, informed by the context in addition to more traditional statistical analysis, are often required. Perhaps through these forms of progressive approaches, less time would be spent solely crunching numbers or protecting Eurocentric myths of equal accessibility and affordability within society.

Rather than lacking context, through increased implementation of Afrocentric education, we may gain the ability to reprioritize our collective efforts more efficiently and productively. Evidence of such a paradigm shift may include more contextual analysis and suggested solutions, less demonization of different demographics, and less emphasis on cancel culture and more concentration on canceling student debt! Active methods of engagement help to deliver positive results for the increasingly diverse populations throughout the nation. These connections are aided by increased opportunities to use the connectivity of common humanity, fueling familiarity while implementing relevant cultural knowledge to create community through culturally infused service. Proactive, holistic Afrocentric expressions and structures, which embrace and educate around the escalating levels of diversity and cultural complexities, will continue to be bolstered by sound research studies, surveys, and simple gestures of sincere humanity.

Cultural competence must be increased to truly encourage greater degrees of agency rather than simply extending access and tolerance. Anti-African euro century scholars have long been guilty of intentionally mischaracterizing, classifying, and linguistically identifying all things pro-African and Afrocentric. From marking the invasion of the Hyksos and the changing the names of lands, pharaohs, and gods, anti-African alteration has been ever present. Theories like those popularized by Pythagoras yet first demonstrated in Africa by Africans elucidate just one example of the myriads of misapplied cultural and scientific credits taken from Africans and unjustly bestowed upon undeserving European figures throughout history. The Berlin conference represents the physical manipulation of African geographic realities for disorienting, dislocating, and exploiting the revolutionary potential as well as natural resources of the entire continent of Africa. Men such as Cecil Rhodes DeBeers and Leopold would all capitalize off the calcified consciousness of African people sadly subjected to the multi-faceted infectious illusion indicative of European colonization.

When Africans were enslaved in the Lens later turn colonies, which became the Americas. A new name was forced upon them, which reflected the all-encompassing power of colonial oppression while simultaneously serving to separate African prisoners of war from the power of their continental cultural connections. This attempt to dislocate and dehumanize was partly portrayed in the classic depiction of enslavement presented by Alex Haley in his novel-turned film *Roots*. In the film, the protagonist Kunta dangles nearly lifeless after defiantly declaring his African name over the suggested Toby Moniker, which enslavers were trying to whip into his soul. After a determined and noble display of cultural resistance to repression, Kunta appears broken and nearly lifeless as he reluctantly begins to acquiesce and affirm the colonizers perceptions of him over the fully human self-determined African, he once was.

## AFROCENTRIC AGENCY AT THE CENTER OF FUTURISTIC THOUGHT

When the question is asked, where do we go from here, the answer I offer is, back to ourselves, toward our center and deeper into our spiritual realities. The Eurocentric illusory academic matrix of decentering by deception has proven to be a formidable cultural cancer, which requires rigorous resistance and the fierce weaponization of truth to adequately counter its harmful effects. In the game Jenga, wooden blocks are configured atop one another forming a disjointed yet tightly packed tower. Competitors remove blocks from lower portions of the tower and place them on top without collapsing the larger structure. If the tower is compromised and falls, the game is over, and whoever is responsible for the toppling is declared the loser.

Some instances occur throughout the game like the dexterity implemented by many great Afrocentric scholars. Jenga competitors, at times, have successfully removed the bottom foundational block without completely jeopardizing the structure upon which it once rested. This reflects the type of academic surgical precision with which historical forces are neutralized, and agency is restored without sacrificing the entire school system upon which such deceptions for erected. The both—and principles are present in much of African culture. The promotion of the Eurocentric perspective as the universal standard that all other perspectives are made to yield in the presence of while simultaneously being encouraged to aspire to emulate creates a tragic paradox of aspiration. Seeking to be other than yourself when that is all you can be creates a self-deceptive and self-destructive cycle of false possibilities predicated upon unrealistic visions of cultural and intellectual attainment. In a world of Fake news and flawed scholarship, the need for Afrocentric location is vital.

Contemporary society has been inundated with so much misdirection and misinformation that we need clarity, agency, and truth more than ever. Afrocentricity has been described as a pathway to regain the sanity threatened by deliberate historical inaccuracies, and many ethnic groups have schools that teach various aspects of the culture. In Chinatowns and other Asian communities, several examples of culturally founded institutions displaying self-determination and agency, with signs written in Mandarin, just as you find, office buildings and schools adorned with Hebrew characters representing Jewish cultural centers, holocaust museums, and your Chivas. Afrocentricity represents the single best hope for creating a nation imbued with this level of self-determination. We must be able to see the world through our own eyes.

The tremendous intellectual and sociological pioneer William Edward Burghardt Du Bois warned of the potential negative impacts of perceptual dislocation if we as a people persist in seeing ourselves through the eyes of the other (Singer, 2024). Afrocentricity encourages Black people to be logically self-directed and self-affirming, having Black thoughts, Black power, Pan-African consciousness and undying love for Black people and the willingness to soldier and sacrifice for the sake of our collective liberation. Molefi Kete Asante is the first person in the world to create a PhD program in African American studies which occurred at Temple University (1988). He also holds the distinction of being the founding editor of the *Journal of Black Studies*. The Afrocentric philosophical approaches to education and other concepts have been his disciplinary focus for over four decades.

Asante argues that the horrific ramifications of my offer, which included some of the most brutal and explicative practices in the history of humanity, served to severely dislocate African people psychologically, culturally, economically, and geographically. This completes the centering of a people scattered throughout foreign lands under the control of those who have no understanding of them and no regard for their humanity. The narratives we existed according to were other than our own. The myths, parables, and heroes we received were transplanted from the history, imagination, and aspirations of others. African people were left to struggle to awkwardly assimilate. The African cultural superstructures that pre-dated the existence of all the peoples on the planet were deliberately callously exchanged with the psychosocial Mal nourish Eurocentric matrix. Due to being forced to feed from this trifling trough of lies, Eurocentric hierarchical racial designs and problematic patriarchy, we suffered greatly and continue to do so.

The contemporary manifestations of this confusion are evident in the division of self-hatred and difficulty with unity and self-determination, which persist in many African American/Diasporic communities today. Through the Afrocentric approach to the historical and cultural regeneration of African empowerment, scholars in the discipline paths back to self and to balance with nature. The principles of MAAT and Sankofa are rigorously implemented through using Afrocentricity as a weapon of resistance to racist anti-Black propaganda.

## SUMMARY

When statistics are presented in the absence of context, describing racial disparities, the likelihood of pathologizing demographics can increase exponentially. A lack of nuance, context, and full recognition of people's humanity may be effectively correlated to remedy disparities in access, inclusion, academic performance, and quality of educational experience. Context matters, and the diversity and emphasis on agency that Afrocentricity promotes offers an appreciation for nuance and diversity of perspective, which can enlighten and help heal a nation.

As Asante's theory encourages scholars to locate authors politically and culturally, it is becoming increasingly imperative to apply similar standards to institutions, including colleges and universities. Geography and reputation also inform the contextual realities of disparities in higher education. People from a college in the heart of the once-Confederate South may have different outlooks and perspectives than those from modern Northern institutions. Location may influence differences in the acceptance or inclusion of added levels of historical transparency as it informs causes and potential resolution of disparate treatment. A college's status or reputation could motivate change concerning greater degrees of Afrocentric context.

In other instances, they could serve as cultural hindrances to more contextually constructed analysis, if additional information threatens the existing idea(s) about the institutional identity of a university. Every approach does not require radical shifts, some would benefit greatly from subtle expansions of scope through greater Afrocentric understanding. We often find Pyric victories and symbols of progress where more significant structural changes are required. Afrocentricity has long challenged the fairness and accuracy of existing Eurocentric institutions by questioning their morality and validity when necessary. However, when effectively confronted we hear more about diversity equity and inclusion programs to increase basic awareness and sensitivity coupled with an occasional apology for poor behavior and disparate systems of privilege and access than actual systemic adjustments within institutions

The recognition that universities need to change is often not accompanied by structural or organizational implementation, which could facilitate the necessary evolutions: An Afrocentric means of addressing these concerns moving forward will be to emphasize the specific work done by Molefi Kete Asante in curriculum development working with several universities and school districts throughout the nation. It is imperative that we as keepers of this culture to some extent ensure that the legacy of celebration surrounding Molefi Kete Asante is practically applied and institutionally infused in ways that impact the lives of knowledge seekers daily in meaningful and lasting ways. The objective has always been to create space for conscious human beings who are, by virtue of their centeredness, committed to sanity. The idea of conscientization is at the center of Afrocentricity because this is what makes it different from Africanity. One can practice African customs and mores and not be Afrocentric. Afrocentricity is conscientization related to the agency of African people. One cannot be Afrocentric without being a conscious human being.

"This is the key to re-orientation and re-centering. Africans have been negated in the system of white racial domination. This is not mere marginalization, but the obliteration of the presence, meaning, activities, or images of the African. This is negated reality, a destruction of the spiritual and material personality of the African person" (Asante, 2005), p. 154).

Unfortunately, the progress in some of the aforementioned areas of education and life appears negligible. To close gaps in education along racial lines, I argue that it is incumbent upon institutions at a foundational, organizational level to move from surviving to thriving in valuing and making accessible, increased Afrocentric context to explain and rectify such disparities. We need to be as progressive around issues of context as many of us have been concerning computers with consistent updates and upgrades.

When our desire for greater Afrocentric context more closely mirrors our appetite for tech, we can exponentially advance in the pursuit of educational parity and a truer more achievable approach to academic equity, especially considering the abundance of obstacles faced in this regard historically: legislative penalties against enslaved Africans learning to read and write, the government provisions of land for land-grant colleges, exclusions from colleges and universities based on race abound. Tracing the exponential growth of universities and their endowments, while weaving the larger story of racial exploitation together with the history of inequality within the university system, is just one way that an Afrocentric comparative analysis could be beneficial. The implementation of earnest policies and initiatives becomes increasingly vulnerable to failure when predicated upon a tone-deaf, anti-historical foundation of half-truths and analytical vacuums devoid of relevant context.

Without the much-needed balance of perspectives and related truth, I am highly concerned about the possibilities of the uninformed developing a default posture of pathologizing African American achievement, potential, and existence. Such unfortunate outcomes could result from a lack of valuable nuance and historical perspective which, when skillfully implemented, could enable those from various new thought in Africology seeks to bring into existence a perpetual revolution toward a paradigm shift to defeat all forms of oppression. It is referred to as new thought because it is not like old thought, which sought to accommodate ignorance and the offshoots of ignorance such as racism, sexism, homophobia, and colorism; it seeks to obliterate them with a steady dose of reality.

In effect, the work of the critical thinker Ana Monteiro Ferreira demonstrated the value of such powerful shift in her book the demise of the inhuman (Ferreira, 2014) "(...) New Thought challenges, confronts and conflicts with those who maintain their psychosis of racism" (Asante, 2020, p. 62). Afrocentric scholars continue to interrogate and value perspectives from diverse walks of life to broaden their understanding of educational disparities, in a manner that could increase mutual empathy and transformative progressive change. In addition to contextual conundrums, there are concerns about understanding existing disparities, which fall along racial lines without the more complete context typically present from an Afrocentric perspective.

# REFERENCES

Asante, M. K., & Karenga, M. (2005). *Handbook of Black studies*. Sage Publications.

# List of Dr. Molefi Kete Asante's Books Published by Universal Write Publications

## INDEXICALITY: *An Africological Method of Inquiry*

*Indexicality: An Africological Method of Inquiry* (Book 1, Volume 1, LBBS, 2025) by Molefi Kete Asante presents a definitive methodological framework for Africology, advancing the discipline's ability to analyze African phenomena from a distinctly Afrocentric perspective. Building on the foundational work of Kemet, Afrocentricity, and Knowledge and the subsequent contributions of Africology scholars, this book addresses the critical need for methodologies.

## LYNCHING BARACK OBAMA: *How Whites Tried to String Up the President*

When President Barack Obama was elected as the first Black president of the United States of America in 2008, stereotypes and racism were considered history. However, as Molefi Kete Asante demonstrates in *Lynching Barack Obama: How Whites Tried to String Up the President* (2016), racism still permeates every sector of society.

## THE AMERICAN DEMAGOGUE: *Donald Trump* (Revised Edition)

The revised edition of *The American Demagogue: Donald Trump in the Presidency of the United States of America* expands and deepens the original 2017 analysis, drawing on the clarity of hindsight and the gravity of post-presidency consequences. While the first edition served as a prescient critique written in real time, mapping Trump's early use of demagoguery, rhetorical manipulation, and racialized populism, the revised edition goes further, incorporating evidence from his full term, including the Capitol insurrection, federal investigations, global diplomatic ruptures, and the lasting erosion of democratic norms.

## THE AMERICAN DEMAGOGUE: *Donald Trump in the Presidency of the United States of America* (2017, 1st Edition)

The 2017 first edition of *The American Demagogue: Donald Trump in the Presidency of the United States of America* offers an urgent, contemporary analysis of Donald Trump's early presidency through the lens of classical demagoguery, Afrocentric critique, and rhetorical deconstruction. Written at the dawn of Trump's administration, the original edition captures the raw immediacy of his ascent, documenting the rapid erosion of political norms, the weaponization of media platforms, and the racialized fear-mongering tactics used to consolidate power.

## 400 YEARS OF WITNESSING: *A Memoir of a People, 1619–2019*

What is a person to do with the pain, anger, fear, frustration, and dismay of Black defamation and demise due to White supremacy's racism and Anti-Blackness? Even more, how does one celebrate the triumph of surviving and escaping enslavement, establishing civil rights, creating and promulgating renaissance after renaissance as social movements, while inspiring the world to take note? Wonder no more. Dr. Molefi K. Asante has eloquently penned an emotional spectrum of poems that truly reflect the spirit, soul, and humanity of Black people in *400 Years of Witnessing: A Memoir of a People, 1619–2019* (2019).

## REVOLUTIONARY PEDAGOGY: *Primer for Teachers of Black Children* (2nd Edition)

The second edition of *Revolutionary Pedagogy: A Primer for Teachers of Black Children* builds upon the seminal foundation of the first, expanding its scope to meet the heightened urgency of post-2020 educational realities.

In this revised edition, Dr. Molefi Kete Asante deepens his Afrocentric methodology by incorporating new chapters on urban violence, trauma-responsive teaching, and the pervasive effects of dysconscious racism in educational institutions. This edition offers expanded lesson plans, first-hand classroom experiences, and revised strategies that make the theory-to-practice connection more transparent and more actionable for today's educators.

## REVOLUTIONARY PEDAGOGY: *Primer for Teachers of Black Children* (2017, 1st Edition)

*Revolutionary Pedagogy: A Primer for Teachers of Black Children* (1st edition) offers a foundational rethinking of how education must serve, affirm, and center Black children, particularly those navigating the inequities of urban school systems. Dr. Molefi Kete Asante articulates a compelling Afrocentric framework that places identity, cultural consciousness, and historical context at the heart of educational practice. Through the introduction of five pedagogical pillars—ethics, values, literacy, and reasoning—Asante equips educators with guiding principles to transform classrooms from sites of passive learning to spaces of critical consciousness and intellectual liberation.

## AFRICAN PYRAMIDS OF KNOWLEDGE: *Kemet, Afrocentricity And Africology* (2015)

*African Pyramids of Knowledge* by Dr. Molefi Kete Asante presents a transformative epistemological framework that repositions Kemet as the intellectual and cultural foundation of Africana thought. Rooted in the discipline of Africology and driven by the Afrocentric paradigm, the book challenges Eurocentric hierarchies of knowledge, asserting the legitimacy of African worldviews as rigorous, scientific, and philosophically rich. The book calls for epistemic justice by emphasizing cultural pluralism, re-centering African contributions to human civilization, and establishing Afrocentricity as a disciplined method for inquiry, pedagogy, and liberation. This work is essential for scholars, educators, and cultural workers committed to decolonizing education, advancing Black intellectual traditions, and restoring ancient African models of wisdom to their rightful global stature.

## BEING HUMAN BEING: *Transforming the Race Discourse*

Universal Write Publications is honored to have published Dr. Molefi Kete Asante's 100th book, *Being Human Being*.

*Being Human Being* depicts the importance of education in combating those who benefit from and promote racism. Educating the masses would enable the achievement of multicultural, pluralistic societies in a practical way. The authors suggest that humanity is hindered by its disunity and that, through concepts like Ma'aticity, the ancient way of becoming human, society can achieve its highest potential. Featuring an array of examples, illustrations, and theoretical models, *Being Human Being* (2021) demonstrates that the only race is the human race. Throughout his career, Dr. Asante has published one hundred book titles.

## RADICAL INSURGENCIES

*Radical Insurgencies* (2020) draws and translates wisdom from Africology, history, sociology, and philosophy to stitch together various social and political concerns presented by Asante in different academic settings. The book presents selected portions of significant speeches, an adaptation from the author's *The American Demagogue*, and a selection of conference papers presented in British Columbia, Zimbabwe, and at the 2011 Chinese Communication Conference.

## THE PRECARIOUS CENTER or *When Will the African Narrative Hold*

*The Precarious Center or When Will the African Narrative Hold?* dispels the Western romanization of Greek, English, French, German, Spanish, and Portuguese to the detriment of African ideas and ideals. This text *re-centers the African world* and dispels the dominant myths and memes of Greek society, which have obscured all other approaches with the false notion of European superiority in a multiethnic and multicultural world.

*The Precarious Center* (2021) strengthens global communication equality and frees the human spirit by challenging the assertive memes of the West, allowing spaces for other cultural postures to thrive.

## WE WILL TELL OUR OWN STORY:
### *The Lions of Africa Speak* (2017)

These authors, all deeply dedicated to telling an African story, are committed to righting the wrongs of intellectual inquiry by setting upright the standards, criteria, and assumptions often avoided by Eurocentrists, regardless of their complexion. Without the "lions of Africa" speaking and writing about their narratives, the fields of literature, philosophy, social science, history, and psychology, evidence would cede to those without the slightest idea about the African knowledge base or how to add to it. Thus, the authors in this volume speak loudly and write deftly and definitively to erect a new phalanx of liberated minds.

## THE DRAMATIC GENIUS OF CHARLES FULLER (2015)

Charles Fuller is a preeminent American dramatist, yet few critics have examined his work seriously or even discussed his philosophy, style, originality, and brilliance. Despite winning some of the nation's highest awards, his work, like that of many other Black writers, has fallen outside the scope of contemporary literary and dramatic discourse. This book brings a critical reading and sympathetic location of Fuller's drama at the center of African American dramatic and social history.

## AFROCENTRICITY: *Generations of Theory in Practice* (2025)

Inspired by Dr. Molefi Kete Asante's pioneering work, *Afrocentricity* offers a bold framework that re-centers African people within their narratives. This collection brings together the insights of leading Afrocentric scholars from across the African diaspora, highlighting their contributions to fields like Africana Studies, cultural movements, and discussions on identity and liberation.

# Book Overview

## *About the Editor*

### Aaron X. Smith (bka, Jabali Adé)

It wasn't long ago that Dr. Aaron X. Smith was a student at Temple University's North Philadelphia main campus, merely grateful for an opportunity in higher education. The foundation of his opportunity was his God-given athletic talents and a thirst for knowledge gifted to him by his parents. As he progressed through his academic life, he realized the opportunity for higher education was not readily accessible for most, and even more difficult to attain for the underrepresented and underprivileged members of his communities. This realization shaped his purpose to dedicate his life to uplifting a new generation of young people, to help them unlock the transformative power of education, and to recognize the potential of investing in one's personal growth.

Dr. Smith currently serves as an Assistant Professor in the Department of Africology and African American Studies at Temple University. He is the author of "The Murder of Octavius Catto," featured in the *Encyclopedia of Greater Philadelphia* (2015). Smith has also published multiple entries in the *Encyclopedia of African Cultural Heritage* (2015) and a chapter on James Baldwin titled, "Boundless Baldwin" published in *Contemporary Critical Thought in Africology and Africana Studies*. In 2015, he received the Molefi Kete Asante Award for academic excellence and innovation in the field of African American Studies. Most recently, Dr. Smith edited *Afrocentricity in Afrofuturism*, published by Mississippi University Press (2023).

His innovative, artistic presentation style has gained him the name "The Rapping Professor." During his short tenure at Temple University, Dr. Smith has quickly been recognized as a dynamic and innovative speaker, educator, artist, and facilitator who uses his vast wealth of knowledge, uncanny energy, and unique oratorical abilities to translate hip-hop culture into a universal language of leadership, learning, and love. During his professorship, he has been focused on developing unique and dynamic ways to actively engage the Gen Z students of today to solidify their love of learning.

# REFERENCES

Asante, M. K. (1997). Afrocentricity and the quest for method. In J. L. Conyers (Ed.), *Africana studies: A disciplinary quest for both theory and method* (pp. 69–90). McFarland.

Asante, M. K. (2004). The Afrocentric idea. In R. L. Jackson (Ed.), *African American communication & identities: Essential readings* (pp. 16–28). Sage Publications.

Asante, M. K., & Karenga, M. (2005). *Handbook of Black studies*. Sage Publications.

Asante, M. K. (2006). Afrocentricity and the Eurocentric hegemony of knowledge: Contradictions of place. In J. A. Young & J. E. Braziel (Eds.), *Race and foundations of knowledge: Cultural amnesia in the academy* (pp. 145–153). University of Illinois Press.

Asante, M. K. (1990). *Kemet, Afrocentricity and knowledge*. Africa World Press.

Asante, M. K. (2007). *An Afrocentric manifesto: Toward an African renaissance* (p. 3). Polity.

Asante, M. K. (2017). Afrocentricity: Notes on a disciplinary position. In J. L. Conyers (Ed.), *Afrocentric traditions* (pp. 1–14). Routledge.

Asante, M. K., & Dove, N. (2021). *Being human being: Transforming the race discourse*. Universal Write Publications LLC.

Asante, M. K. (2020). *Radical insurgencies*. Universal Write Publications LLC.

Asante, M. K. (2007). *An Afrocentric manifesto: Toward an African renaissance*. Polity.

Asante, M. K. (2003). *Afrocentricity: The theory of social change*. African American Images.

Asante, M. K. (2015). *African pyramids of knowledge: Kemet, Afrocentricity and Africology*. Universal Write Publications LLC.

Conyers, J. L. (Ed.). (2017). *Molefi Kete Asante: A critical Afrocentric reader*. Peter Lang Publishing Incorporated.

Barnett, R. (2020). Leading with meaning: Why diversity, equity, and inclusion matters in US higher education. *Perspectives in Education, 38*(2), 20–35.

Beavers, D. (2018). *Diversity, equity and inclusion framework*. The Greenlining Institute.

Crenshaw, K., Gotanda, N., Peller, G., & Thomas, K. (Eds.). (1995). *Critical race theory: The key writings that formed the movement*. The New Press.

Monteiro-Ferreira, A. (2014). The demise of the inhuman: Afrocentricity, modernism, and postmodernism. State University of New York Press.

McLean, S., & Dixit, J. (2018). The power of positive thinking: A hidden curriculum for precarious times. *Adult Education Quarterly, 68*(4), 280–296.

Nes, L. S. (2016). Optimism, pessimism, and stress. In *Stress: Concepts, cognition, emotion, and behavior* (pp. 405–411). Academic Press.

Peale, N. V. (2007). *The tough-minded optimist*. Simon and Schuster.

Singer, A. J. (2024). Teach NY: WEB Du Bois's 1901 study of Black life in New York City. *New York History, 104*(1), 179–193.

White, M. J., Bean, F. D., & Espenshade, T. J. (1990). The US 1986 Immigration Reform and Control Act and undocumented migration to the United States. *Population Research and Policy Review, 9*, 93–116.

Yu, Y., & Luo, J. (2018). Dispositional optimism and well-being in college students: Self-efficacy as a mediator. *Social Behavior and Personality: An International Journal, 46*(5), 783–792.

.

# Index

www.ingramcontent.com/pod-product-compliance
Lightning Source LLC
Chambersburg PA
CBHW052110030426
42335CB00025B/2914